D0762002

The Garland Library of Medieval Literature

Title page woodcut by Hans Baldung Grien from Johannes Grüninger's 1515 edition of Eulenspiegel's adventures.

TILL EULENSPIEGEL
His Adventures

translated,
with introduction
and notes, by

Paul Oppenheimer

Volume 74
Series B
GARLAND LIBRARY OF MEDIEVAL LITERATURE

Garland Publishing, Inc.
New York & London
1991

Library of Congress Cataloging-in-Publication Data

Eulenspiegel (Satire). English
Till Eulenspiegel : his adventures / translated by Paul Oppenheimer.
p. cm. — (Garland library of medieval literature ; v. 74. Series B)
Translation of: Eulenspiegel.
Includes bibliographical references.
ISBN 0-8240-5754-6 (alk. paper)
1. Oppenheimer, Paul. II. Title. III. Series: Garland library of medieval literature ; v. 74.
PT941.E8E5 1991
833'.3—dc20 90-26368
CIP

Printed on acid-free, 250-year-life paper
Manufactured in the United States of America

To Julie (ancora) and Ben too

CONTENTS

Preface of the General Editors

The Garland Library of Medieval Literature was established to make available to the general reader modern translations of texts in editions that conform to the highest academic standards. All of the translations are originals, and were created especially for this series. The translations attempt to render the foreign works in a natural idiom that remains faithful to the originals.

The Library is divided into two sections: Series A, texts and translations; and Series B, translations alone. Those volumes containing texts have been prepared after consultation of the major previous editions and manuscripts. The aim in the edition has been to offer a reliable text with a minimum of editorial intervention. Significant variants accompany the original, and important problems are discussed in the Textual Notes. Volumes without texts contain translations based on the most scholarly texts available, which have been updated in terms of recent scholarship.

Most volumes contain Introductions with the following features: (1) a biography of the author or a discussion of the problem of authorship, with any pertinent historical or legendary information; (2) an objective discussion of the literary style of the original, emphasizing any individual features; (3) a consideration of sources for the work and its influence; and (4) a statement of the editorial policy for each edition and translation. There is also a Select Bibliography, which emphasizes recent criticism on the works. Critical writings are often accompanied by brief descriptions of their importance. Selective glossaries, indices, and footnotes are included where appropriate.

The Library covers a broad range of linguistic areas, including all of the major European languages. All of the important literary forms and genres are considered, sometimes in anthologies or selections.

The General Editors hope that these volumes will bring the general reader a closer awareness of a richly diversified area that has for too long been closed to everyone except those with precise academic training, an area that is well worth study and reflection.

James J. Wilhelm
Rutgers University

Lowry Nelson, Jr.
Yale University

TRANSLATOR'S PREFACE

This is in most important respects a new book and not simply a new edition of my translation of Till Eulenspiegel's adventures published in 1972. The translation has been extensively revised, the notes on the tales extended in what I hope will prove to be ways helpful to those interested in late medieval and Renaissance culture, and the Introduction much altered to take account of recent scholarship. If I have retained the theory of assertional language (under Artistic Achievement in the Introduction), I have done so in the trust that it holds as much validity today as it did when it was first conceived by a twenty-eight-year-old apprentice scholar.

I am deeply grateful to many people for many sorts of help: to my editor, Lowry Nelson Jr., who has offered numerous valuable suggestions for improving the manuscript; to James J. Wilhelm, for encouragement, important advice, and assistance; to Paula Ladenburg, my editor at Garland Publishing; to Dean Paul Sherwin of the Humanities Division of the City College of New York, for making his office with its facilities available to me; to Laryssa Barboza; and to Maria Correa, who has worked tirelessly to make this a better-appearing book. I am indebted as well to the staffs of The British Library, The New York Public Library, and The Library of the City College of New York for cooperation and assistance; and to Princeton University Library, from whose copy of the Schröder facsimile of the Grüninger edition of 1515 the woodcuts for this edition were reproduced. I also wish to acknowledge yet again the major corrections offered on very early versions of this book by the late W.T.H. Jackson, and by Howard Schless, both of Columbia University. The wealth of contributions from other scholars is, I trust, fully acknowledged in the text and bibliography. I am, finally, most grateful to Andras Hamori and Francesca Simpson Pedler, whose friendship and constant stream of good suggestions have enabled me to make this a better book than it otherwise would have been.

New York
November 1990

P.O.

INTRODUCTION

DATE AND AUTHORSHIP

Europe's most famous jester is himself the creation of a jester. His book is in many ways itself a jest. Whether the author is Hermann Bote (ca. 1467-ca. 1520), as certain investigators of these tales lately wish to maintain, burying his name as a mangled acronym in his text, or someone else whose surname begins with N., as the author announces in his Foreword, it seems clear that he is busy on a well appointed medieval-Renaissance stage in acting out elaborate charades before his audience. His inconsistencies thus become his calculated consistency. His humility becomes a special sort of bravado. His disdain of hypocrisy belies his obvious enjoyment of it. His highest personal value is no doubt his invisibility. In this, his curious reticence about himself, he matches the curious invisibility of his jester-hero.

Till Eulenspiegel is both spectacularly famous and paradoxically unknown. Regarded with delight as Germany's, if not much of the world's, jester *par excellence* for the past five hundred years, he has suffered the frustrating indignity, over the last two centuries, of being reduced to infantile proportions as the childish hero of a children's book. If every German is weaned on Eulenspiegel's adventures, so to speak, and believes that he knows who Eulenspiegel is, he has probably not read his adventures in their original, highly scatological forms at all, but instead run into one of their numerous bland adaptations. The satire too has been censored, or so toned down, that its native hue of sophistication, and adult and often merciless instrument, has been sicklied o'er with the pale cast of mortification. Lately this situation has been changing, perhaps because in the new social climate of Western cultures prudishness itself is readily regarded as an impropriety. Wolfgang Lindow's impressive re-editing of the earliest complete edition of Eulenspiegel's adventures, that of 1515, in 1966, opened a green and fruitful period in Eulenspiegel scholarship. His volume was succeeded, in 1969, by an event even more remarkable. Peter Honegger, a Swiss jurist and Eulenspiegel enthusiast, announced the discovery of a lost fragment of either the first or second edition of the Eulenspiegel stories, published in Strassburg in 1510-11. Ingenious detective work, done on the basis of this discovery, prompted Honegger to declare, in 1971, that the entire book had been written by Hermann Bote, a Low Saxon author of repute, who had concealed his name in code among his penultimate six Late Middle High German chapters, possibly because he feared reprisals from scurrilous local officials. The book could thus no longer be regarded as anonymous. Nor was it, as quite a few scholars had believed, a *Volksmund* product, a "communal" effort over decades to link in picaresque fashion the elements of a popular or "people's" legend reaching back to 1350, the year of the "real" Eulenspiegel's supposed death. The legend, which certainly existed, and which sustains an amazing vitality to this day, had been supplied with an organic unity by a single writer.

With this said, it must be added that Honegger's ideas are both intriguing and replete with difficulties. The difficulties, especially, require elucidation. What needs to be understood first by the reader new to Eulenspiegel's adventures, however, is that Honegger's discovery as well as his ideas led to an explosion of scholarly and critical interest over the next eighteen years, a veritable flood of fresh articles and books. This flood continues unabated. There may in fact be no area of *Germanistik* that has experienced so rapid and fascinating a recent expansion, or with such constructive results. The expansion is appropriate and long overdue. The importance of the subject demands it. The truth is that Till Eulenspiegel – the Eulenspiegel of this book – occupies a position of secret happiness in the German soul. It is a position, as well, of impudent glory. It rivals – not in grandeur but in magic, influence, and mystery – the positions of King Arthur in the soul of England and the Roland of *La chanson de Roland* in the soul of France. Like these legendary figures, Eulenspiegel exerts a magnetism that has been felt not only by many subsequent authors writing in German and other European languages, but also by composers and artists, including brilliant ones such as Hans Baldung Grien, who was a friend of Albrecht Dürer and who made a number of the woodcuts for the earliest editions (these are reproduced here and will be discussed below). Eulenspiegel's attraction for millions has also expressed itself in even more obvious signs of public self-perception. As of 1983, at last count, at least twenty-one public statues, carvings, painted figurines affixed to houses, plaques, and other *Denkmäler*, some of them quite recent, commemorated Eulenspiegel's exploits, in Germany, Flanders, and Holland (Sichtermann, 310). The jester whom Germans always felt to be far more than a jester – who was, and is, an actor, thief, liar, prankster, devil, saint, sadist, philanthropist, and indeed (as I shall try to demonstrate) an early and interesting linguistic philosopher – still mesmerizes and enchants. The fact, therefore, that this new, full, and collated translation of the editions of 1515, 1519, and recently discovered fragments (see also Editorial Policy for this Text and Translation, below) is the first complete one done into English in several centuries must be seen as rather astonishing. As will become clear to the most casual reader of Eulenspiegel's adventures, the absence of an English version has shuttered a lucid window through which to view ordinary life in the later Middle Ages and the Renaissance. The absence has also prevented an encounter with one of the most original and compelling authors to have written in Late Middle High German.

Whoever composed, compiled, and wrote these tales, and in the process created the complex jester who survives today, lived in a pre-national Germany during the Age of Christian Humanism. This historical context, which is also political, economic, social, philosophical, and to some extent religious, needs to be understood if the questions of authorship and the dates of the writing are to be resolved in a satisfactory way. The grand German castles, fortresses, and palaces – ten thousand of them in German-speaking duchies at the start of the sixteenth century – need to be reimagined, not in their present ruins but in their previous magnificence. The stones still sang of a dying knightly splendor. The crossbow, with its steel-tipped missiles, remained a ubiquitous obsolescent weapon. Artillery, a creature of the feral European battlefields for over two centuries by 1500, roared against the awkward clashings of obsolescent armor. Cavalry horses, to be sure, would continue to mass, glitter in their protective steel casings, and charge until the invention of the tank, and beyond, some four centuries later. In a time when printing books with moveable type was a spreading novelty, new coal and iron mines in Saxony and Bohemia lured thousands of worker-colonists from across Europe. Cities such as Strassburg, together with the growing urban communities of the German south, formed a nexus of trade, banking, and a more sophisticated cultural life than elsewhere in Germany. In Strassburg alone, where Eulenspiegel's adventures were first published, at least eighteen publishers produced dozens of books per year by the end of the fifteenth century, on an armada of subjects that included the classics, collections of *fabliaux*, and beer-making.

The intellectual climate consisted of revolutionary storms and arid frigidity. The quest of the new, often inspired by the rediscovery of the old, encountered a gelid rejection. The dismissal of Church Latin and medieval scholasticism – reflected in N.'s remark in his Foreword to the tales, "I am, I'm sorry to say, unfamiliar with written Latin and am a simple layman" – is part of the humanist author's typical pose as an advocate of the vernacular. Where today a classical education is viewed as broadening, fifteenth-century humanists, opposed to mere catechistical uses of Latin, often saw it as constricting. "Ciceronianism," as this sort of learning was called, was mere slavish imitation, albeit one condemned by writers who had certainly studied their Ovid and Virgil. The tolerance of the new Renaissance art and humanistic scholarship in one district matched the fierce repression of both in the next. At the same time, the loose and often squabbling confederation of German princes under the Holy Roman Emperor Maximillian I (1493-1519) permitted the flowering of an inquisitive literature, humanist in character, whose intellectual vigor, satire, and bitter assaults on priestly corruption helped to stimulate the coming Reformation. Conrad Celtis (1459-1508) produced a popular erotic poetry full of physical images and candor. Ulrich von Hutten (1488-1523) wrote anti-clerical diatribes whose teasing satirical tone contributed to the rebellions among German knights in 1522. (Curiously, both men died of syphilis, a disease introduced, it is likely, by travelers returning from the New World.) Johann Reuchlin (in 1506) published a book, *On the Rudiments of Hebrew*, in which he argued that Hebrew was the only proper language for Christian theology. His bizarre position led him to reject anti-Semitic theologians on the one hand, and Martin Luther on the other. Rudolf Agricola (1443-85), probably the first major German humanist, though he was born in Holland, wrote a life of Petrarch, a textbook on logic (in which he sought to make logic the basis of grammar), and the *Mensa philosophica*, at least one of whose witticisms, found in the adventures of Till Eulenspiegel, suggests that the author of the Eulenspiegel stories was familiar with Agricola's work (see the note on Chapter 57). In the darkened recesses of the great German and Austrian cathedrals, among the rich new altarpieces lit by candles and by sunlight distilled through windows of medieval and Renaissance stained glass, the Church seemed to await, in mistrustful patience, the waves of popular disgust soon to rise against it. A lush choral music could nonetheless be heard in the cathedrals, as well as in the town and city streets outside. Sacred and secular polyphonic songs, by Hofhaimer, Finck, Isaac, and Senfl, have survived in two major collections, called *Liederbücher*. Part-singing was most favored, and many of the songs reveal influences of the medieval *cantus firmus* technique and the *Minnesänger*, often in a melodic line whose "Germanness" is distinguishable less as a smoothness – a quality more typical of Dutch and French compositions – than as an awkward, alien intensity. Wandering professional musicians, plying their trade in the large market places and on feast days, made intricate use of the transverse flute, so called because when played it was held across the face. This instrument had been invented in Germany in the twelfth century. While its manufacture had spread to other countries, it retained a special popularity in Renaissance German duchies, landgravates, and margravates.

In such an atmosphere, mixing skepticism, entrepreneurial daring, technological and aesthetic innovation, fierce liberalism, and fierce conservatism, jest-books, or *Schwankbücher*, found a ready audience. To judge from the popularity of jest-books such as that of Till Eulenspiegel, nearly everyone who could read was prepared to laugh at everyone else. Nationalism, in the modern sense of national consciousness or even nation-worship, was hardly an impediment to national jeering. Nationalism did not exist, any more than did Germany as a nation. Christianity itself, as an institution, invited contradictory responses. An early German example of the jest-book genre is *Der Pfaffe Amis*, a rhymed

Volksbuch of the thirteenth century (Lambel, 22-102). More influential on the medieval-Renaissance tradition of these books, though, is Poggio's *Facetiae* (1438-52), which is discussed with *Der Pfaffe Amis* in Sources and Influence, below. Gian Francesco Poggio Bracciolini was born on Feb. 11, 1380, in Terranuova (Italy), and died on Oct. 30, 1459, in Florence. He spent much of his life in making scholarly discoveries. He found, for instance, "lost" manuscripts of Quintilian, Cicero, and Lucretius (his *De rerum natura*) in monastic libraries at Cluny, St. Gallen, and Cologne. The inventor of "humanist" script, which later served as the basis of roman type fonts, he turned Roman citizen himself, becoming secretary to Pope Boniface IX. Poggio's obscene and scatological *facetiae* certainly affect what becomes an international humanist tradition of *Schwankliteratur*, or "fool's literature" in the broadest sense. This tradition, influenced by folktales and medieval *fabliaux*, includes *Das Narrenschiff* of Sebastian Brant (published in 1494, with illustrations by Albrecht Dürer; translated into English in 1509 as *The Ship of Folys of the Worlde*, by Alexander Barclay), Thomas Murner's poem *Die Narrenbeschwörung* (1512), and Erasmus' *In Praise of Folly* (in Latin, 1509). Eulenspiegel's book and its author belong squarely in this quixotic stream of humanist satirical writing. The international spread of the jest-book genre – its indifference to mere territorial passions – is in fact crucial to understanding it, and to understanding Eulenspiegel and his literary creator as well. Local details, especially in the Eulenspiegel stories, are often sketchy, though valuable as cultural indices. They emphasize, rather than detract from, the author's ambitions to mock and satirize the pretentiousness of mankind generally. The foreign settings of some of Eulenspiegel's adventures complement this fact. So too does the author's concern with the great themes of his Renaissance-humanist as well as his (later) Reformation contemporaries – Martin Luther, Castiglione, Machiavelli, and Rabelais, as well as Erasmus. Luther's passion for a Christianity purified of corruption shows in traces here and there, as do Castiglione's perception that cultures without rules of civilized behavior cannot survive, Machiavelli's exposure of the mechanics of political power, Rabelais' ridicule of megalomania and fatuous language, and Erasmus' fascination with folly born of greed. The achievements of Luther, Rabelais, and particularly Erasmus exhibit precisely that delight in philology – an international study by definition–which lies at the center of the Eulenspiegel stories, as will be shown below, and which is typical of humanist scholars. The Renaissance *homo universalis* was in fact first a philologist and second an artist and encyclopedist. In a pre-Copernican universe in which God was still regarded as an abstraction, a word or *verbum* (a concept derived from the beginning of the Gospel of St. John, "The Word was God"), this philological *Wanderlust* was not in the least surprising. Beyond these typically internationalist concerns of the humanists, the author of the Eulenspiegel stories shares another, perhaps personal quality with them and other Renaissance thinkers: his contradictions. Like Rabelais, he combines vulgarity and sensitivity. Like Machiavelli, he mixes elegance and (as in Machiavelli's comedies) poor taste. Like Benvenuto Cellini (1500-71), he displays violence and sympathy. Like Poggio, he marries eloquence and scatology. The author of the Eulenspiegel stories also makes no effort to resolve his contradictions, or those of his hero, into some sort of unctuous ideology. In this too he resembles Machiavelli, Cellini, Rabelais, and Erasmus–or for that matter, Hamlet. If he never offers anything resembling their larger visions, he certainly seems bent on suffusing his work with a mischievous genius of individualism and independence. These contradictions are likewise apparent in the character of another humanist contemporary who may supply an explicit link between the author of Eulenspiegel's adventures and humanist satire: Willibald Pirckheimer. Pirckheimer (1470-1530), a wealthy Nuremberg physician, was a widower who lived with several mistresses in succession and the bastard children he had by them. He was a classicist of note. He corresponded with Erasmus. He was a friend of Albrecht Dürer, whose most famous assistant, Hans Baldung Grien, created (as has been remarked above) a number of the woodcuts for the first editions of Till Eulenspiegel's adventures.

In the Foreword to the tales, which is the only part of the book written in the first person singular, the author tells us these facts about himself: that his initial is "N."; that he is writing in the year 1500; that he has been asked to "compile" [zesammenbringen] these "accounts and tales" by various people who would have been "pretty grateful" to him for doing so; that he lacks sufficient "intelligence and understanding" for the job; that he believes, or strongly suggests that he does, in God; and that he does not know how to write Latin. He also makes his ambition clear: "to create a happy feeling in hard times, so my readers may experience good, pleasant entertainment and fun." His work will, if successful, give the greatest pleasure to people who are lonely in winter, when the "hours grow short." This information is skimpy enough, and while reading the tales tells a good deal about the author's interests, it tells nearly nothing about him biographically. The peculiar quarrels among scholars over the identity of the author have, at least until recently (and even here the results are questionable), added little to the information about him.

Scholarly investigation of the tales begins properly with the monumental and generally superb work of J.M. Lappenberg, whose *Dr. Thomas Murners Ulenspiegel* (Leipzig, 1854) is the first critical edition of the publisher Johannes Grüninger's text of 1519 (Lappenberg did not know of the existence of Grüninger's earlier editions). As his title indicates, Lappenberg believes that the tales were written by Thomas Murner, four of whose books were actually published by Grüninger: *Logica/memoratiua/Chartiludiu Logice* (1509); *Ein andechtig geistliche/Badenfart/des hochgelerte Herre Thomas Murner* (1514); *Murner Der Keiserl. stat rechen ein ingag* (1521); and *Murner. Von dem grossen Lutherschen Narren wie in doctor Murner beschworen hat* (1522) (Kristeller, 87-106). Lappenberg's ascription of authorship to Murner is no longer taken seriously, first, because the only explicit connection between Murner and the tales is to be found in a scarcely creditable sarcastic remark by a contemporary, and second, because Murner's style is utterly different from the style of the Eulenspiegel stories (cf. Schröder, "Gleitwort," 37-8; also Lemcke, who offers detailed philological arguments against Murner's authorship). Other blind alleys in the quest of authorship have been discovered in abundance. One of these presents a different date for the actual writing of the book, 1483 as opposed to 1500. 1483 shows up without explanation in the Foreword to the Strassburg edition of 1531, as well as in nine more editions published in the sixteenth century, in Cologne, Augsburg, and Frankfurt. While the likelihood is great that each of these last nine editions simply copied the first, the date 1483 nonetheless seemed a correct one for the composition of the tales. It fits in rather well, or almost does, with the date alluded to in the first tale, that of the "destruction of the wicked thieves' castle at Magdeburg . . . more than fifty years ago." The castle was destroyed in 1425 (see the note on Chapter 1). There may have been some confusion in the author's mind with 1433, the year in which (fifty years earlier) Ampleben, the village in which Eulenspiegel is baptized, purchased the castle (Flood, 164, n29). 1483 therefore seemed to many scholars the proper date for what was perhaps the earliest version of the tales. This substitution of dates – 1483 for 1500 – also reinforced a conviction, held by Krogmann and others, that the version of "1500" was in fact a translation from Low German into Late Middle High German, an idea inspired by various Low German forms of words and phrases that could be found in Grüninger's editions of 1515 and 1519. As Honegger (126) points out, however, what is far more likely is that the printers of the subsequent ten editions, all of which in other respects duplicate Grüninger's earliest editions, simply changed 1500 to 1483 to allow their work to conform with N.'s assertion in Chapter 1 that the book dates from fifty years or so after 1425, or the destruction of the robber-baron castle at Magdeburg. In any case, the sentence in question literally reads "somewhat more than fifty years ago," which may allow for the discrepancy. 1500 is today, as N. announces it in his Foreword, the date of composition that is universally accepted. Also accepted today is that the book was originally written in Late Middle High German, but by an author accustomed to writing in Low German (hence the Low German words and phrases). It is not, as had been believed, a translation at all.

Two other issues of importance in the quest of authorship have been the relations of the 1515 edition to the edition of 1519, and the possibility that more than one author may have had a hand in writing the tales. The question of the relations of the two earliest complete editions, along with the relations to them of the newly discovered fragments (including an almost complete version of Grüninger's 1510-11 edition, found by Bernd Ulrich Hucker in 1975), are considered in more detail below, under Editorial Policy for this Text and Translation. Schröder ("Geitwort," 5), noting differences between the 1515 and 1519 editions, not only speculated on the existence of a previous edition, a correct idea indeed, but on the possibility of an earlier version of the tales by an author different from "N." What seems to be the case, as is discussed below, is that the edition of 1519 is a slightly rewritten improvement, by the same author, of the 1515 edition (contrary views appear in Scherer, 83; Walther, 26; and Krogmann). Honegger, who also takes note of typographical divergencies between the two editions, describes them, notwithstanding, as "sister editions" (19).

The possibility of more than one author is trickier. It reaches interestingly into the development of the Eulenspiegel legend itself, long before Grüninger's published versions. It also lends itself, with equal interest, to textual examinations of the versions and fragments that have survived, in an effort to see whether, on textual grounds alone, it can be demonstrated that they are the work of a single author. As far as an Eulenspiegel legend is concerned, references to one abound. All but two references, however, date from well after Grüninger's editions. (Some of these are mentioned in the notes on specific tales.) The two prior references to an Eulenspiegel legend are also surprisingly inconclusive. Neither of them is directly contemporary with Eulenspiegel's "life" in the fourteenth century or his "death" in 1350. In 1932, to cite the first reference, Hermann Heimpel drew attention to an allusion to some sort of written "Ullenspeygel" in two personal letters in Latin, both dating from 1411 (Heimpel, 232). An "Ullenspeygel" text is mentioned, in connection with "works" of Socrates and Cicero, and that is all. The second, equally enigmatic reference is by Hermann Bote himself (for Honegger it serves as part of the evidence that he wishes to gather to show that Bote is the "N." of Grüninger's published versions). It appears in a manuscript that has come to be called "Weltchronik" (Bote produced more than one of these), written after 1493. Here Bote lists, among various events for the year 1350, the death of an "Ullenspeygel" at "Mollen" (perhaps the Mölln of the last chapter of Grüninger's editions). Sichtermann (15) believes that Bote was thus acquainted with the "Eulenspiegel manuscript" mentioned in the Latin correspondence of 1411. Despite the skeletal bareness of these references, they certainly argue for some sort of Eulenspiegel legend before 1500. They also seem to prove that when N. describes himself as a "compiler" in his Foreword, he is only telling the truth. He is indeed putting together tales that were already in existence and well known. None of this, it may be added, proves that a "real" Eulenspiegel, who died in 1350, actually existed.

As to the question whether a single author wrote the versions that remain from the early sixteenth century, mere examinations of their attitudes, in a search for personal commitments whispering through the writing, prove distinctly unhelpful. Kadlec (187-88), who wishes to discover a series of views indicating the voices of more than one author, points out that the first paragraph of Chapter 28, in which John Huss and the students of the University of Prague are treated with disdain, reflects bitter opposition to the Hussites and Protestantism. He concludes that a new voice may be heard in the tales at this point, one whose sophistication jars against the simpler, disinterested tone of earlier tales. Werner Wunderlich, who supports Honegger's belief that Hermann Bote must be the author, maintains, in an important essay summarizing old and new criticism, that the author is a "conservative moralist," who sought through his hero to "supply an ominous, rousing example" for his audience (Wunderlich, 11). Neither of these conclusions is supported by the text. In fact, to deal directly with the latter of them, a striking feature of the text is its omission of all conventional moralizing. Certain values are affirmed by implication, but this is a very different thing from the sort of pointed, explicit moralizing to be found in a great many other contemporary *Schwankbücher*, in which a sentence or two at the end of a "jest" makes plain, in the style of the medieval *exemplum*, the moral instruction that the reader was expected to assimilate (cf., for instance, the *Trecento novelle* of Franco Sacchetti). The fact is that all of the tales are shot through with attitudes, and whether these are "simple," "sophisticated," or mutually exclusive and contradictory remains in the end a matter of opinion. It is also one of the book's richest sources of entertainment. What is indeed remarkably consistent – though this too proves nothing – is the text's, and Eulenspiegel's, seemingly unrelenting contempt, which falls into at least these acute categories: contempt for dishonest Christianity and other sects or religions; contempt for dishonest scholars; contempt for dishonest tradesmen, hotel-keepers, and farmers; contempt for dishonest officials and nobles; contempt for dishonest citizens and politicians; contempt for dishonest doctors; and contempt for stupid people generally. This contemptuous attitude seems often to reflect a greater hostility toward those who are newly prosperous than toward those who have always been poor (as long as they are not stupid) or whose desire for power has always been satisfied. The intention in Chapter 34, for example, cannot be to ridicule the pope but to demonstrate the hypocrisy of the Christianity of Eulenspiegel's innkeeper. The pope, clearly a figure of power in the story, is described as without blemish and even as extraordinarily generous. On the other hand, here as in the rest of the book the studied contempt is simply too familiar to indicate anything personal about the author. The same "commitment" or "attitude" appears in a great many other contemporary works, or nearly contemporary ones, including the medieval German drama, Chaucer's *Canterbury Tales*, and the tales of Hans Sachs. What is therefore clear is that proofs of the contributions of one or more authors are exceedingly difficult, if not impossible, to establish by these methods. Indeed, it is only when Eulenspiegel's adventures are examined on textual and aesthetic grounds, and when their uses of words and ideas are compared with their probable literary sources, that the originality of N.'s accomplishment, the unique accomplishment of a single author, begins to emerge. Looked at in this way, the book reveals at least seven areas of novel, and perhaps even profound, distinction.

First, a self-evident feature of these tales is their focus on the birth, life, and death of a single hero. Of the eight likely sources of many of the tales only three–*Les repues franches*, the tales of Pfaffe Amis, and the tales of Pfaffe vom Kalenberg–deal exclusively with one hero; and of these only the latter two can be described as having had any extensive influence on the tales of Till Eulenspiegel. Wilhelm Henning, in his introduction to his translation into modern German of *Die Geschicht des Pfarrers vom Kalenberg*, speaks interestingly to this point:

> One can thus divide the *Schwankbücher* into two large groups: the *Schwankzyklen* [jest-cycles], which group themselves around a central figure, and the collections of single jests. . . . [The *Schwankzyklen* find] their prototype in the *Pfaffe Amis*, a

> satirical jest-poem of around the middle of the thirteenth century, written by Der Striker. The Middle High German poet here fastened onto the form of the French *fabliaux*. Except that with the *fabliaux* it is a matter of single, unconnected jests; what is new in the *Pfaffe Amis* is precisely the form of the *Schwankzyklus* (5).

As Henning observes, *Till Eulenspiegel* belongs clearly among the *Schwankzyklen*, a fact which in itself separates N.'s work from all those extra-German *Schwankbücher* which probably had some literary influence on it.

Second, the narrative or descriptive language of the tales, from one end of *Eulenspiegel* to the other, is, in contrast to all the sources, strikingly and curiously lacking in nearly all conventional figures of speech and rhetoric (N.'s Foreword is an exception here; it will be considered later). There is in fact scarcely an instance of metaphor, hyperbole, personification, metonomy, alliteration, *suggestio falsi*, zeugma, syllepsis, anticlimax, apostrophe, pleonasm, litotes, meiosis, hypallage, histeron proteron, asyndeton, and euphemism to be found in any narrative passage in the original. Two similes do occur in Chapters 2 and 7; similes may also, but most rarely, be found in a number of other chapters. Anaphora, which takes the form of a constant use of "and" to run sentences and even transitions together, occurs with great frequency. Its purpose is to create a feeling of casualness (as the effect of the constant repetition of "and" in English prose is to create exactly the opposite effect, to produce instead a clotted English, I have usually omitted it from my translation). The absence of the usual figurative and rhetorical devices of most literature, moreover, becomes fascinating once it is noticed that while N. may have eliminated them from his narrative passages, he has not eliminated them from his passages of conversation and dialogue. Here, in fact, metaphors and similes abound, while other rhetorical devices, such as hyperbole, appear with real frequency. What is even more fascinating is that Eulenspiegel's own speech, along with his behavior, usually glosses, interprets, and satirizes the metaphors, similes, and hyperboles addressed to him by others. He thus appears in many of his adventures to be acting as a clever and ruthless translator and psychologist for people who cannot speak precisely and intelligibly–who constantly speak in metaphors, similes, and hyperboles whose true meanings they blithely ignore. In Chapter 23, for instance, Eulenspiegel is told by the King of Denmark, who enjoys his pranks and wishes to reward him for them, to have his horse shod with "best" horseshoes, and that the royal treasury will pay the cost. The King, as Eulenspiegel at once realizes, is exaggerating: he does not mean "best" at all–the term is an obvious hyperbole–but "good, new, and conventional." Eulenspiegel takes the King at his word, however, and has his horse shod with gold shoes and silver nails. When the King finds out and is presented with an outrageous bill (he seems to have been an unusually tolerant king), he is merely amused. He even acknowledges his exaggerated command by saying to Eulenspiegel, "You're the most valuable of all the people at my court: you do what I tell you!" The point, though, is that the king appears to have learned a lesson of speech and fact. Once he admits his mistake, Eulenspiegel has the gold shoes taken off, and remains with the king to "the end of his days." This not the case, by any means, with the hero of the probable literary source of this tale, Pfaffe vom Kalenberg, in the *Volksbuch* cited above. There the priest is told by a prince to buy himself, at the prince's cost, a new pair of shoes. His own look too shabby to be worn by a priest. Pfaffe vom Kalenberg refuses. It is, he explains, immodest and unwise to spend much money on mere physical decoration. He would prefer simply to have his old shoes repaired. The prince compliments him on his piety. But Pfaffe vom Kalenberg has really been lying. When he finally has the repairs done, he turns the work over to a goldsmith, who covers his shoes with gold enamelling. Pfaffe vom Kalenberg's purpose, as the tale makes plain, is pure deception. He is perfectly willing to allow the prince to pay for the gold on his shoes, and makes no offer, once his mischief is found out, to replace the gold. The contrast with Eulenspiegel's tale could not be clearer. Where Pfaffe vom Kalenberg enjoys the deception for its own sake, Eulenspiegel seems to care, in this adventure at least, about the language people speak, and about the relations between that language and clarity between human beings. The same may be said of more than half of Eulenspiegel's adventures, in which, with impressive obviousness, he spends his time in reacting to the metaphors and hyperboles of others (and as often as not making no money in the process) or in showing others, through rhetorical devices of his own, how language deceives as well as reveals. In Chapter 49, for example, he calls together a convocation of tailors to tell them, as he puts it, something that would "help them and their children forever, for as long as the world lasted." The tailors assume, quite naturally, that he plans to divulge some novel skill, and crowd into a meadow to hear what he has to say. All Eulenspiegel does, however, during a deliberately labored speech, is to tell them to be careful, when threading their needles, that the thread does not slip out. The tailors are understandably furious, but Eulenspiegel has kept his word. What he has told them is indeed something that will help them and their children, even if they knew it beforehand. N.'s idea, again, seems to be that figures of speech and rhetoric often confuse human perceptions of reality–an obvious enough notion in itself, but one that rapidly suggests important questions that reappear throughout N.'s text. The first is: how is humanity to speak at all without such devices? The second, perhaps equally important, is: can linguistic deception be avoided between human beings? These questions, as shrewd as they are implicit in nearly every episode, form one of N.'s grand themes. They are, moreover, almost never, and certainly never as consistently, thematic in any of the literary sources of Eulenspiegel's adventures. The distinguishing mark of N.'s book, in contrast to other jest-books, is that he sets up two worlds for his reader, a world of metaphor or trickery in conversation and dialogue, and a world of spare, straightforward language in his paragraphs of description. The one comments on the other, and both create the literary and even philosophical meanings he has in mind (what these may be are discussed more fully below, under Artistic Achievement). While word plays, puns, and figures of speech abound in all of the literary sources of Eulenspiegel's tales–from Poggio's *Facetiae* to Heinrich Bebel's *Schwänke* to *Les repues franches* to *Il novellino* and the *Schwankbücher* of Pfaffe Amis and Pfaffe vom Kalenberg–the heroes of these tales invariably use their victories in games of words for personal profit and almost never for linguistic and psychological illumination. N.'s two decisively separated worlds, of unadorned language in his narrative passages, and of figurative speech in his conversational passages, not only do not appear in these other texts but it is surely the case that they are unusual in literature generally.

The third distinguishing feature of *Till Eulenspiegel* is its emphasis throughout on the word "truth" and on Eulenspiegel's telling the "truth" or on his having done what his employers have "told him to do," thereby literally or "truthfully" carrying out their instructions. Thus in Chapter 30 he describes himself as one who practices "telling the truth"; in Chapter 14, a crowd of onlookers remarks of him that he is "a charlatan. Still, he spoke the truth"; in Chapter 46, he says, "Isn't it terrible? I do everything that people tell me to – and never seem to earn much thanks at all"; in Chapter 50, he tells a wool-weaver who is furious with him, "I'm doing what you told me"; in Chapter 63, he says, "Isn't it a great wonder? I do everything I'm told – and still earn gratitude nowhere"; and so on, through more than sixty percent of the tales. The persistent emphasis on the word "truth" and on the literal or absurdly precise following of instructions does not appear in the sources of Eulenspiegel's tales. In the sources, again, the stress is on the pleasure of deception, as a sport to be enjoyed for its own sake, rather than on its more serious implications (these will, again, be taken up in more detail below, under Artistic Achievement).

The fourth indication that *Till Eulenspiegel* is a specimen of uniquely complex satire, and that its single author is refashioning the work of his predecessors to suit his own more interesting purposes, appears when it is realized that *Eulenspiegel*, alone among comparable *Schwankbücher* and *Volksbücher*, contains, of all things, no sexual experiences. At least it contains none in which Eulenspiegel himself clearly participates. In Chapter 38 he cheats the priest of Kissenbrück out of his horse by telling him that he has slept with his maid, but the maid denies it, and we get the distinct impression that Eulenspiegel has invented the story to deceive the priest. The title of the story, but not the story itself, describes Eulenspiegel's confession to the priest here as "false." This is actually one of the saddest tales in the book: the suspected maid is beaten, and the priest, who loves her, loses both his maid and his horse. In any event, this is the only incident in the book which refers even mildly to Eulenspiegel's sexual life. Does he, indeed, have a sexual life? Or is he to be thought of, a bit like Swift's Gulliver, as a hero with a massively and satirically anal experience of the world, and with–perhaps as a result–no experiences of either sex or love? Both *Die Geschicht des Pfarrers vom Kalenberg* and *Die Geschicht des Pfaffe Amis* contain not only tales in which the hero seduces various women and shows a delighted interest in sex, but also woodcuts in which the hero appears in bed with the women he seduces. Nothing equivalent is to be found in *Eulenspiegel*, and this despite the fact that all of the other sources of the tales also contain many stories whose theme is sex and that they invariably present sexual experiences in a rather happy-go-lucky manner. Of course, the elimination of sex might not in itself be so striking, were it not for the constant, contrasting appearances, throughout the book, of anal experiences of all types. The word "shit" is liberally used–it may be found in more than fifteen tales–and in many other tales equivalent expressions, such as "excrement," often smile, or grin knowingly, at the reader. To be sure, "shit" shows up in many of the sources as well: the tales of Pfaffe Amis and Pfaffe vom Kalenberg, and the *Facetiae* of Gonella, offer ample documentation of the anal fantasies of the late Middle Ages and the *quattrocento*. All these sources, however, manage to balance their anal episodes (as does Chaucer) with their sexual ones. Their emphasis never lies, as it unmistakably does in *Eulenspiegel*, on the anal to the exclusion of the sexual. Is it not then more than likely that N. deliberately omits the delights of sex, as well as love, precisely so as to focus on a peculiar and unusual "excremental vision" of humanity? In discussing this very possibility with respect to Swift's *Gulliver's Travels*, Norman O. Brown has argued famously that Swift anticipates Freudian theories of anal eroticism in a number of his satirical poems as well as in Gulliver's adventures. Brown writes (190): "But above all the Yahoos are distinguished from other animals by their attitude towards their own excrement. Excrement to the Yahoos is no mere waste product but a magic instrument for self-expression and aggression." The same may be said of Gulliver himself (who, for example, puts out a fire in the palace of the Lilliputian queen by urinating on it) and of Eulenspiegel (who in Chapters 80, 87, and 90, to cite but a few instances of his rather typical behavior, uses his excrement as an obvious means of satire and aggression).

The fifth point is simple but perhaps crucial to what has just been said. This is that more than sixty percent of the tales in

Grüninger's editions of *Eulenspiegel* have no apparent antecedents and must therefore be considered original. This fact gains in importance once it is noticed that most of N.'s excremental tales (such as Chapters 10, 12, and 15) are probably original. It is perhaps possible by now to suggest that part of N.'s accomplishment, as well as his signature, in *Eulenspiegel* lies in his "excremental" slant on the human experience, prior to Swift's. To this it should be added that many of the accompanying woodcuts are similarly "excremental," a fact which indicates that the artist may have understood the tales along these same lines.

The sixth distinguishing quality of *Eulenspiegel* is that, again in contrast to its sources, it presents connected treatments and elaborations of subjects rather than mere anecdotes. Entire groups and professions, such as farmers, carpenters, furriers, tailors, and priests, are treated repeatedly, with various chapters devoted to each one. As a result, mere anecdote, or observation, becomes a series of digressive explorations of human society. Thus Eulenspiegel's encounter with a furrier, in Chapter 52, is purely anecdotal, and its pleasure lies in Eulenspiegel's making a fool of his employer. Eulenspiegel more or less repeats his behavior, though, in Chapter 53. By Chapter 54, in which he sells a group of furriers a live cat sewn into a rabbit skin for a live rabbit, a cumulative effect can – typically – be felt. A whole profession has been laughed out of court. This is the sort of technique that recurs throughout the book, and it extends eventually beyond groups and professions to humanity as whole. On the other hand, N. condenses those tales that he borrows from *Pfaffe Amis* and *Pfaffe vom Kalenberg*, eliminating or cutting sharply the content of the long speeches in verse to be found in them. It is, moreover, precisely those very tales that N. borrows from these two sources that do not receive any elaboration.

The seventh piece of evidence that *Eulenspiegel* is to be thought of as the largely original creation of one unique imagination is to be found in its organization. Honegger (101f) has proposed a revised ordering of the tales, in which Eulenspiegel's life, as well as his encounters with various professions, assumes a chronological and thematic clarity. Sichtermann (335f) supports this alteration. (A chart showing their changes, and a discussion of them, appears below, under Editorial Policy for this Text and Translation.) However, even without so drastic a reshuffling of the tales, the organization of the texts as they stand rapidly becomes clear to the reader. Chapters in the surviving complete editions of 1515 and 1519 – far from piling on each other in some random fashion, as they do in the sources – are frequently, though not always, grouped according to their subjects and their possible psychological effects. For example, N. has evidently taken pains to ensure that we sympathize with Eulenspiegel. Unlike the heroes, such as Pfaffe Amis, of the major sources, Eulenspiegel is presented as by no means invincible, as by no means the constant victor in his exploits. He becomes in fact not only a sympathetic character but also a more interesting one because of his carefully timed defeats. These occur throughout the book, and they seem to be spaced in such a manner as to guarantee that we will think of him as both successful and human in the vast majority of those other tales in which he obviously triumphs. He is ridiculed in Chapters 2 and 3 (and the ridicule seems to create our sympathy for his rather sadistic behavior in Chapters 4 and 5), and utterly defeated in Chapters 7, 18, 66, and 74. In a large number of other stories, moreover, he is cast as an avenger, as a righter of wrongs inflicted on him, and this fact, again, permits us to sympathize with behavior whose sadism we would normally find repulsive. In Chapter 37, for instance, he makes a priest nauseous because the priest has stolen his sausage; in Chapter 39 he wrecks the bed and roof of the house of a smith who tries to overwork him; in Chapter 40 he ruins a smith's tools because the man has offered him excrement to eat; and so on. To be sure, many of the other tales exhibit a sheer sadism which has no basis in any injustice, but the point is that N. seems to be trying, through a deliberately timed series of misadventures, to organize our sympathy with his hero's usual behavior. It is also clear that the volume has a well developed symmetry. Eulenspiegel's mother, who disappears in Chapter 9, reappears in Chapter 89; his youth, during which he seems often to be made the butt of the cruel jokes of others (as in Chapters 1, 2, 3, and 7), seems to be complemented by his old age, during which his victories over smug hypocrites follow without interruption (in Chapters 89 through 94); and the sole episode of what may be termed his "false death," two chapters in which the citizens of Lübeck try to hang him, falls in almost the exact middle of the book (as Chapters 56 and 57), becoming in a real and aesthetic sense the centerpiece of his life:

the priest who confesses him on his death bed, in Chapter 91, refers to this episode as typical of Eulenspiegel's cleverness. The book, in other words, is far more than a compilation and is much better organized, with a higher degree of psychological sensitivity, than one might at first suspect.

What should be clear from these paragraphs is twofold: first, that *Eulenspiegel's* textual and aesthetic evidence strongly indicates, though it does not because it cannot absolutely prove, the presence of a single author here, with a forceful, original imagination; and second, that this author seems to have been torn, not always to his disadvantage, between the desire to write a "pure" *Schwankbuch* and a "pure" satire. N.'s sensibility seems to vacillate between the sort of pure jest or *Schwank* that, finally, lacks the moral and philosophical perceptions of conscience, and serious social mockery of the sort to be found in high satires such as *Gulliver's Travels*. This is why the book seems full so of ambivalence. It is also one of the reasons that it has produced controversy among critics and scholars. It is neither pure *Schwankliteratur* nor pure satire but both, and unique because it is both. It is also not a picaresque novel. With the exception of Eulenspiegel himself, there is nearly no effort to delineate characters in these tales, a feature of the picaresque novel despite its often random-seeming events. Yet *Eulenspiegel* is not in the end a ragged book. To read the tales at one sitting, and to consider all the pieces of evidence cited above, not singly but collectively, is to receive an impression of genuine coherence. The final effect of *Eulenspiegel* is one of delight in humanist contradictions, deliberately left authentic because unresolved, and a modernistic, even dramatic unity. One becomes aware of reading a dramatic work of some sort, rather than simply a series of unconnected adventures. One is aware as well that if the author often seems medieval in his nearly slavish surrender to some of his sources, he also seems utterly modern in his frequent inventiveness and the liberties he grants to his own voice and *Weltanschauung*.

The first suggestion that Hermann Bote might be the author of the tales was made by Christoph Walther in 1892 (Walther, 1-79). While Walther died before publishing his evidence, Honegger has attempted to reconstruct his probable lines of thought, while adding considerably to the already established body of knowledge about Grüninger's texts. Most of this work is extremely valuable. All of it, in its thoroughness, daring, and logic, has resulted in an illumination of many dim and dark areas surrounding the Eulenspiegel legend and its history in print – surely the chief aim of the finest scholarship.

Fishing significant Low German expressions and words out of a number of tales, and examining in detail the locations and descriptions of places to be found in quite a few others, Honegger (presumably like Walther) comes to the conclusion that the author must have been a native of Brunswick [Braunschweig]. In fact, the book's geographical range is relatively narrow. With the exceptions of a tale each set in Rome, Prague, Denmark, and Poland, and references to Eulenspiegel's having visited Flanders and "other countries," which are never named (a reference to Paris in the title of one tale is ignored in the tale itself; see the note on Chapter 64), his adventures take place in and around this Hanseatic city. Even Prague and Denmark, not terribly far away, would hardly tax an inveterate wanderer of Eulenspiegel's ilk. The author's repeated announcement that Eulenspiegel travels widely – as when we read in Chapter 88, that he has "run around through every country" – is less a statement of fact than a literary device. It emphasizes an international quality, and possibly a humanist's broad perspective, that develops as an aura, a subtle tincture, and an atmosphere. The subtitle of Grüninger's editions of 1515 and 1519, moreover, refers to the district or "country" of Brunswick as Eulenspiegel's birthplace. Chapters 19, 44, and 55 are set in Brunswick itself.

These vague indications are merely the beginning of Honegger's case. It is built on a number of skilfully connected facts and complex investigations, some of them by other scholars, and for the sake of new readers should be summarized here (see Honegger, *Ulenspiegel*, 84f). Honegger establishes the date of publication of his newly discovered fragment of the tales largely on the basis of the woodcuts known to have been made by Hans Baldung Grien (29f). These include the title-page woodcut as well as those (whose attribution to Baldung Grien is more questionable) for Chapters 1, 5, 6, 8, 10, 11, 12, and 22. (None of these actually appears in Honegger's fragment, though they do in Bernd Ulrich Hucker's larger fragment found in 1975; Honegger assumed, correctly, that because the typography of his fragment is

Grüninger's, and because in most other respects, such as certain other woodcuts, his fragment is identical with Grüninger's other Eulenspiegel texts, these woodcuts did appear with it.) Hans Baldung Grien, who illustrated several of Grüninger's books, to wit, *Die zehen Gebot*, was definitely in Strassburg in 1509. Allowing for the customary lapse of a year or so between the commissioning of illustrations and the appearance of the printed book, as evidenced by Grüninger's and other publishers' known business practices, it seems reasonable to conclude that Honegger's fragment dates from 1510-11, and that it is probably a specimen of the first published edition of the tales (the edition differs in slight but revelatory textual ways from the 1515 edition). Honegger is led to believe that Hermann Bote must be the author of this edition by what he terms "a stunning number of parallels" between phrases in the text and various works now attributed to Bote. Some of these will be taken up directly below, along with Honegger's conviction that Bote actually "signed" his name to the book in an acrostic – the clincher, so to speak, of Honegger's argument. First it may be useful to recount what is known about Bote himself.

Almost completely unfamiliar to the reading public in Germany and elsewhere up to the present moment, though described by the critic Joseph Nadler in 1939 as the "most gifted poet of the fifteenth century, perhaps of the whole Low Saxon stock," Hermann Bote was the son of a Brunswick blacksmith. By 1488, when Bote would have been in his twenties, he was working as a custom-house clerk. In around 1493, he took a job as a bailiff, and thereafter as manager of the Brunswick Altstadt-Ratskeller. From 1497 till 1513, he apparently worked again as a customs clerk. Between 1516 and 1520, when he died, he worked as the manager of a municipal tile factory, producing tiles for roofs. Honegger would set his birth date as early as 1463 (85), and his death date as late as 1525, but what is clear is that, allowing for a few brief trips to other cities such as (perhaps) Strassburg, he spent his entire life in Brunswick. He could have done far worse. At the close of the fifteenth century, Brunswick was a commercial center of importance and a member of the Hanseatic League (see also the note on Chapter 49). Its magnificent town hall and St. Martin's Church, in Gothic style, were already regarded as masterpieces. The town hall, particularly, opposite the church, with its L-shape and two open arcades, was, and is, a triumph of pomp and utility. The arcades were built in 1393 and 1447 respectively, and designed with delicate plumes of tracery that provided an inspirational and sensual backdrop to ordinary business transactions. They formed two spectacular sides of the market place. In Bote's day, in cities such as Brunswick, urban life was thus shrewdly setting in place a security and prosperous independence well removed from the nervous protection of the cloister and the castles of the frequently repressive nobility. The cathedral, as well, boasted several examples of the finest Romanesque sculpture. A striking Romanesque statue, the noted bronze lion of Brunswick, free-standing on an outdoor pillar, still complements in its hints of a startling new realism the marble effigies of Henry the Lion and his duchess Matilda, made in about 1240, with their drapery that seems ruffled by breezes and their faces that are surely portraits from life. Artisans' and craftsmen's guilds, too, played influential roles on the city's political and economic stages. This fact has some relevance to the little that has so far been unearthed about Bote (there is as yet no full biography). In 1488, for allegedly mocking the power of the guilds, he was punished with house-arrest and lost his job as a customs clerk. In 1513, during a rebellion of the guilds against civil authorities, Bote nearly lost his life (Sichtermann, 10). To be sure, Brunswick, like other German cities, was frequently the site of violent struggles between the increasingly avaricious commercial and artisans' guilds and the municipal government. It thus comes as no surprise that Bote, who sided with his citizen-employers, or "Patricians," found himself threatened, out of work, and almost the victim of a murderous retribution.

His virtual anonymity as an author comes as no surprise either, though it poses thorny questions, especially in trying to decide whether he wrote the Eulenspiegel stories. Fears of censorship, imprisonment, and execution led many authors of the Middle Ages and Renaissance to omit their names from their works. Latin satirical literature of the eleventh and twelfth centuries is often anonymous, but here, as W.T.H. Jackson points out, the reason was often simply that the writer "was not thinking of impressing an audience" (53). In Bote's case, with the works that can confidently be seen as his, the matter of attribution seems often to involve discovering and decoding the acrostical games that he likes to play with his readers. In fact Bote's connection with a great deal that is now regarded as authentically his has been managed by this curious method, combined with circumstantial evidence. Werner Wunderlich's commentary on one of these works, *Dat boek van veleme rade* (or *Das Radbuch*, *The Book of Wheels*), ca. 1492-93, offers a list of twenty-four lyric poems, chronicles, and narratives, including *Till Eulenspiegel*, considered as possibly Bote's. A couple of these, *Dat narren schyp* (1497) and *Reynke de vos* (1498), remain extremely dubious. Lacking an acrostical means of identifying Bote or any other author, they are thought to be probably by Bote simply because they are bound together with other works, such as *Der Koker* (ca. 1520), which do exhibit Bote's characteristic acrostics.

The verbal parallels that Honegger discovers between known works of Bote and *Till Eulenspiegel* consist of four sentences from *Der Koker*, one from a *Weltchronik* by Bote, a number of phrases from the Foreword to Bote's *Radbuch*, and eight phrases from a single tale in Bote's *Schichtbuch* (1510/13-1514), a tale that itself echoes Eulenspiegel's adventure with the furriers of Leipzig, in which he sells them a cat in a rabbit skin for a live rabbit (Chapter 54). Typical of the parallels cited by Honegger is this from the *Koker*: "We dar verladen ist mit schelken de mach sine slippen afsniden" (711/12), which he pairs with this from Chapter 44 of *Eulenspiegel*: "Wer mit schalkßleuten beladen ist/der sol den schlupff abschneide" [Whoever's bothered by tricksters should cut the traces]. The ideas here are close enough, but once it is realized that the author is merely repeating what is probably an old saw, or popular saying of some sort, the relationship seems less impressive. In fact *Der Koker*, or *Köker* in High German, is simply an anthology of such sayings (see also Chapter 18, with its note, for another equally unpersuasive example of the same thing). The parallel Honegger cites from Bote's *Weltchronik* is with a sentence in *Eulenspiegel's* Chapter 89, "Als einß menschen lebe ist/so ist ouch sein end" [A man dies as he has lived], and is again simply and obviously a popular maxim rather than a set of phrases whose literary originality reveals a distinctive style. These are, indeed, the types of statements that one actually expects to find in many sorts of books, and whose very omission would be a surprise. *Eulenspiegel* contains quite a few of them. Most do not echo Bote. None, certainly, and Honegger himself admits as much, amounts to a convincing proof of authorship. The same may be said of the phrases cited from Bote's serpentine and fascinating *The Book of Wheels*. This is a complex poem in rhyming couplets, blocked out in eleven sections, each illustrated with a woodcut. As Wunderlich observes (149), it comes straight out of a surviving medieval tradition of allegory. Bote here seizes on a slew of ancient ideas about wheels, including such fairly obvious ones as the mill wheel ("the oldest known machine") and the wheel of fortune, and describes them as symbols of human ethical perils. The tone throughout is didactic, unrelieved by irony, unspiced with humor, or for that matter, with *Eulenspiegel's* jests, stories, and *exempla*. The author's attitude, which is consistent from section to section, remains grim. It would be difficult to imagine a piece of writing more opposite, in style and heavy-handed approach, to the casual and punning light-heartedness of *Till Eulenspiegel*. Despite these drastic differences, Honegger maintains not only that the books are by the same author, but that the Eulenspiegel stories represent a "completion" of the themes in Bote's *The Book of Wheels*. They do this, he suggests, by playing a satirical game with them. This is an idea that seems as odd and questionable as Honegger's speculation that the wagon wheel on which Eulenspiegel seats himself in Chapter 82 is no mere literary coincidence: it too must verify a connection between the books. How or why this is the case is not made clear by internal evidence. The same occurs with the similar or identical phrases. These likewise turn out to be literary conventions or idiomatic expressions (these conventions in N.'s Foreword are taken up under Sources and Influence, below). The words that Honegger adduces are simply too ordinary to demonstrate shared authorship. Eulenspiegel's adventure with Leipzig's furriers, which does strongly resemble a tale in Bote's *Schichtbuch*, proves equally refractory. The phrases cited, none of them particularly original, imply that Bote may have read *Eulenspiegel*, or vice versa, that N. may have read Bote. But few people, it may be imagined, would seriously maintain that because a number of Holinshed's episodes and expressions correspond with Shakespeare's, that Holinshed must be the author of *Macbeth*.

As noted above, Honegger recognizes these problems. He is far too solid a scholar to base his case on mere flimsy threads. He bases it on Bote's acrostics. These occur – but do they occur in

Eulenspiegel? The acrostics that occur in Bote's *Book of Wheels* and his *Köker* are of two types. One consists of an arrangement of the initial capital letters of various sections in a run-through of the alphabet. The other, which appears in his *Book of Wheels*, uses the ten initial capital letters at the start of ten of the book's chapters to spell out HERMEN BOTE. Honegger claims that both types are present in *Eulenspiegel*. The alphabet, which for Bote would have consisted of twenty-three letters (with I, U, and X omitted), shows up in four run-throughs, followed in (Chapters 90 through 95, according to the original numbering) by ERMANB, or what Honegger regards as an acrostic of Bote's name. As will be seen, both types present serious problems. The problem with the second, for example, is of course that it is not there. The first letter of Bote's first name is missing. The last three letters of his surname are also missing. A similar problem arises with the alphabetical "acrostics." These are not present either. The Foreword begins with A (in *Als*), and is followed, in Chapter 1, by the initial capital B (in *Bei*). This arrangement appears in both the 1515 and 1519 editions. It is followed, in both editions, by a nearly total disruption of the sequence. A number, though very few, of the letters in the remaining three alphabetical sequences show up in their proper places. The letter A begins Chapter 48, for instance, with a capital B succeeding it in Chapter 49. Chapter 72 begins with an A, while Chapter 73 starts off with a B. Quite spectacular gaps occur in all four sequences, however, and letters such as A, which appears at the beginning of twelve chapters, and B, which is the initial letter in eleven, pop up with an uneasy, defeating frequency. Seven letters simply refuse to start off any chapters at all (K, O, P, Q, T, W, and Y). 39 of 96 possible initial capital letters actually conform to Honegger's proposed patterns, including Bote's "acrostical name" at the end of the book. 57 do not. To be sure, Honegger offers complex and intriguing solutions to these disturbances of his acrostics. A couple of his solutions are not only intriguing but fairly drastic. The question is whether they can be accepted (a number of scholars do accept them), whether they seem plausible.

This is not an issue that can be completely laid to rest. Suffice it that for the time being at least prickly doubts must reasonably persist about the solutions as well as the acrostical methods. What Honegger proposes is (a) that the tales are sloppily misarranged, and (b) that the original capital letters at the beginnings of a great many chapters have been altered, or ignored, probably by Grüninger's printer. Honegger justifies these beliefs on the basis of three assumptions: (1) the clear connections between various tales have been severed and must be restored; (2) the geography of Eulenspiegel's adventures has also been rendered senseless through a disorderly presentation; and (3) the "true" *Weltanschauung* of the book, which is the same as Bote's in his *Book of Wheels*, has similarly been obliterated through misarrangement and must be reestablished. A fourth assumption, unmentioned, is that the entire book must be straightened out, so to speak. It is to be subjected to a *scrutin épuratoire*, in which, with tidiness as the rule, order will be made to appear. Eulenspiegel's exploits with carpenters will follow each other without interruptions. His references to his trip to Rome will be neatly linked. A strictly moral viewpoint, unapparent in the book as it stands, but very much like Bote's in its relentless revelations of sin and doom, will shine forth with a ghastly light. It perhaps needs scarcely to be mentioned that the surviving complete texts of Eulenspiegel's adventures not only make no such demands but suggest exactly opposed lines of thought. There is no intrinsic reason to assume that an author who was creating a literary hero out of legendary fragments, who was, as he says, "compiling" adventures, saw any particular need of this sort of orderliness and tidiness. He may only have seen a need of the sort of loose and baggy, but pleasant, monster that now exists. In an important essay criticizing Honegger's belief that the tales reflect some sort of strictly theological morality (Honegger, "Eulenspiegel und die sieben Todsünden"), Hans Wiswe not only shows how numerous tales contradict this hypothesis but also questions how Bote, whether he wrote the book or not, could possibly have written it in the versions that have survived (Wiswe, 180-81). Wiswe argues that there was certainly no need for Bote, who conventionally wrote in Low German, to shift to High German in any case. Low German was a perfectly acceptable business and literary form of the language. Wiswe speculates that someone else may have translated the book into Late Middle High German. This itself is a dubious hypothesis: there is no reason to believe, simply on the basis of a scattering of words present in the texts from Low German, that the book was not written in High German.

Honegger certainly seems convinced that it was, and also that Bote resorted to an acrostical misspelling of his name in *Eulenspiegel* to conceal his identity, presumably from enemies among his fellow Brunswickers. Aside from the purely speculative nature of this proposition – there is simply no evidence to support it – it seems to make little sense. One does not conceal a name by revealing it. Nor does it make much sense, if one wishes to reveal a name, to do so incompletely. Honegger suggests that a missing tale may account for the absent H at the beginning of Bote's name, but evidence to support this idea is also missing. Lindow (*Korrespondenzblatt*, 31-2) cites parallel Low German texts and phrases in urging that a Low German H, in the 89th tale, was altered to yield the N, in the word "Nun," with which the tale now begins. While this speculation is certainly interesting, it remains a speculation. Honegger's own speculations that a large number of capital letters at the beginnings of chapters have been carelessly changed or replaced, and that the order of the tales has been violently reshuffled, are rather weakly supported by such evidence as he advances. It may indeed be true that the letter E, for instance, in Chapter 4, should be inserted before the J in JN, with which the tale begins (so that it will read "Ein"). What, however, is one to make of his radically changing the word order at the beginnings of chapters to allow them to fit into the proposed acrostical patterns? This is what is offered for no less than eight chapters (4, 5, 6, 29, 32, 33, 53, and 60), along with a rearrangement of twelve chapters (or over eleven percent of the book). Other obvious questions remain. If the tales are so misarranged, why was the disorder never noticed? Why was it repeated in print and not only by Grüninger in 1519, but in many editions thereafter? Why would Grüninger, who presumably saw the tales in their "correct" sequence, tolerate such a remarkably different one? The absence of clear answers to such questions, to date, leaves a great deal up in the air. Certainly the case for Hermann Bote's authorship is unproved. It is a possibility, no more, at this point. Nor, of course, is the initial N, with which the author introduces himself, terribly helpful. Probably it is not an initial at all, but simply the first letter of "*Name*," as in "name to be inserted."

What should probably be remembered at this point is that a major and obvious theme of the book is disguise. The hero disguises himself constantly. Peculiarly, the author does too. The result is an atmosphere of invisibility. It is precisely this atmosphere that dovetails so neatly with Eulenspiegel's infinite gift for escaping the consequences of his acts. He nearly always escapes at once, and always escapes later. Even his death involves an escape. His last little trick consists of leaving his friends, the town council of Mölln, and the priest who confesses him a chest full of stones. He gets away with tricking these people while satirizing their appetite for his supposed "treasure" by being safely dead and buried, or invisible. By then the author too has disappeared. Not only is his book finished, or as finished as he apparently wishes to leave it, but he has managed to write ninety-five brief tales without surrendering more than a few solid facts about himself. This in itself is a *tour de force*, and certainly a triumph of modesty over authorial vanity. What he leaves behind is his delectable puzzle. If some puzzles are solvable equations, while others are permanently secret labyrinths, still others are spotlights, casting an irradiant glow over their creators and their age. The puzzle of authorship here is a spotlight. It illuminates the contradictions, sense of humor, and impudence of the age of humanism in Germany and elsewhere, while its glow is so bright that it leaves its creator a mere silhouette.

SOURCES AND INFLUENCE

Whoever wrote *Eulenspiegel* must have been widely read and a good listener. At least thirty-three of the tales appear to be taken directly from earlier authors, and many of the rest contain echoes, phrases, and aphorisms found in previous texts. Popular sayings and maxims are rife (these are considered in the Notes on the Tales). N.'s recipe is typical of his medieval and Renaissance literary contemporaries, and he mixes a familiar if often heady brew. It freely distills the plots and themes of numerous stories, along with well known motifs, in an age when plagiarism, in the modern sense of literary theft, scarcely existed as a vice. The older and more recognizable the textual source, the more likely it was to be "true." As C.S. Lewis observes, "Almost the typical activity of the medieval [and

Renaissance] author consists of touching up something that was already there; as Chaucer touched up Boccaccio, as Malory touched up French prose romances which themselves touched up earlier romances in verse. . . . The predecessor is usually much more than a 'source' in the sense in which an Italian novel may be the source of a Shakespearian play" (209). The voice, however, or *langue personnelle*, in the phrase of Edmond de Goncourt, is always N.'s.

Lappenberg, Lindow, and other scholars trace the adapted tales and the Foreword to nine sources: Pfaffe Amis, Pfaffe vom Kalenberg, Gonella, Poggio, *Le cento novelle antiche*, Morlini, Heinrich Bebel, *Les repues franches*, and the prose romance *Wigoleis vom Rade*. Kadlec, in his still useful investigations of the sources, usually follows Lappenberg. His improvements, like those of more recent investigators, are greater thoroughness and sometimes greater accuracy of critical judgment, these due chiefly to the revisions of opinion necessitated by Schröder's important discovery of Grüninger's edition of 1515 and his publication of a facsimile of it in 1911 (the discovery is taken up below, under Editorial Policy for this Text and Translation). Kadlec (9) proposes that Chapters 14 and 23 derive from *Die Geschicht des Pfaffe vom Kalenberg*, which first began to circulate as a rhymed *Volksbuch* toward the end of the fifteenth century. Chapters 17, 27, 28, 29, and 31 are traceable to *Der Pfaffe Amis*. N.'s Foreword has come under careful scrutiny by John Flood, who in an illuminating essay argues that it must, regardless of contemporary attitudes toward plagiarism, in fact be a pilfering of the foreword to the prose romance *Wigoleis vom Rade*. Flood adduces correspondences of phrases and tone to support his thesis, which also provides independent confirmation that *Eulenspiegel* dates from post-1493, when Wirnt von Grafenberg's thirteenth-century verse romance *Wigalois vom Rade* first appeared in its prose version. While this is quite possible, it must also be noted that N.'s *Eulenspiegel* is equally indebted, and in similar ways, to the foreword of the Pfaffe vom Kalenberg stories. The truth is that all three forewords are outfitted with commonplace literary conventions. These become a costume and a mask. They are an invitation and a smokescreen. Readers of the Middle Ages and Renaissance would certainly have felt, amid strikingly familiar expressions, the comforts of recognition. Thus the author of the Pfaffe vom Kalenberg stories presents himself in his opening lines as someone who is not widely read, is lacking in literary skills, and cannot speak well (lines 1-6), feints which are rather neatly echoed in N.'s introductory sentences. In line 8, the Kalenberg author uses the term "suptile," as he rather suspiciously bemoans his lack of clever and flowery words [suptile and gelumpte wart]. The same word, in a nearly identical context, appears in N.'s Foreword, in which he says, "Es ist auch in disem meinem schlechte schreiben kein kunst oder subteilichkeit" [Also there is in this my rather plain writing no art or elegance]. In line 9 of the Kalenberg book, the Greco-Latinate "rhetorica" is tossed in casually as the author falsely disclaims all knowledge of rhetoric. It performs the sort of ironic task that N. assigns to his occasional latinisms, letting the reader know that the author is far more sophisticated than he pretends to be and that his book is some sort of jest. The word "subtile" also appears, and again in a nearly identical context, in *Wigoleis vom Rade*, in which the author likewise denies, as one might expect, his abilities in written Latin. Of the nine parallel phrases and instances that Flood cites in *Eulenspiegel* and *Wigoleis*, six are either also imitated from the Kalenberg *Vorrede*, or – and this is far more significant – recommended as correct authorial practice by Matthieu de Vendôme in his *Ars versificatoria*. Matthieu's book, which dates from the late twelfth century, was an extremely influential and widely read manual on the art of rhetoric in poetry. Matthieu suggests, among other things, that an author deny his learning and beg to be excused for his failures (*veniae petitionem*). Both of these conventional approaches to readers are present in *Eulenspiegel*, as they are in *Wigoleis* and the Kalenberg stories, a fact that, combined with the lighthearted tone of all three, argues less for successive acts of plagiarism (though this is perfectly possible) than for authors following an accepted formula. Even the opening phrases of Eulenspiegel's adventures (ALs man zalt von Crist geburt), which appear almost word for word in *Wigoleis* (ALs man zalt von der geburt Christi), are obviously conventional, and may be found, for instance, in Hans Sachs' "Summa all meiner gedicht vom MDXIIII jar an biß ins 1567 jar": "Als man zelt viertzehundert jar." So may the disclaimer of learning, with Sachs describing himself, in lines 251-2, as "einem ungelehrten mann,/Der weder latein noch griechisch kan" [an uneducated man,/Who knows neither Latin nor Greek]. The denial of classical learning, as a humanist convention by the time *Eulenspiegel* came to be written in 1500, also suggests the humanist leanings and sympathies of its author. At any rate, the fact that N. uses standard conventions of rhetoric in his Foreword makes it an act of uninspired daring to draw any large conclusions about him from what he says here. He writes in jest.

Kadlec believes that Chapters 24, 26, 35, 70, and 86 of *Eulenspiegel* are similar to certain adventures of Gonella, the court fool of Count Niccolò d'Este and his son Borso, Duke of Ferrara. These were collected in *Facecie del Gonella composte per maestro Francesco, dicto maestro Raynaldo da Mantua* (Bologna, 1506). The adventures are indeed similar, while the date may indicate that in 1506 the author of the Eulenspiegel stories was still at work on his job of compilation. An example of the similarity is to be found in Gonella's encounter with the Duke of Ferrara's servant (stanzas 3-9), which may be compared with Eulenspiegel's exploit at the court of the King of Poland (Chapter 26). Gonella, in this *facezia*, is a boy of seven and already a favorite of the Duke. The boy pretends to fall ill, and the Duke asks him what he needs to recover. Gonella at first refuses to tell him, but when pressed, answers, "Voria de un stronzo, habenche e dishonesto" ["I'd like a piece of shit, even though it's disgusting"]. The Duke's servant, Gonella complains, concealing his rivalry, would never fulfill his request. The Duke summons his servant, terrifies him with threats of torture, and forces him to do whatever Gonella wants. Gonella naturally asks for the "stronzo," which, after some delay, the servant manages to produce. Gonella now orders the servant to chew the "stronzo" a bit to prepare it for him, and the servant does this too. When the servant finally tries to offer the awful stuff to Gonella, though, the child-buffoon, much to the delight of the Duke and his household, says,

"Tu li ciciasti ogni sapore,
Et or a me me porgi la vinaza.
Mo mangial tu; che'l mal pro si te faza!"

["You've chewed up all the good stuff here,
And now you're giving me the refuse.
Better you eat it. May it make you sick!"]

Kadlec describes the interesting correspondences between this tale and Chapter 26 of *Eulenspiegel*: the competition between two servants, both of whom are eager for a reward from a powerful noble; the noble's recklessness, his tolerance of wild and obscene behavior; the focusing of the reader's attention on Gonella and the servant, with the noble and his household functioning as mere background figures; the eating of human excrement as a humiliating test; and finally the rogue's triumph. While it is impossible to prove any direct relationship between Gonella and Eulenspiegel (Kadlec stubbornly denies one, citing the parallels expertly enough), it seems likely that one exists.

Lappenberg, Kadlec, and Lindow point to similarities between a number of Eulenspiegel's tales and those of Poggio Bracciolini, the Italian humanist, classicist, and author who died in 1459 (see also the reference to him, above, under Date and Authorship). Poggio's *Facetiae* was published in Nuremberg during the 1470s, and shortly afterwards the book became well known throughout Germany. Versions of it were definitely available in Strassburg by 1511 (Fubini, v, n). The influence of Poggio on German *Schwankliteratur* of the sixteenth century was considerable, and in Eulenspiegel's case extended into one of the sources of Eulenspiegel's adventures as well as into the adventures themselves. The author of the tales of Pfaffe vom Kalenberg appears to have read Poggio, and Chapters 14, 17, 29, and 61 of Eulenspiegel's adventures parallel episodes in Poggio as well as in this German source. Whether N. himself read Poggio is unknown, though it is hard to see how he could at the very least have escaped hearing about his work.

Le cento novelle antiche, also known as *Il novellino*, the Italian collection of facetious tales, perhaps by more than one author, dating from the last decade of the thirteenth century, seems also to have had some influence. Lappenberg doubts that N. had actually read this book, though he does not dismiss the possibility (360). Kadlec discovers relations between Novella IX and Chapter 79 of Eulenspiegel's adventures, as well as between Novella X and Chapter 90 of the edition of the tales published in Erfurt in 1532 (this chapter does not appear in Grüninger's editions, and is thus part of the "Zusatzgeschichten"). Kadlec traces Chapter 79, in which Eulenspiegel pays an innkeeper with the sound of his money, even further back, to Plutarch and to India (see also the note on this tale).

Another detectable influence is that of Morlini, whose exceedingly rare *Opus Morlini complectans novellas, fabulas et comoediam* was first published in Naples in 1520. Lappenberg believes that Chapter 2 of Eulenspiegel's tales is a modified version of Morlini's Novella XLIV, and that several other tales bear comparison with Morlini's Novella LXXIII, in which a servant interprets his master's instructions literally. Kadlec, who prefers to think of the literary Eulenspiegel, as well as the possibly legendary one, as utterly German, as a type of *Volksmund*, rather predictably argues against any borrowings (73f). He also rejects Lappenberg's suggestion (248) that Chapter 34, in which Eulenspiegel meets the pope, has any literary relation to Morlini's Novella XII, "De colono, qui ut regem alloqui posset, quadrupedem se fecit." It is impossible to tell whether Kadlec is right or wrong here, but it is a fact that both motifs are common to early folktales of many parts of Europe, among them Hungary and England (Kadlec, 77; on the motif of the servant who interprets his master's instructions literally, see also Thompson, 195, and below, under Artistic Achievement).

Heinrich Bebel, the autodidact, humanist, professor at Tübingen, and author (who died in 1514), exerted a solid influence on German *Schwankliteratur* of the sixteenth century. It has frequently been assumed that Bebel influenced *Till Eulenspiegel* as well, though in the light of Honegger's recent discovery this possibility must now be considered doubtful. Lappenberg, for instance, believes that Bebel is the source of Chapters 35, 69, 79, and 81, while Kadlec wishes to see the influence as running in just the opposite direction, with the same chapters serving as models for four jests in Bebel's *Facetiae*, first published in 1512. The chronological priority of Grüninger's first edition of Eulenspiegel's adventures, as established by Honegger, shows the probable correctness of Kadlec's view. Chapter 79, as remarked above, also finds a likely source in *Le cento novelle antiche* (see the note on this tale).

The last major source that needs mentioning here is *Les repues franches*, an anonymous collection of tales, with the poet François Villon as hero, first published before 1493. Lappenberg argues that Chapters 6, 57, 61, 62, and 72 are derived from this work. Kadlec agrees to similarities between these chapters and various tales in the French collection, but denies any literary relations. Joseph Bédier, in 1925, apparently believed in some sort of literary relations, and there is certainly no reason now to dismiss the possibility. What should be clear, in this as in other cases of sources, though, is that the question of borrowings, whether of phrases, plots, situations, or all three, simply complements N.'s announcement in his Foreword that he has been asked to compile or collect various tales. Nor is there any true question of plagiarism involved in any of these instances, at least not in the modern sense of the word. Plagiarism implies secrecy. For N. and his Renaissance audience the pleasure certainly lay in the open retelling of popular anecdotes, episodes, and stories. Often the pleasure also lay in the transposition of a tale from one setting or hero to another, accompanied by the happy introduction of a new sensibility. N. constantly extracts honey from rich public hives. A good deal of the entertainment in what he does, as when Ovid retells a famous myth, lies in watching a shrewd honey-bear at work.

Even more striking than the numbers of sources that contribute to *Eulenspiegel*, and which combine with the author's remodeling of them, is the book's enormous influence. As has been suggested, it endures to this day. It reaches into literature, art, music, philosophy, and dance. It also digs even deeper, into national consciousness and character, into the mysteries of ancient linguistic community. To be sure, the proposition that national characters exist is itself a Pandora's box full of doubts and eclipsing confusions. Probably no serious investigator would maintain that people need to read to acquire a national character. On the other hand, powerful works of art obviously produce ripples and waves. People who rarely read, or do not read at all, and who may never have heard of a particular work, are influenced by it. Turner's sunsets are seen by thousands, perhaps millions, who have never seen Turner's pictures. Hemingway's clipped prose is spoken and written by masses of people who have never heard of his novels. E.E. Cummings' massacre of punctuation has led to hundreds of volumes of mispunctuated poetry, many of them no doubt produced by authors who have never read a line of Cummings' poems. The idea that the culture and character of a people are both revealed and formed by language, myth, and certain enduringly popular works of art is at least as old as Vico (1668-1744). It leads to the important, if presently obvious-sounding, formulation of Herder (1748-1803) that one of the deepest human needs, often deeper than material satisfaction, is "to belong to identifiable communal groups, each possessing its own unique language, traditions, historical memories, style and outlook" (Hausheer, xxxvi). While the idea of nationhood is implied by this concept, nationalism, in the modern sense of group superiority, or in its extreme forms the adoration of the nation or state as a replacement of religious experiences, is not. As Isaiah Berlin observes (341), "In this sense, nationalism does not seem to exist in the ancient world, nor in the Christian Middle Ages." Prejudice alone is not patriotism. Xenophobia is not ideology. Nor is the mere popularity of a work of art an indicator that it is a teacher of more than fleeting habits. Popularity and endurance are what count. It is the vast appeal over centuries of Dante's *Commedia*, tenuous though that popularity was from 1400 to 1750, that suggests that the *Commedia* has become a friendly and magisterial tutor and shaper of Italian consciousness and character. Nor is this idea meant to open yet another Pandora's box, this time one full of murky metaphysical terminology. It is meant only to underline the obvious fact that Dante's *Commedia* necessarily affects Italian readers in special ways. It surely offers them a more intense and personal cultural intimacy than it offers to non-Italian readers, to whom, simply and marvelously, it may present an eternal fastidious glory. By the same lights, *Don Quixote* echoes and creates part of what may be termed a Spanish national character. *Huckleberry Finn* and *Walden* have created American attitudes, or part of America's national character, as much as they winnowed them from the country at large. The issue here is the truth of Oscar Wilde's proposition that nature imitates art. Nor can Wilde's insight realistically be seen as indifferent to biological, geographical, linguistic, and social contexts. It merely confirms his *mot* about *Hamlet*: "Before Shakespeare wrote *Hamlet*, there was no such person. Afterwards, there were thousands." In fact, of course, this cannot literally be true. After Shakespeare wrote *Hamlet*, there were no more Hamlets than before. What was new was a style of perception and a fashion. National character, as distinct from nationalism, is nothing but a series of peculiar autochthonous fashions. In large measure, these are invented, or at least given memorable forms, by popular and enduring works of art. As a result, to suggest that *Eulenspiegel* has been playing an important attitude-creating role among Germans, a bit like the role of Malory's *Le Morte D'Arthur* among the English, is not at all far-fetched. To believe that it is one finely ground lens among many through which to observe the development of a modern German national character may not be so far-fetched either. The fact that nearly everyone in Germany has read Till Eulenspiegel's adventures, albeit for the most part in childishly truncated and censored versions, doing so for five centuries by now, surely suggests that this is a strong likelihood. So do the literally thousands of cases of *Eulenspiegel's* recorded influence on the arts.

The most famous, and certainly one of the most eloquent, of these in modern times is Richard Strauss' tone poem *Till Eulenspiegels lustige Streiche* [*Till Eulenspiegel's Merry Pranks*] (1895), which is played in concert halls the world over. Strauss' fifteen-minute composition for orchestra captures accurately, and even deliciously, the accents of Eulenspiegel's foolishness, mischief, courage, and scorn. The composer's choice of the rondo form is also entirely appropriate to N.'s essentially picaresque demi-novel, which contains many minor climaxes and many unconnected episodes, but no main climax and no main plot. The scampering twists and turns of the music mimic well N.'s style, with its mix of informality, roughness, slang, lightness, and, here and there, formal speech. A similarly happy and significant influence is to be found in Wilhelm Busch's *Max und Moritz*, again a work that is universally known, especially among Geman-speaking children, and quite possibly in Nietzsche's *Also sprach Zarathustra* (see the notes on Chapter 8 and 3, respectively; a great many of the literary influences, especially on Renaissance authors, are mentioned in the notes on the tales, below). Claudia Ross Pierpont refers to a "Tyl Eulenspiegel" ballet by Nijinsky, which failed to survive its first season, and is known only through a few photographs and descriptions (Pierpont, 88). Nor are these recent instances of *Eulenspiegel's* continuing penetration into the cultural life of German-speaking peoples and elsewhere terribly surprising. Within seventy years of Grüninger's first editions of the tales, they were translated into Dutch, English, French, Latin, Danish, Polish,

Czech, and probably Italian. Between the seventeenth and nineteenth centuries, translations appeared in Swedish, Russian, Hungarian, Serbo-Croatian, Norwegian, and Romanian. In the twentieth century alone, editions have appeared in Afrikaans, Chinese, Estonian, Finnish, Japanese, Italian, modern Greek, Serbian, Spanish, Thai, four Indian languages (Hindi, Bengali, Marati, and Urdu), and Esperanto. Sichtermann (17) records over 350 German editions since the first ones (to 1980), with over 150 of these, including those designed specifically for children, published since the Second World War. Possibly the best known version of Eulenspiegel's adventures remains the severely bowdlerized adaptation by Charles Theodore Henri de Coster (Brussels, 1867), a sanitized and idealized treatment, translated on occasion into English, that bears only a limp relationship to the original.

In addition to Renaissance artists, such as Hans Baldung Grien, who contributed to the earliest editions and whose woodcuts are discussed under The Woodcuts, below, Eulenspiegel has figured importantly in the art of Josef Hegenbarth, Alfred Kubin, Frans Masereel, and A. Paul Weber (Sichtermann, 23 n40). Scholarly and critical publications, as noted earlier under Date and Authorship, have multiplied in recent decades. The *Eulenspiegel-Jahrbuch*, published in Schöppenstedt, where the Till Eulenspiegel Museum is also located, has appeared regularly since 1960. Since 1967, the *Jahrbuch* has been issued by the Freundeskreis Till Eulenspiegels. While a complete listing of all of *Eulenspiegel's* influences in many fields, including drama and film, has not yet been compiled (a film by Christa Wolf is cited in the Bibliography), it is safe to say that works shaped and influenced in some fashion by N.'s *Volksbuch* number in the several thousands. With all this attention lavished on a book written in Late Middle High German in 1500 or so, by an author whose identity is obscure, it is obviously appropriate to ask how and why, to inquire into some of the sources in the book itself of the enduring platinum radiance of its attraction.

ARTISTIC ACHIEVEMENT

Till Eulenspiegel is one of the most scandalous characters, and one of the queerest fish, in the history of German fiction. Even his name, which in modern German means "owl glass" or "owl mirror" or "wise mirror" or, metaphorically, "wise reflection," but which also had more sinister meanings in the sixteenth century, has provoked controversy among scholars who question whether his name has any meanings at all. He is a creature, and largely literary creation, of infinite contradictions and skirmishing paradoxes. He died, or so the last chapter of his adventures announces, in 1350, but it is a puzzle whether he ever lived. He practices, or so he says in Chapter 30, the telling of the "truth," but his definition of "truth" is odd, and by any usual standards he must be judged a liar. His incessant need to expose human gullibility, superstitious fears, and naive frailties – this, if anything, is the theme of his life – has so horrified translators and adaptors of his tales that they have consistently mistranslated, misadapted, misrepresented, and mischristened them, subjecting them to a prudishness that would no doubt have made Eulenspiegel and his sixteenth-century audience laugh with derision. George Bollenbeck, in his important book on the disperate studies and treatments of Eulenspiegel since the Renaissance, notes that he has been variously regarded as an avenger of peasants, a representative of the oppressed, a romantic loser, a rebel, a nihilist, a callous judge of humanity, an embodiment of German motherwit, a critic of language, a good-for-nothing, a cataloguer of Low German humor, a symbol of Satan, a parasite, an incarnation of the "cold spirit" of materialism, an enlightened explorer of the "I-Thou" relationship, a traitor to humanity, a cynic, and a representative of a new age, or modern times (Bollenbeck, 1). The contradictions here certainly indicate his tenacious and complex vitality. If many of these views seem absurd and completely divorced from the texts, revealing little about Eulenspiegel, they may at least show a good deal about the hallucinations of private enthusiasms disguised as literary criticism. In fact Eulenspiegel's import, as a paradoxical character with clever ideas about the world, has been frequently, though not always, overlooked. Far from being a "representative" or "symbol" of this or that fad or trend of the moment, or from being simply a fool, clown, rogue, and example of the medieval literary type of the buffoon and rascal, he is, as the texts demonstrate and as I shall try to show, a protean and original linguistic philosopher.

Startlingly, and with the connection so far unnoticed, the literary Till Eulenspiegel, who is also a vagabond and explorer of sorts, steps onto the public stage in a Renaissance society full of vagabonds and fascinated with explorers. This social context is certainly vital to illuminating his contradictions, various facts about his name, and humanist aspects of his character, such as his passionate interest in language. Vagabonds and wayfarers were well known in Europe since at least the eighth century, when Charlemagne issued an edict against "magones et cogciones qui sine omni lege vagabundi vadunt" [peddlers and hucksters who wander about lawlessly as vagabonds], tricking and deceiving people right and left. Undeterred by Charlemagne's attitude, vagabondage increased hugely. By 1250, it was an organized way of life. By 1400, it had become an established, if risky, profession of sorts, especially east of the Rhine, with masses of itinerants, many of them rogues, knaves, thieves, and mendicant frairs, as well as quack doctors and idle mercenary soldiers, flooding the roads. They benefited from obligatory religious alms-giving and also, as N. points out in Chapter 36, from rustic innocence: "People were not always as sophisticated as they are now, especially country people." The *Liber Vagatorum: Der Bettler Orden* (Augsburg, 1509) suggests through its popularity alone (eighteen editions appeared before Martin Luther wrote a preface to it in 1528; it has been translated as *The Book of Vagabonds and Beggars with a Vocabulary of their Language*, by D.B. Thomas) a vast public concern with what had become a large shady subculture. In his preface to this book, Luther distinguishes between paupers and homeless women with children, on the one hand, and "outlandish and strange beggars," who "ought not to be borne with," on the other. The second of these groups, as Reinhold August Dorwart (94f) points out, multiplied rapidly in the centuries following the Crusades. Its members, including robber barons and "emancipated" monks, chose to live by guile, lacing flattery with mockery for the sake of quick profits, turning themselves into social exiles and outsiders, and as often as not eliciting sympathy from impoverished farmers and peasants who admired their freer lives and offered them shelter. Eulenspiegel clearly belongs among and comes from this company of potential Bardolfs, Falstaffs, and Lords of Misrule, in Thomas Nashe's famous phrase. In tale after tale (see, for instance, Chapters 15, 16, 36, and 65), Eulenspiegel appears as a tramp and vagabond, as a type that would have been easily visible and familiar to N.'s audience, defeating the harshness of incessant penury and the fierce cold of winter with a native predatory brilliance.

He is a type of explorer as well, not only of places and countries but of groups and classes of people (as has been remarked earlier), and this aspect of his nature must be seen in the light of a growing German and European enchantment with explorers generally, and especially with explorers of the New World. His Continental adventures complement their American adventures. His ridicule of the mundane matches their worship of the fantastic. His wanderings and practical jokes mirror in reverse their visits among alien tribes and their efforts at economic exploitation. By 1500, according to a number of studies (see especially Fredi Chiapelli, ed., *First Images of America: the Impact of the New World on the Old*, and Johann Scheible, ed., *Die fliegenden Blätter des XVI. und XVII. Jahrhunderts*), printed broadsides, sold in major German cities such as Brunswick and Augsburg and serving as the newspapers and magazines of their day, depicted the unusual and often fanciful customs of Brazilian indians, their "many" wives, their devotion to magic, their "purity," and their "simplicity" (anticipating Rousseau's conception of "natural' and unspoiled man two and a half centuries later). The illustrations accompanying these broadsides were big and colorful, the captions lengthy. The broadsides sold right alongside others that depicted and recounted *facetiae* such as those in *Till Eulenspiegel*. Popular enthusiasm for the two ran in tandem, as if the muses of history and comedy, Clio and Thalia, were sharing a new frontier.

Much of N.'s method can be seen in his combining qualities of the vagabond and explorer in the Eulenspiegel that he creates out of the materials of folklore. His method is to synthesize. In fact he synthesizes several contemporary types, the court jester, the clown, the medieval-Renaissance vagabond, the Renaissance explorer, the actor, and the rogue, with at least two familiar humanist interests, satire and philology. The result, his achievement, is a spectacularly complex, fresh, and vibrant character. Even the hero's original name, Ulenspiegel, seems to show this method at work. It too appears to be a fortuitous synthesis of meanings, a couple of which have only lately been recovered through scholarly investigation. Early scholarship was concerned with the question of the "real" Ulenspiegel (with the name spelled in confusingly different ways). While this question may never be completely resolved, it is obvious, on the basis of the many intermingled sources of Eulenspiegel's adventures, that the Eulenspiegel who survives is primarily a literary creation (see also the note on Chapter 1, and Lutz Mackensen's lucid discussion (242-43), in which he writes, "Above all, one thing is clear: the hero of these jests cannot have lived. It is also not the case that the man who put together the *Volksbuch* was writing the biography of a beloved folk-hero"). The problem for early twentieth-century scholars such as Schröder (cf. his "Gleitwort," 29-30) was that "the author of the *Volksbuch* also nowhere makes a connection between the name and the character of the hero: whether he did not concern himself with its meaning, or whether he took it as self-evident . . . we do not know." This reading, however, is a shade too literal. In Chapter 40, for instance, we find:

> Now, Eulenspiegel had this custom whenever he did some mischief where he was unknown: he took chalk or coal and drew an owl and a mirror over the door, and underneath wrote, in Latin, *Hic fuit*.

It may be true that the stories supply no explicit connection between the character of the hero and his name, but this description, which clearly links his name with his customary behavior, indicates (a) that Eulenspiegel himself sees his name as meaningful, and recognizably so, and (b) that his audience also knew what his name meant and probably expected, as a result, a certain sort of mischievous behavior from him. Two other points should also be made. The first is that Chapter 94 describes Eulenspiegel's gravestone as having an owl and a mirror carved into it; the second, a signal of a widespread view surely, is that two contemporary woodcuts, of Eulenspiegel himself, on the title page, and of his gravestone, also show the owl and the mirror. What, then, did his name mean? The answer is that it fairly glowed with meanings for N.'s audience, these ranging from the socially cutting to the mythic to the scatalogical to the bloodthirsty. The "mirror book" (in Latin, *speculum*; in German, *Spiegel*) was extremely popular in the late Middle Ages and into the Renaissance. Such books sought to "mirror" various activities and classes, such as confessions and wives, and usually overflowed with ripe ethical and moral instruction. Whether *Eulenspiegel* belongs in this tradition has always been a matter of dispute, chiefly because "Ulenspiegel" is also an identifiable family name (see the note to Chapter 1), though it is probably not the hero's, and because the name can also be understood as "Ul'n speghel," a command or invitation to "wipe one's arse" (Honegger, 129f; Wunderlich, 10f) in contemporary hunter's jargon (from "ulen," to sweep or wipe clean, and "spiegel," arse or behind). Beyond this lies the metaphorical idea of the owl in Eulenspiegel's day. According to the *Etymologicum Teutonicae Linguae* of Cornelius Kilianus (1598) the Dutch "wl," which is the source of "ul" or "ulen," was a symbol of the "homo stolidus et improbus," or the stupid and evil or wicked man (cf. also Honegger, 130). The book, and the hero's name, may thus at least be understood as the "mirror of the stupid and wicked," together with the less delicate image of arse-wiping or cleaning implicit in it. The owl in the Middle Ages was also regarded as the "devil's bird," a perhaps appropriate symbol for a sometimes diabolical-seeming hero who turns all sorts of conventional values and morals upside down (see Wunderlich, 19 n17). Dieter Arendt (55) speculates that the owl image, a conventional symbol of lost wisdom, indicates enlightenment as well. The ancient "owl of Minerva," goddess of crafts, became in fact a symbol of the new craft of book publishing. "Ulenspiegel" or "Eulenspiegel" may easily, in addition to its other meanings, have referred to the book as a "mirror of wise enlightenment," in which readers, seeing their stupidity and evil reflected in Eulenspiegel's adventures, were to be led into a new and better condition. To this it must be added that the text itself never actually says or suggests anything of the sort.

What all this wealth of meanings clearly reveals is what any reader at once realizes, that Eulenspiegel is far more than a mischief-maker, far more than a supremely entertaining practical joker. Goethe's one recorded statement about him is quite to the point:

> Eulenspiegel: alle Hauptspäße des Buches beruhen darauf, daß alle Menschen figürlich sprechen und Eulenspiegel es eigentlich nimmt (1045, 218). [Eulenspiegel: all the chief jests of the book depend on this: that everybody speaks figuratively and Eulenspiegel takes it literally.]

Goethe's statement applies directly to about half the tales in the book and in many of the rest it is clear that figurative speech and Eulenspiegel's interpretation of it influence the action. He wins a barrel of beer from a priest who fails to shit, as he promises, in exactly the middle of his church (Chapter 12); he bakes owls and long-tailed monkeys for a baker who jokingly tells him to bake them (Chapter 19); he presents a soapy sausage to a priest who wants to eat till his mouth "simply foams" (Chapter 37); he breaks through the roof of the house of a smith who tells him to get up and out of his house (Chapter 39); he cuts animals out of the leather of a shoemaker who tells him to cut "large and small," like those the swineherd runs out of town (Chapter 42); he brews a dog called Hops instead of hops (Chapter 46); he leaves his shit in a wool-weaver's dining room when the wool-weaver tells him to put it "where no one will have it" (Chapter 50); and so on. When the response to his typical behavior is a foul-faced explosion, his mild reply is that he has only done what he was asked to do. As has been suggested, Eulenspiegel is enthralled with two cudgeling features of human relations: their need for the sort of figurative language that amounts to dishonesty, and their frequent collapse into violence when "the facts," or any truth at all, come to light. He is a jester and mythical buffoon on a crusade against evasiveness and confusion.

Enid Welsford distinguishes neatly between the professional buffoon, the court fool, and the mythical buffoon as definite types. The professional buffoon, whose origins she locates in ancient Greece, is the parasitical entertainer willing to heap any absurdity on himself for a meal. He is "neither the unconscious fool, nor the conscious artist who portrays him; he is the conscious fool who shows himself up, chiefly for gain, but occasionally at least for the mere love of folly" (27). Examples of such historical figures are the Germans Hans Clawert and Friedrich Taubmann, of the sixteenth century, and the sixteenth-century Italian Fra Mariano. The court fool, on the other hand, is either a clever and nasty rogue, entertainer, and sometimes politician; or the sort of pitiful cripple whose physical and mental deformities would, in the twentieth century, require medical attention; or he is the court dwarf. All three were kept as pets in a sense, though the first of these types enjoyed a freedom proportionate to his cleverness (Eulenspiegel frequently plays this sort of court fool). The mythical buffoon, by contrast, is a fictional character often comprised of the materials of legend. His humorous, vicious, and sometimes charming behavior results less from a desire for money than, as might be expected in fiction, his attitude: a palatial, chilly skepticism. As Welsford observes (50-51), Eulenspiegel is just such a buffoon and rascal:

> Almost all of us feel an instinctive pleasure in an occasional reversal or topsyturvydom, an occasional reminder that no human barriers are unbreakable, no human judgments final. And so we get the Marcolfs and the Eulenspiegels, the incorrigibly impudent rogues, the irrepressible mischief-makers. There is one quality about this kind of buffoon, however, that is most disagreeable and that is his complete heartlessness. Regard Eulenspiegel as a real man, dealing with real men capable of feeling pain, and he becomes a purely odious figure. Buffoons can only flourish, jest-books can only be written, in a society where the general level of sensitiveness and sympathy is not very high. Nevertheless, although a certain amount of callousness must be assured if the book is to be enjoyed at all, yet the remarkable quality in Eulenspiegel is not his power of causing trouble, but his skill in evading consequences. To identify oneself with Eulenspiegel is to feel for a moment invulnerable. True, one must regard other men as puppets of sawdust, but then identification with Eulenspiegel does, for the time being, delude one into the intoxicating fancy that other men are made of sawdust, that sensation is not real, that fact is not inexorable, and that pain itself is comic.

Despite the aptness of her comments on the topsyturvydom of many of the tales, Welsford's notions about invulnerabililty cannot be considered quite accurate (as has been pointed out,

Eulenspiegel is defeated in a number of tales), and her belief in Eulenspiegel's "complete heartlessness" is questionable. What is striking about Eulenspiegel (in contrast to the sources of his adventures, such as *Pfaffe Amis* and *Pfaffe vom Kalenberg*) is that, far from simply playing tricks on the naive, innocent, and gullible, he very often sets out to deceive the dishonest, harsh, cruel, stupid, conceited, obnoxious, boring, and pretentious. There is little of the strutting fop in N.'s hero, and nothing of the pavonine aristocrat. It is usually hypocrisy and inhumanity that N. and Eulenspiegel wish to debase, never the arrogance of class. Eulenspiegel thus moves through what often seems a pitiless world, in which his own ethics and compassion appear all the more wondrous for their rarity, like green oases among murderous dark dunes. If his behavior is generally sadistic, it is also, in this sense, moral. A full exposure to his adventures offers the choice pleasure, unobtainable in life but possible in art, of seeing wrongs perfectly righted and punishments perfectly suited to crimes. He frequently, as well, displays an interest in justice, as in Chapter 70, when he twice comes to the rescue of some blind men while baffling and duping a greedy innkeeper and a duplicitous priest (stock characters whom N.'s audience would automatically have suspected of treachery in any case). Eulenspiegel is, however, interested in a special sort of justice. He has in mind not a legalistic idea of compensation, but justice as a child's passion for symmetry, logic, and retribution would like them to be, and as an unfair world only rarely allows them to be. Where more pliant people are satisfied with approximations of justice, Eulenspiegel advocates a fierce, literal precision. He is an eccentric mathematician of human reality, believing as much in the possible absolute perfection of the human world as a mathematician must believe in the absolute truth of the infinitesimal calculus. Eulenspiegel's near obsession with this sort of justice, like his devotion to "truth" and to telling the truth, mentioned earlier, gathers with an erratic, accelerating force through chapter after chapter, impressing the reader eventually with the realization that his is a career with a definite intellectual dimension. The dimension, it turns out, and this at a time when German itself was rapidly maturing into a modern sinewy expressiveness, is not only ethical but linguistic and even philosophical. Eulenspiegel is revealed as an explorer not only of groups of people but also of the effects of ordinary colloquial speech. He is apparently fascinated with the idea that vast numbers of injustices, along with misunderstandings, disputes, and struggles, result from errors in speech, as well as from the nature of language itself. In these senses, which need to be discussed in a philosophical context, Eulenspiegel steps before his audience as both a humanist and a modern linguistic philosopher. His passion is to explore the mechanisms of psychological and what I wish to call assertional language. He yearns for information that can be trusted.

The trouble, from Eulenspiegel's point of view, is that the reality of most speech, and most literature, is psychological rather than informational. It is more concerned to recreate and reveal recognizable states of mind than to communicate "facts." In doing so, such speech adds to "the stock of available reality," in Richard Blackmur's phrase (337), with the emphasis here falling on the word "available" and on the idea that "reality" becomes available only when endowed with language. "A rose is a rose is a rose," for example, neither makes, nor intends to make, a statement about roses. It is not informational. Neither is it meaningless. Rather it is what may be called psychological and what I would term, in a broader sense, assertional. It depicts perfectly a state of mind, one that mocks logic and perception, and that does so through an unexpected exaggeration or extension; in other words, by simply asserting itself. It thus lets us look at a sort of stop-frame photograph of logic and perception. In valuable ways, it also sets us free to examine logic and ourselves. Its surprising repetition becomes an ambushing delight. Most of what we call conversation and imaginative literature is assertional in this way. It is more concerned to reveal or "photograph" complex states of mind than merely to disclose the outside world. Swift's *Gulliver's Travels*, Lear's raging that seems to induce an actual tempest, and Dante's circles of Hell are each logically absurd if they are considered as offering logical or true propositions about conditions in the physical world. However, their intentions are not at all to offer logical or true propositions about the world. Their interests lie in depicting states of mind and states of internal conflict.

The language of imaginative literature, and of most speech, is thus only seldom the language of propositions. Indeed, the very word "proposition," especially as it is used by certain philosophers, seems often to be confused with what is in fact assertional language. Bertrand Russell's definition of the term, for instance, in "On Propositions: What they are and how they mean" (*Logic and Knowledge*, 285), is this: "A proposition may be defined as: *What we believe when we believe truly or falsely*." While this definition, as Russell demonstrates, has a perfect application to sentences that explicitly demand true or false belief, because they have to do with facts, it is questionable whether the definition remains compatible with our usual uses of "proposition" once we move into other areas, such as ordinary human speech and imaginative literature. This poses the question whether Russell's definition has not been deliberately made so narrow as to exclude a number of areas of language that it could illuminate. Swift's *Gulliver's Travels*, for example, may be looked at as consisting of a series of propositions (or statements in the indicative which propose, present, and propound). Are we to believe in them as if they were simply true or false, or is another demand, a psychological and emotional one, unrelated to truth and falsity, being made on us? Is it Swift's intention to convince us that what he is saying is factually accurate or to change our way of looking at ourselves and the world? Cannot language be used to do this? J.L. Austin, in *How to Do Things with Words*, proposes that words may be "performative" as well as true, false, and meaningless. This notion, which leads into the related theory of assertional language presented here, is in fact an outgrowth of Russell's approach to propositions in his narrower sense.

The distinction becomes sharper if one considers Russell's well known example of a proposition that he regards as either true, false, or meaningless (in his essay "On Denoting"), "The present king of France is bald," in which it is granted *a priori* (a) that there is no present king of France, and (b) that he cannot therefore be bald. In fact this sentence does not ask for a discrimination between truth, falsity, and meaninglessness, as would be the case with a sentence such as "If x contains y, and y contains z, then x must contain z." While the second sentence is propositional in Russell's original sense, because it proposes a logical consequence which can be deduced from its grammar and syntax, the first sentence is assertional because, disinterested in logic and fact, it makes an irrelevant or fictional announcement. What is the announcement about? How is it to be understood? Clearly, it is not "about" the "outside" or physical world but about the "inside" world of our emotions, and it is there that we as readers are forced instantly to test not its "truth" but its impact. If the sentence causes us to smile, because we know that it cannot be true informationally or "propositionally," or false either, then we confirm its emotional "truth," or value. Beyond this, it may be argued that sentences which contain propositional truth are most unlikely also to contain emotional "truth," or impact. The two categories appear in most cases to be mutually exclusive. This is why art, and a good deal of conversation, are deliberate nonsense and lying, in the conventional sense, and also why art must remain so. Art's exposure of how to perceive and feel the world seems to result from its asserting conditions out of the emotional and psychological arena rather than proposing them out of the inanimate or even social world. Where science organizes what is speechless, art explores whoever is articulate. The artist (and most people probably attempt to become artists in at least their conversational lives) is more concerned with a statement's being right than with its being true. A revealing mirror of some recognizable psychology, and this blithely presented or asserted, is what counts.

It is precisely this revealing mirror that Eulenspiegel rejects and shatters wherever he finds it. In all of those tales in which he reacts literally to metaphors or hyperboles or emotional phrases, he seems deliberately to disregard the psychological and assertional qualities of the language addressed to him. In chapters in which he seeks to impose a perfect "justice" on someone who has treated him harshly, he often exposes the innocent cruelty of the psychological and assertional language which we all speak and cannot do without. A single example, of many possible ones, may illustrate what is meant by this. In Chapter 50, Eulenspiegel becomes a wool-weaver's apprentice, and does his work absurdly, as is his habit. The wool-weaver tells him sarcastically, "If you want to beat the wool that way, you could just as well do it sitting down on the roof instead of standing up here on this ladder." So Eulenspiegel climbs onto the roof and beats the wool up there. When the wool-weaver catches him on the roof, he remarks, again with obvious sarcasm, "If you want to beat wool, beat it. If you want to fool around, fool around. Climb off the roof and shit in the wool basket." So Eulenspiegel shits in the wool basket. But the point is that when Eulenspiegel takes the wool-weaver's "instructions" literally, he ignores their assertional content. The purpose of the wool-weaver's statements is clearly to ridicule and to assert the state of mind of ridicule. It is not at all to inform or instruct. The wool-weaver, who is here using the assertional and psychological language of the artist, though admittedly in a rather shallow way, is himself ridiculed by someone who refuses to recognize the possibility of such language, and who in fact treats all language as if it were "propositional," informational, and logical. It is also clear that Eulenspiegel acts as he does deliberately, rather than whimsically or petulantly. His shrewdness and intelligence are hardly in question here.

What then are we to conclude, if not that Eulenspiegel is deeply fascinated with speech and language? His usual rejection of assertional and psychological language simply emphasizes his avid sensitivity to it. What is more, modern linguistic philosophers such as Russell and Wittgenstein exhibit an interest in the relations between speech and psychology which, in illuminating ways, exactly matches Eulenspiegel's. Here, for example, are Russell's comments on the establishment of a definition of "one":

> This development in the principles of mathematics suggested that philosophical puzzles are to be solved by patience and clear thinking, the result being, in very many cases, that the original question is shown to be nonsensical [because it has been proposed psychologically rather than logically]. Carnap maintained at one time that *all* philosophical problems arise from errors in syntax, and that, when these errors are corrected, the problems either disappear or are obviously not soluble by argument. I do not think he would still maintain quite so extreme a position, but there can be no doubt that correct logical syntax has an importance which was not formerly recognized, and which logical positivists have rightly emphasized (*Logic and Knowledge*, 370).

It should be added that much of Russell's great achievement in philosophy consists, as is well known, of clarifications of what were supposed to be genuine intellectual problems through an elimination of their psychological terminology, with the result that, as he here remarks, "the original question is shown to be nonsensical." Thus in "On the Notion of Cause" (*Mysticism and Logic*, 174f), he demonstrates not only that science does not deal with cause and effect, but that the concept of "cause and effect" is itself fallacious; in "The Relation of Sense Data to Physics" (169f), he shows how the term "existence" is meaningless when used in metaphysics; and in "Logical Atomism" (*Logic and Knowledge*, 328), he writes, "The ontological argument and most of its refutations are found to depend upon bad grammar."

Clearly, the conflicts in many of Eulenspiegel's tales arise, as in the philosophical problems here described by Russell, because of nonsensical, or psychological, or purely assertional language. But is there, except in exclusively logical realms of thought, such as mathematics, any alternative to such language? Would not any alternative be finally less essential to us personally than its psychological and assertional opposite? The dilemma is incapable of resolution, except the provisional resolution of continuously remaining sensitive to its existence. This is what Eulenspiegel manages to be. A great deal of Eulenspiegel's life is spent in revealing the nature of the linguistic trap in which everyone thrives, fails, flourishes, struggles, and occasionally thrashes about. His life also reveals ways of becoming free within the trap, through his frequent enthusiasm for justice, and through his apparent conviction that many of the fictional, or linguistic, confusions of life can be made to vanish, or turn into pleasures, if only they are met with clear, often humor-filled thinking. His is a linguistic philosophy like a running midnight brook that flashes at the moon here and there, as its waters trick between strange, thick trees.

EDITORIAL POLICY FOR THIS TEXT AND TRANSLATION

The earliest known complete version of Eulenspiegel's adventures, the printed quarto published by Johannes Grüninger in Strassburg on St. Adolph's Day (August 29), 1515, is the basic text of this translation. It is presented in combination with elements of Grüninger's text of 1519 and Honegger's recently discovered fragment of Grüninger's earlier text of 1510-11. Grüninger's quarto measures 20 by 30 millimeters; contains 260 pages, or according to the book's own reckoning, 130 leaves; has 81 different woodcuts; and offers 95 (instead of the announced 96) tales of Till Eulenspiegel. Exactly one copy of Grüninger's volume survives. It is located in The British Library. A British Museum stamp, unused for the past one hundred fifty to two hundred years, and found on the title page, indicates that the book has been among the Library's collections for about that long. The volume is bound with *Der schelmen zunft Anzeigung alles Weltleüffigen/mutwils/Schalckheite un Pribereyen diser Zeyt/Durch doctor Thomas Murner von Strassburg/schympflichenn erdichtet/unnd zu Franckfurt an dem Meyn geprediget*. Murner's book was printed in Strassburg by Grüninger's colleague in publishing, Johannes Knobloch, in 1516.

Grüninger's 1515 edition is only slightly more faded than the excellent photographic facsimile made of it by Edward Schröder in 1911. Schröder's facsimile (with reproduction by Emery G. Walker, London, the paper reproduced to match the original by J. Batchelor & Son, Ford Mill, Little Chart, and zinc plates and printing by Graphische Kunstanstalt, F. Bruckmann, A.-G., Munich) has been used throughout. Also used have been Honegger's fascimile of his fragment ("Faksimilewiedergabe des Fragmentes S 1510/11 aus der Offizin des Johann Grüninger zu Strassburg"); Lappenberg's *Dr. Thomas Murners Ulenspiegel* (which, as mentioned earlier, is a scholarly and editorial treatment, in full, of Grüninger's edition of 1519); and Wolfgang Lindow's scholarly and critical edition of the 1515 volume, published in 1966 (see also the Bibliography, below). Honegger's fragment consists of 32 printed pages with woodcuts (included in his *Ulenspiegel: Ein Beitrag zur Druckgeschichte und zur Verfasserfrage* (1973)) and has been compared wherever possible with the editions of Schröder,

Lappenberg, and Lindow. Scholarly and critical comments by Sichtermann and others, acknowledged in the Notes on the Tales, have provided inestimable assistance in establishing the sense of various opaque phrases.

Grüninger's edition of 1519 is not simply a second printing of the book, though the texts correspond exactly in most important respects and details. A great many of the textual differences, together with my resolutions of them in the translation, are taken up in the Notes on the Tales. The texts differ typographically in a number of interesting ways (Honegger, 19f), with the initial and ornamented letters of chapters exhibiting diverse styles, and more important, with the edition of 1515 having 26 lines per page, while that of 1519 has 28 (the number of pages is nonetheless identical). Honegger's fragment, which runs from Chapter 27 to 53, with many chapters incomplete, differs from both of the complete texts in having 30 lines per page, another woodcut for Chapter 44 (45 in the original because of a printer's error; see the note on the title page for an explanation of this misnumbering), and lettering that also differs slightly in styles and sizes. The typography of the fragment is definitely Grüninger's, however, and it is worth noting that all three texts offer different woodcuts for Chapter 44 (45). The edition of 1515 is the only one of the three to repeat the woodcut for Chapter 81 (82) here. On the basis of these discrepancies, Honegger speculates that still another edition, most likely printed in 1512, but not yet recovered, must have existed as well. This idea is perfectly acceptable, but where Honegger wishes to attribute the textual changes in the surviving complete editions to Grüninger's printer, who was, Honegger believes, constantly trying to improve his texts and working from a manuscript that he may have had difficulty in reading, I would be far more inclined to attribute them to the author himself. The changes between the texts of 1510-11, 1515, and 1519 usually amount to literary improvements. Information is added. Spelling is clarified. Even when, as is infrequently the case, the edition of 1519 reverts to phrasing in the 1510-11 version, what seems to be happening is that an experiment, or an experimental improvement, has been rejected. All of this is the sort of thing that one expects of an author who is revising and correcting, and possibly grateful for the opportunity to do so, where a printer would surely have hesitated. In Chapter 66, in which an old woman steals Eulenspiegel's purse, for instance, the 1515 text describes her as going "to sit by the river." The 1519 texts tells us that she also sat down over the purse, a crucial detail. In Chapter 77, the merchants who hire Eulenspiegel to humiliate a pompous innkeeper promise him mere money in the 1515 edition, but money and provisions in that of 1519, adding a detail that enriches the plausibility of the story. In Chapter 79, when Eulenspiegel moves "to one end of the table" and "when he basted the roast till it was ready" (phrases which do not appear in the 1515 edition), his attitude and reaction are made clearer. The simplest explanation of these types of changes, and one that seems most credibly to take account of the facts, is that among the complete editions and the fragments of the tales we can watch an author's revising mind at work. Steven Urkowitz, in his important essay "Good News about 'Bad' Quartos," proposes a similar line of defense for Shakespeare's quartos, which have usually been regarded as "corrupt" or mere actors' remembered versions of Shakespeare's plays. The quartos too are most likely earlier stages of the texts, which Shakespeare himself later revised. The present translation itself is a substantial revision (I naturally hope for the better) of the one I did in 1969, which appeared in print in 1972. Every effort has been made to produce a version in fluent, modern English that is also respectful of N.'s style and loyal to the original texts. As in my previous version, I have eliminated a few obvious errors, such as occur in the numbering of the tales, and dropped the leaden phrase "The [blank] chapter tells," with the "blank" replaced by a Roman numeral, from the chapter headings. Also eliminated are typographical errors, the more important of which I cite in the Notes on the Tales. Their relative frequency suggests that Grüninger may have put the book together rather quickly.

Enough is known about Johannes Grüninger to be certain that he was clearly a master printer among the earliest European printers who followed Gutenberg (1400?-1468), while his personal contacts with Albrecht Dürer and Willibald Pirckheimer (see also the note on Pirckheimer under Date and Authorship, above), plus the staggering variety of his published books, show that he was probably aware of working in a novel industry that was busy changing the world. The spirit of intellectual and spiritual unity in the early Renaissance reaches an apotheosis with the invention of moveable type. This invention also speeds the collapse of medieval unity. If the first aim of book publishers was to preserve ancient and valued texts, doing what the monastic scribes had done for centuries, only better, this aim was rapidly realized. Attention turned elsewhere. By 1500, when *Eulenspiegel* was being written and prepared for the press, tens of thousands of editions of books, many of them on humanist, medical, architectural, and scientific subjects, attracted expanding legions of readers across Europe.

Grüninger's father's name was Reinhard, a name which, with variations such as Reinhardi de Grüningen, he signed to a number of his books. He himself was born in Grüningen in Württemberg (hence his signatures, in other books, of Grüninger, Greyninger, and Grieninger; I have opted for the High German form throughout). By 1480 he was living in Basel, at the house of a goldsmith named Erhart, whose widow later sued him for ten guilders for his keep. In the record of the law suit he is already referred to as a "Meister," from which Voulliéme (153) concludes that by this time he had established himself as a printer and that he went to Basel expressly to learn printing. On October 2, 1482, he became a citizen of Strassburg. He now set up shop in earnest, forming a partnership with a "Meister Heinrich von Ingweiler," about whom nothing is known except that the partnership must have dissolved almost immediately: von Ingweiler's name appears on only a few of the extant copies of their first book, the *Petrus Comestor Historia scholastica*, published on August 28, 1483. Grüninger now worked on alone, his reputation and success increasing rapidly. Paul Kristeller, in his study of Grüninger's professional career (87-106; for Kristeller's discussion of Grüninger see 24-50), reveals that between 1494 and 1530 Grüninger published 139 books, in Latin, German, and Italian; Charles Schmidt puts the number as high as 251, while Honegger (17 n22) argues that the number was at least 270. Among them were Brant's *Ship of Fools*, cited earlier; editions of Horace, Virgil, and Boccaccio; various missals, diurnals, and breviaries; and volumes of Roman history, alchemy, surgery, folk history, liquor making and literature – all of these, of course, in addition to the three or four editions of *Eulenspiegel*. His last known publication bears the date of March 10, 1529, though another book, by Amandus Farkal and dated 1530, is described as having been made "in Kosten Grüningers" (Kristeller, 105). Many of Grüninger's books were illustrated, and there is interesting evidence that he valued their aesthetic impact quite highly. In 1525, in a letter to Pirckheimer, he writes, "Albrecht Dürer knows me well. He also well knows that I love art. So much the worse for me that he dismisses my product. I didn't publish it as a work of art" (Kristeller, 49). It is thus impossible to agree with Schröder's view ("Gleitwort," 6) that he knows "of no work of the Grüninger House that was as carelessly printed as the *Eulenspiegel*." To judge from the meticulousness with which Grüninger selected his illustrations alone, the book reflects pride and attention. The book may have been done in a hurry, or as Lindow remarks (269), with some of the haste of a broadsheet, and this perhaps due to popular demand. Clearly, though, it was done with respect. It appears even today as a cheery consecration of early printer's ink, adorned with often superb woodcuts whose independent wit comments on the jests in the tales themselves.

Sichtermann (335f), as mentioned earlier, provides a revised ordering of the tales, basing his revisions on Honegger (110f). This is partly reproduced here. The columns below show Sichtermann's changes only. "G" at the head of a column indicates the original position of a chapter; "S" indicates Sichtermann's new placement of it. An asterisk means that a tale has been divided into two tales.

G. S.	G. S.	G. S.	G. S.	G. S.
11=13	22=21	49=48	59=58	68=67
12=14	39=40	50=49	60=59	69=68
13=15	40=41	51=50	61=60	70=87*
14=16	41=42	52=51	62=22	70=88
15=17	43=74	53=52	63=11*	71=69
16=39	44=71	54=53	63=12	72=70
17=89	45=44	55=54	64=63	74=86
19=61	46=45	56=55	65=64	86=72
20=62	47=46	57=56	66=65	87=20
21=19	48=47	58=57	67=66	88=90

THE WOODCUTS

Woodcuts illustrating books were still a bright new invention in 1510. There is evidence that both artists and the public regarded them with awe. If one was wealthy and could buy what one pleased, one would have been familiar with the dazzling color illuminations of medieval manuscripts, the Dutch tradition of which reached its apex in a series of posh, elegant books produced in the fifteenth century, coincidental with the invention of moveable type. The developing literate classes, who bought the first printed books with woodcuts, knew little, it may be assumed, of their colorful predecessors. Most of the new buyers and readers were not rich. A black and white illustration, printed on a portable world of pages, was therefore, apart from its aesthetic qualities, an object of intense, novel, and miraculous pleasure. If modern people can carry about with them, in tiny electronic boxes, the ghostly voices and moving image-ghosts of singers, dancers, and actors, the Renaissance audience for printed books, with their woodcuts, could suddenly pocket an entire universe, reduced to squiggly lines, human forms, and white space made voluptuous and plastic by a gifted use of black ink.

The virtual inventor of the illustrative woodcut was Albrecht Dürer (1471-1528). To be sure, he was not the very first to work in a medium that began to look recognizably more and more modern as early as the 1470s. Fine woodcuts illustrating books, by Schongauer and Israhel van Meckenem, were already announcing an interest of artists, as opposed to mere craftsmen, in what would soon mature into a startling new art form. Their influence, however, except on fellow artists such as Dürer himself, remained spotty and scant. An older conservatism prevailed. At the end of the fifteenth century, as Charles Ilsley Minott observes (8), most illustrations for printed books were "votive, decorative, or even practical" (in the sense that they were mostly of the how-to variety, showing the intricacies of tools, wells, machines, and catapults). As a result, the decorative initial letter, an import into printed books from the realm of the illuminated capital letters of medieval manuscripts, gleamed on the new printed pages with an isolated, ebony grandeur. The problem, and one quickly solved by Dürer and his successors, was a universal artistic obedience. If the art that accompanied most illuminated manuscripts was not always interlaced with the text, still it almost always obeyed the text. The sensibility of the artist had simply surrendered. The aesthetically eccentric had bowed to the literary. The concrete details of text and miniatures, usually corresponding exactly, or intended to do so, collaborated on an illuminated page that, with its designs, colors, and human figures, became, like the universe of medieval theologians, a single harmonious language itself, waiting to be read by all who knew the allegorical style of the Word, or *verbum* of God. If the books produced in the climate of this repressive attitude toward artists were nonetheless often quite thrilling, they were so in the nervous, expectant sense in which prison-literature and concentration-camp art may also be thrilling. Against all odds, and in spite of imperial strictures, an individual artist's temperament has managed to express its vision and to blossom.

Dürer almost singlehandedly swept aside all questions of surrender. What had been merely a buoyant aesthetic game for Schongauer, that of making pictures for the amazing printed books, became for Dürer a billowing, serene mission. His point was of course to illustrate the books rather than to illuminate their texts. For the first time, the artist would forge ahead with stylish abandon. He would set sail on his own, across seas and in directions scarcely or not at all revealed among the words. Impelled by this novel concept, writes Panofsky in his biography of Dürer (4), "his prints set a new standard of graphic perfection for more than a century, and served as models for countless other prints." An unexpected outcome of Dürer's rebellion, as can be seen in his own illustrated volumes, was that the pictures, whether woodcuts or etchings, often took precedence over the text altogether. His woodcuts, especially, became commentaries and assertions in their own right, a natural enough step in his case, if only because the chief catalyst of his adventurousness was humanism, the iconoclastic, testing outlook which, through his friends Erasmus and Pirckheimer, guided his entire career.

It is a matter of pure speculation whether Dürer did any of the woodcuts for *Till Eulenspiegel*, all of which are unsigned (see also Lindow, 285). The possibility cannot simply be dismissed, for several reasons. Dürer's relationship with Grüninger, apparently extending over a number of years, may have been professional as well as personal. Panofsky records Dürer's contribution of a very small woodcut, *The Four Horsemen*, to Grüninger's *Bible* (Strassburg, 1485); other scholars question the attribution. Dürer was actually in Strassburg in 1493, where he cut his extraordinary *Crucifixion*, published in a Strassburg missal, and where he may have met Hans Baldung Grien, who would later move to Nuremberg to work as an apprentice in his studio. Dürer's enthusiasm for jest-books, including specifically *Till Eulenspiegel*, is also well documented. In 1489-90, he contributed at least seven, and perhaps more, woodcuts to Philip Frankfurter's *Die Geschichte des Pfarrers vom Kalenberg*, published in Nuremberg by P. Wagner (Kurth, 9; Hutchison, 26), one of the sources of the Eulenspiegel stories. While in Basel, in 1494, Dürer cut an entire sequence of woodcuts for Brant's *Ship of Fools*, published by Bergmann von Olpe on Carnival Day (February 11). By 1499, the popularity of this book, due in part to its jest-filled woodcuts, had led it into eight reprints, plus three German and three Latin editions. Dürer also did a splendid woodblock portrait of Brant, showing him kneeling in prayer, for his *Varia carmina*, published in 1498. More significant, though utterly enigmatic, is a note in Dürer's diary for his trip to the Netherlands. The diary runs from July, 1520 to July, 1521. Here, for August 27, 1520, he lists, among his usual voluminous purchases of paintings, clothes, and bibelots: "I paid 3 st. for two buffalo horns and 1 st. for two Eulenspiegels" ["1 Stüber für zween Eulenspiegel"] (Dürer, *Writings*, 102; cf. also Lindow, 285). Werner (*Writings*, 102) takes this to mean that Dürer bought two copies of Grüninger's 1519 edition of *Eulenspiegel*. Lindow's more plausible guess is that the purchase involved Eulenspiegel broadsides or a couple of Eulenspiegel "illustrations." Grüninger, it should be added, was also the publisher of Dürer's close friend Pirckheimer, whose translation of Ptolemy's *Geography* was issued by his house in 1525. Suggestive, though certainly problematic, similarities between Dürer's authenticated woodcuts and a number of those in the 1515 edition of *Eulenspiegel* seem to exist as well, particularly for Chapters 2, 4, 7, 9, and 72. The first four of these present birds in flight, like black darts and arrows against a white sky, in ways that bear comparison with Dürer's *Samson Killing the Lion* (1488?); "The Angel with the Key Hurls the Dragon into the Abyss," from his *Apocalypse* (1498, with Dürer mentioned as the printer); and *The Schoolmaster* (1510, with accompanying verses by the artist). The woodcut for Chapter 72 of *Eulenspiegel* shows a knight in armor, in the side-bar section, that is reminiscent of Dürer's small woodcut showing eight knights and soldiers (plate 135 in Kurth) both in the details of the armor and the pose of the central knight. The entire issue of Dürer's possible contributions, as Lindow and Honegger also propose, thus plainly awaits further study. Details of Dürer's management of his studio may prove helpful in any investigation. Hutchison (109) reports that "in the case of the book illustrations, none of the woodblocks was signed when an outside publisher was used [as would have been the case if cuts were made for Grüninger]. When Dürer acted as his own publisher, he initialed all the cuts, whether or not he had designed them himself." Did Dürer do all of his own woodcutting in any event, after making preliminary drawings? Is it the case that various woodcuts in *Till Eulenspiegel* reveal only his influence, his characteristic mingling of slashing, bold lines with others of an ineffable, almost Mozartian sweetness? The usual practice of an apprentice in training, such as Baldung Grien, was conscientiously to imitate the style of his master-teacher. Dürer, as one might expect, given his humanist sympathies, abandoned this practice and let his apprentices cultivate their own styles. Traces of Dürer's style were bound to persist, however, and these may be what glimmer among scattered patches in the *Eulenspiegel* woodcuts.

When Dürer died, on April 6, 1528, Pirckheimer said, "I have lost the best friend I ever had on earth." Hans Baldung Grien begged Dürer's widow for a lock of his hair. Baldung Grien (1484-1545), whom Dürer had nicknamed "Grienhans," had long since moved to Strassburg, become a citizen there, gotten himself elected to the town council, and been appointed official painter for the Strassburg episcopate. H. Perseke first attributed nine of the woodcuts in *Eulenspiegel*, including that of the title page, to Baldung Grien back in 1941. Perseke's authentication, confirmed in 1962 by Maria Consuelo Oldenbourg, takes off from Baldung Grien's use of a vine leaf as a sort of personal emblem on his woodcuts until 1512 (see also Honegger, 30 n45). The vine leaf appears in the lower right-hand corner of the title page. The tales illustrated by Baldung Grien (1, 5, 6, 8, 10, 11, 12, and 22, as listed in Date and Authorship earlier) do not show the vine leaf, but do offer up gestures, scenes, and even faces that strongly echo Baldung Grien's other woodcuts. The woodcut for Chapter 5, for instance, in which Eulenspiegel serves his robber-baron boss shit for mustard, looks like a scatological parody of one of Baldung Grien's religious cuts, showing two priests celebrating mass before an altar, done for his series "beschlossen Gart." Still, the stylistic divergencies between groups of other cuts in *Eulenspiegel* indicate that as many as five artists, altogether, probably worked on the book, with the remaining three or four unidentified. This likelihood tallies with what is known of Grüninger's business practices. Kristeller (47) writes that after 1500 a change came about in his dealings with artists. Instead of retaining them indefinitely, regardless of the work on hand, he now began to hire them, often two or more at a time, by the book. Kristeller (120) himself believes that the woodcuts, possibly all of them, were made by Urs Graf. This notion is virtually contradicted by the facts of Graf's fickle, passionate, and violent life as well as by his career as a brilliant artist. Graf worked in Strassburg only from 1502 to 1507, where indeed he knew publishers of books, among them Johannes Knobloch, for whom he completed one of his masterpieces, the Ringmann *Passion*, illustrated with twenty-five woodcuts, in 1506. In 1507, however, Graf moved to Zürich, and by 1509 he had returned to Basel, the city of his apprenticeship. There is no evidence that he ever returned to Strassburg or ever collaborated with Grüninger on any of his books. Thus the only artist identified with certainty to date remains Hans Baldung Grien. Behind him, as in a five-hundred-year-old twilight, may perhaps be discerned the ghost of his friend and teacher, Albrecht Dürer.

The woodcuts themselves present their own grab-bag of puzzles, beauties, and revealing interpretations of the tales. Six woodcuts are repeated, with those for Chapters 16, 36, 45, 49, 53, and 59 turning up again in Chapters 51, 66, 81, 54, 77, and 60, respectively. The woodcut for Chapter 20 also appears in Grüninger's earlier volume of Horace, published in 1498. The edition of 1519 substitutes different cuts for Chapters 16, 44, 56, and 57. 67 woodcuts are accompanied by side-bar motifs, of which 63 are architectural designs and the remainder human figures. The side-bar woodcuts differ considerably from one another, with no clear pattern apparent in their differences. The larger, or chapter, woodcuts, though, almost invariably depict Eulenspiegel himself at the very moment when he plays his prank in the tale that they illustrate. The woodcuts are clearly meant to catch him in the act.

Interestingly, none of the depictions of Eulenspiegel shows him in jester's costume. He nearly always appears in late fifteenth-century riding clothes, in garments so simple, so lacking in the sumptuous and gaudy, as to seem anonymous. The meanings of his plainness of dress will perhaps by now be obvious. On the one hand, he is not merely a jester; or more precisely, the role of jester is only one of the roles that he plays. On the other hand, he is clearly an actor. His simplicity of dress, shown over and over in the woodcuts (here reproduced in actual size), points to the fact that one of Eulenspiegel's chief activities is play-acting. Where Pfaffe Amis and Pfaffe vom Kalenberg almost always play themselves, Eulenspiegel (in more than thirty-six tales) either acts a part or pretends to be someone he is not. On various occasions he plays page-boy, barber's boy, painter, scholar, wandering monk, salesman of religious relics, cleaner of pelts, Abbess' scribe, dying man, blacksmith's boy, shoemaker's apprentice, brewer's apprentice, furrier's apprentice, tanner, carpenter, optician, cook, horse dealer, and sacristan. He deeply enjoys role-playing for its own sake. His role-playing is an instrument of revelation and an escape. Acting allows him to expose human pretensions and to be free. The rogue is hidden.

The woodcuts thus highlight yet another aspect of his nature. For Eulenspiegel, as has been urged more than once in this essay, is far more complex than comparable folk heroes and jesters, emerging as he does from the late Middle Ages into the more modern Age of Humanism. He operates on many levels of psychology, and of theater, and this is no doubt one of the many reasons that he has been so well liked by his German audience. If he plays the devil, he also plays the philosopher of language; if he delights in clowning, deceiving, and provoking, he also not infrequently delights in setting matters straight between people. The final pleasure of Till Eulenspiegel seems in fact to lie in his fearless clawing at the masks of others, in his exposure of their pomposities. He exposes them through language that means what it says, through behavior that refuses to be diplomatic, and often through an aggressive, satirical use of human excrement (as mentioned earlier). Eulenspiegel's ambition, if he believes that any ambition is worth anything at all, is thus to humble, charm, and entertain us by showing us that we are all linguistically and emotionally clumsy animals, animals that always fall on their faces and begin to babble when they aspire to become gods.

BIBLIOGRAPHY

TEXTS

Ein kurzweilig lesen von Dyl/Ulenspiegel gebore uss dem land zu Brunsswick. Wie/er sein leben volbracht hatt. xcvi seiner geschichten. Anon. Text Brit. Lib. cat. no.: C. 57 C. 23. Strassburg: Johannes Grieninger, 1515.

Schröder, Edward, ed. *Ein kurzweilig lesen von Dyl/Ulenspiegel gebore uss dem land zu Brunsswick. Wie/er sein leben volbracht hatt. xcvi seiner geschichten*. Photographic facsimile. Leipzig: Inselverlag, 1911.

Lappenberg, J. M., ed. *Dr. Thomas Murners Ulenspiegel*. Leipzig: T. O. Weigel, 1854.

Lindow, Wolfgang, ed. *Ein kurtzweilig Lesen von Dil Ulenspiegel*. Stuttgart: Philipp Reclam Jun., 1966.

Honegger, Peter. "Faksimile wiedergabe des Fragmentes S1510/11 aus der Offizin des Johann Grüninger zu Strassburg" (*See* Honegger, *below*).

SECONDARY WORKS

Agricola, Johannes. *750 deutsche Sprichwörter*. Mathilde Hain, ed. [Based on the edition of Hagenau, 1534] Hildesheim: Olms, 1970.

Aickol, Johannes. *Till Eulenspiegels Streiche*. Düsseldorf: 1903.

Albrecht Dürer: Das graphische Werk. Catalogue. Frankfurt am Main: Städelsches Kunstinstitut, 1971.

Arendt, Dieter. "Eulenspiegel. Sprachwitz und Widerstand." *Kürbiskern*, (March, 1977), Munich: Damnitz Verlag, 108-16.

______. *Eulenspiegel: Ein Narrenspiegel der Gesellschaft*. Stuttgart: Klett-Cotta, 1978.

Ashe, Geoffrey. *Land to the West*. New York: The Viking Press, 1962.

Austin, J. L. *How to do things with Words*. J.O. Urmson, ed. Cambridge, Mass.: Harvard University Press, 1962.

Barton, Bruce & James Craig. *Thirty Centuries of Graphic Design: An Illustrated Survey*. New York: Watson-Guptill Publications, 1987.

Bebel, Heinrich. *Heinrich Bebels Schwänke*. A. Wesselski, ed. 2 vols. Munich: 1907.

______. *Opuscula nova et adolescentiae labores*. Paris: 1516.

Beckers, Hartmut. "Die Erforschung der Niederdeutschen Literatur des Mittelalters." *Niederdeutsches Jahrbuch*, vol. 97 (1974), 37f.

Bédier, Joseph. *Les Fabliaux: études de littérature populaire et d'histoire littéraire du moyen âge*. Paris: Champion, 1925.

Benz, Dr. Richard. *Geschichte und Ästhetik des deutschen Volksbuchs*. Jena: Diederichs, 1924.

______, ed. *Drei deutsche Volksbücher. Die sieben weisen Meister, Fortunatus, Till Eulenspiegel*. Köln und Olten: Hegner, 1969.

Berlin, Isaiah. *Against the Current: Essays in the History of Ideas*. Henry Hardy, ed. Introduction by Roger Hausheer. Harmondsworth: Penguin Books, 1982.

Blackmur, R. P. *Form and Value in Modern Poetry*. New York: Doubleday, 1957.

Bobertag, Felix. *Narrenbuch*. Darmstadt: Wissenschaftliche Buchgesellschaft, 1964.

Bodensohn, Anneliese. *Die Provokation des Narren*. 2 vols. Frankfurt am Main: Dipa-Verlag, 1972, 1975.

Bollenbeck, George. *Till Eulenspiegel, der dauerhafte Schwankheld: Zum Verhältnis von Produktions- und Reproduktionsgeschichte*. Stuttgart: Metzler, 1985.

Borst Arno. *Lebensformen im Mittelalter*. Frankfurt am Main: 1973.

Bote, Hermann. *Der Köker*. Gerhard Cordes, ed. Tübingen: Niemeyer, 1963.

______. *Herman Botes Radbuch: in Abbildung des Druckes L, ca. 1492-93/mit dem Text nach Herman Brandes*. Heinz-Lothar Worm, trans. Werner Wunderlich, ed. and author of "Nachwort." Göppingen: Kümmerle, 1985.

Brant, Dieter. *Till: es ist nicht leicht ein Narr zu sein*. Stuttgart: Belser, 1988.

Brie, Friedrich W. D. *Eulenspiegel in England*. Berlin: Mayer & Müller, 1903.

Brigden, Susan. *London and the Reformation*. Oxford: Clarendon Press, 1990.

Brown, Norman O. *Life Against Death*. Middletown: Wesleyan University Press, 1959.

Brunkhorst-Hasenclever, Annegrit, ed. *Till Eulenspiegel. Texte zur Rezeptionsgeschichte*. Frankfurt am Main, Berlin, München: Diesterweg, 1979.

Bullock, Allan. *The Humanist Tradition in the West*. New York: W.W. Norton, 1985.

Chance, Jane, ed. *The Mythographic Art: Classical Fable and the Rise of the Vernacular in Early France and England*. Gainesville: Florida Univ. Press, 1990.

Châtellier, Louis. *The Europe of the Devout: The Catholic Reformation and the formation of a new society*. Jean Birrell, trans. Cambridge, Eng.: Cambridge Univ. Press, 1990.

Chiapelli, Fredi, ed. *First Images of America: The Impact of the New World on the Old*. Berkeley: Univ. of California Press, 1976.

Chute, Marchette. *Ben Jonson of Westminster*. New York: Dutton, 1953.

Cleaver, James. *A History of Graphic Art*. New York: Philosophical Library, 1963.

de Coster, Charles Theodore Henri. *Ulenspiegel*. Brussels: 1867.

Cramer, Thomas, ed. *Till Eulenspiegel in Geschichte und Gegenwart*. Bern: Lang, 1978.

Dickens, M.G. *The Age of Humanism and Reformation: Europe in the Fourteenth, Fifteenth and Sixteenth Centuries*. London: Prentice-Hall International Inc., 1977.

Dollmayr, Viktor, ed. *Die Geschichten des Pfaffen vom Kalenberg*. Halle: 1907.

Dorwart, Reinhold August. *The Prussian Welfare State before 1740*. Cambridge, Mass.: Harvard Univ. Press, 1971.

Dürer, Albrecht. *The Writings of Albrecht Dürer*. William Martin Conway, ed. and trans. Alfred Werner, introduction. New York: Philosophical Library, 1958.

Englisch, Paul. *Das skatologische Element in Literatur, Kunst und Volksleben*. Stuttgart: Püttmann, 1928.

Eulenspiegel-Jahrbuch. Siegfried H. Sichtermann ed. since 1966.

Falik, Urii Aleksandrovich. *Concerto* ["for big symphony orchestra, after the legends about Till Eulenspiegel"] Leningrad: Music, 1971.

Faral, Edmond. *Les arts poétiques du XIIe et du XIIIe siècle*. Paris: Champion, 1925.

Faye, C.U., compiler. *Fifteenth-Century Printed Books at the University of Illinois*. Urbana: Univ. of Illinois Press, 1949.

Flögel, Karl Fredrich. *Geschichte der Hofnarren*. Liegnitz & Leipzig: D. siegert, 1789.

Flood, John L. "Der Prosaroman 'Wigoleis vom Rade' und die Entstehung des 'Ulenspiegel.' " *Zeitschrift für Deutsches Altertum und Deutsche Literatur*, vol. 105, 2 (1976), 151-165.

_______. "Besprechung von Honeggers 'Ulenspiegel.' " *Anzeiger für Deutsches Altertum und Deutsche Literatur*, vol. 87 (1976), 134f.

Fournier, Paul. "The Kingdom of Burgundy or Arles from the Eleventh to the Fifteenth Century," *The Cambridge Medieval History*, VIII (Cambridge, 1959): Cambridge University Press, 306-31.

Geiringer, Karl. *Musical Instruments: their History from the Stone Age to the Present Day*. London: George Allen and Unwin, 1943.

"Gleitwort" to the facsimile of the 1515 edition of Eulenspiegel's adventures. *See* Schröder, Edward.

Goethe, Johann Wolfgang von. *Maximen und Reflexionen*. Weimar: Goethe-Gesellschaft, 1907.

Guedes, Max Justo & Gerald Lombardi, eds. *Portugal/Brazil: The Age of Atlantic Discoveries*. Milan: Franco Maria Ricci, 1990.

Hartmann, W., ed. *Salomon und Markolf*. Halle: 1934.

Hausheer, Roger. *See* Isaiah Berlin. [Hausheer as author of Introduction]

Heer, Friedrich. *The Medieval World: Europe 1100-1350*. Janet Sondheimer, trans. Cleveland, New York: The World Publishing Co., 1961.

Heiland, Karl, ed. *Der Pfaffe Amis von dem Striker*. München: 1912.

Heimpel, Hermann. *Dietrich von Niem*. Münster: 1932.

Henning, Wilhelm, ed. *Die Geschicht des Pfarrers vom Kalenberg, Hans Clawerts werkliche Historien, Das Lalebuch; Drei altdeutsche Schwankbücher*. Munich: 1962.

Herrmann, Max. "Das Volksbuch vom Till Eulenspiegel als theater-geschichtliche Quelle." *Neues Archiv für Theatergeschichte*. Berlin: 1929, vol 1, 1f.

Hildebrandt, Hans-Hagen. "Sozialkritik in der List Till Eulenspiegels." Wunderlich (ed.), *Eulenspiegel-Interpretationen* (below), 187-200.

Hinz, Walter. *Katalog der Eulenspiegelliteratur im Eulenspiegel-Museum zu Schöppenstedt*. Schöppenstedt: Freundeskreis Till Eulenspiegels, 1973.

Hippel, Ernst von. "Till Eulenspiegel als Symbol der Neuzeit." *Stimmen der Zeit*, vol. 151 (1952-53), 357-62.

Honegger, Peter. *Ulenspiegel: Ein Beitrag zur Druckgeschichte und zur Verfasserfrage*. Neumünster: Karl Wachholtz Verlag, 1973.

______. "Eulenspiegel und die sieben Todsünden." Wunderlich (ed.), *Eulenspiegel-Interpretationen* (below), 225-41.

Howard, John A., ed. *Wunderparlich und seltsame Historien Til Eulenspiegels*. Würzburg, Bamberg: Könnigshausen + Neumann, 1983.

Hucker, Bernd Ulrich. "Eine neuentdeckte Erstausgabe des Eulenspiegels von 1510/11." *Philobiblon*, XX, 2 (June, 1976), 78f.

______. "Neue Eulenspiegelforschungen." *Eulenspiegel-Jahrbuch*, (1977), p. 3f.

Hutchison, Jane Campbell. *Albrecht Dürer: A Biography*. Princeton: Princeton Univ. Press, 1990.

Jackson, W.T.H. *The Literature of the Middle Ages*. New York: Columbia Univ. Press, 1960.

Jeep, Ernst. "Eulenspiegel." *Mitteilungen des deutschen Sprachvereins*, VIII (1885), 111f.

Junger, Friedrich Georg. *Über das Kömische*. 3rd ed. Frankfurt am Main: Klostermann, 1948.

Kadlec, Dr. Eduard. "Untersuchungen zum Volksbuch von Ulenspiegel." *Prager Deutsche Studien*, 26. Prague: Koppe-Bellmann, 1916.

Kinney, Arthur F., ed. *Rogues, Vagabonds, and Sturdy Beggars: A New Gallery of Tudor and Early Stuart Rogue Literature*. Boston: Univ. of Mass. Press, 1990.

Klahn, Erich. *Erich Klahns Ulenspiegel: Illustrationsfolgen zu Charles de Costers Roman.* [Ausstellung und Katalog, Ulrike Bodemann.] Wolfenbüttel: Herzog August Bibliothek, 1986.

Klinkenberg, Jean Marie. *Style et archaisme dans la Legende d'Ulenspiegel de Charles de Coster.* Bruxelles: Palais des Academies, 1973.

Knappe, Karl-Adolf, ed. *Dürer: The Complete Etchings, Engravings and Woodcuts*. Secaucus: The Wellfleet Press, n.d.

Knust, Hermann. *Till Eulenspiegel. Abdruck der Ausgabe vom Jahre 1515*. Halle: Niemeyer, 1884.

Könneker, Barbara. *Wesen und Wandlung der Narrenidee im Zeitalter des Humanismus*. Wiesbaden: Steiner, 1966.

Kreutzer, Hans Joachim. *Der Mythos vom Volksbuch*. Stuttgart: Metzler, 1977.

Kristeller, Paul. *Die Strassburger Bücher Illustration im XV. und im Anfange des XVI. Jahrhunderts*. Leipzig: Bär & Hermann, 1888.

Krofta, Dr. Kamil. "John Huss," *The Cambridge Medieval History*, VIII, (Cambridge, 1959): Cambridge University Press, 45-155.

Krogmann, W. "Ulenspiegel." *Jahrbuch des Vereins für niederdeutsche Sprachforschung*, LVIII/LIX (Hamburg, 1933), 104-114.

______. *Ulenspiegel. Kritische Textausgabe*. Neumünster: Wachholtz, 1952.

Kurth, Dr. Willi, ed. *The Complete Woodcuts of Albrecht Dürer*. New York: Crown Publishers, 1946.

Lambel, Hans, ed. *Deutsche Klassiker des Mittelalters. XII. Erzählungen und Schwänke*. 2nd ed. Leipzig: F.A. Brockhaus 1883.

Lemcke, H. *Der hochdeutsche Eulenspiegel*. Freiburg: 1908.

Lewis, C. S. *The Discarded Image*. Cambridge: Cambridge University Press, 1964.

Lindow, Wolfgang. *See also under* Texts.

______. "Zum Verfasser des Ulenspiegel." *Korrespondenzblatt des Vereins für niederdeutsche Sprachforschung*, vol. 80, no. 3 (1973), 31-32.

______. "Der Narr und sein Publikum." *See* Wunderlich (ed.), *Eulenspiegel-Interpretationen* (below), 182-86.

Lussky, Geo. "Was bedeutet der Name Eulenspiegel?" *Zeitschrift für deutsche Philologie*, vol. 63 (1938), 235f.

Lüthi, Max. *The European Folktale: Form and Nature*. Bloomington: Indiana Univ. Press, 1982.

Machiavelli, Niccolò. *The Comedies of Machiavelli*. Bilingual ed. David Sices & James B. Atkinson, eds. and trans. Hanover: Univ. Press of New England, 1985.

______. *Teatro: Niccolò Machiavelli*. Guido Davico Bonino, ed. Torino: G. Einaudi, 1979.

Mackensen, Lutz. "Zur Entstehung des Volksbuches vom Eulenspiegel." *Germanisch-Romanische Monatsschrift*, VII/VIII (Heidelberg, 1936): 241-269.

Major, Emil, & Gradmann, Erwin. *Vrs Graf*. Basel: Holbein-Verlag, 1943.

McDonnell, Ernest W. *The Beguines and Beghards in Medieval Culture*. New Brunswick: Rutgers University Press, 1954.

Meiners, Irmgard. *Schelm und Dümmling in Erzählungen des deutschen Mittelalters*. Munich: C. H. Beck, 1967.

Meyer, Albert. *Lustige Streiche Till Eulenspiegels*. Wolfenbüttel: 1921.

Minott, Charles Ilsley. *Albrecht Dürer: The Early Graphic Works*. Princeton Univ. exhibition catalogue. Princeton: 1971.

Morlini, Hieronymi. *Novellae, Fabulae, Comoedia*. 3rd ed. Paris: P. Jannet, 1855.

Musper, H. Th. *Der Holzschnitt in fünf Jahrhunderten*. Stuttgart: W. Kohlhammer, 1964.

Nietzsche, Friedrich. *The Portable Nietzsche*. Walter Kaufmann, trans. New York: The Viking Press, 1954.

Oeuvres de maître François Villon, par Prompsault. Paris: 1932.

Oldenbourg, Maria Conseulo. *Die Buchholtzschnitte des Hans Baldung Grien*. Baden-Baden, Strassburg: Heitz, 1962.

Oppenheimer, Paul. *A Pleasant Vintage of Till Eulenspiegel, Born in the country of Brunswick. How he spent his life. 95 of his tales. Translated from the edition of 1515, with Introduction and Critical Appendix*. Middletown: Wesleyan University Press, 1972.

______. "Eulenspiegel-Interpretationen: Der Schalk im Spiegel der Forschung 1807-1977." *The Germanic Review*, vol. LVI, 4 (fall, 1981), 157-60.

Opus Morlini complectens novellas, fabulas et comoediam. Paris: 1799.

Orgelsdorfer Eulenspiegel. Fort Ogelthorpe, Georgia. Internment camp: Oct., 1918-May, 1919.

Pannier, Karl. *Das Volksbuch von Till Eulenspiegel*. Leipzig: Reclam, 1882.

Panofsky, Erwin. *Albrecht Dürer*. 2 vols. Princeton: Princeton Univ. Press, 1948.

Paul, Herman, & Walther Mitzka. *Mittelhochdeutsche Grammatik*. Tübingen: M. Niemeyer, 1963.

Pauli, Johannes. *Schimpf und Ernst*. Hermann Österly, ed. Stuttgart: Stuttgart literarischer Verein, 1866.

Peleman, Bert. *In het spoor van Uilenspiegel*. Brussels: Heideland, 1968.

Perseke, Helmut. "Baldungs Holtzschnitte für den Ulenspiegel." *Oberrheinische Kunst*, vol. 9 (1940), 162f.

Petzoldt, Leander. "Tradition und Rezeption. Überlegungen zum Wandel des Eulenspiegelbildes in der literarischen und volkstümlichen Tradition." *Schweizerisches Archiv für Volkskunde*, vol. 75 (1979), 203-11.

Phillips, Dayton. *Beguines in Medieval Strassburg*. Stanford: Stanford University Press, 1941.

Pierpont, Claudia Roth. "Maenads." *The New Yorker* (Aug. 20, 1990), 82-91.

Po-Chia Hsia, R. *Social Discipline in the Reformation: Central Europe 1550-1750*. London: Routledge, 1990.

Poggio. *Facezie di Poggio Fiorentino*. Rome: 1885.

Poggius Bracciolini. *Opera Omnia*, con una premessa di Riccardo Fubini. Torino: Bottega d'Erasmo, 1964.

Reese, Gustave. *Music in the Renaissance*. New York: J.M. Dent & Sons, 1954.

Robertson, Charles Laurence. *The Preparation and Performance of the Ballet "Till Eulenspiegel."* [Microform] New York Public Library. New York: 1973.

Rocke, Werner. *Ulenspiegel. Spätmittelalterliche Literatur im Übergang zur Neuzeit*. Düsseldorf: Bagel, 1978.

Röhrich, Lutz. *Lexikon der sprichwörtlichen Redensarten*. 2 vols. Basel, Freiburg, Wien: Herder, 1973.

______. *Der Witz. Figuren, Formen, Funktionen*. Stuttgart: Metzler, 1977.

Roloff, E. A. *Ewiger Eulenspiegel*. Braunschweig: 1940.

Russell, Bertrand. *Logic and Knowledge*. Robert Charles Marsh, ed. New York: Doubleday, 1956.

______. *Mysticism and Logic*. New York: Doubleday, 1957.

Russell, Francis. *The World of Albrecht Dürer: 1471-1528*. New York: Time Inc., 1967.

Sacchetti, Franco *Il trecentonovelle*. Antonio Lanza, ed. Firenze: Sansoni, 1984.

Sachs, Hans. *Meistergesänge, Fastnachtspiele, Schwänke*. Eugen Geiger, ed. Stuttgart: Philip Reclam, 1987.

Sachse, Johann Christoph. *Der deutsche Gil Blas. Eingeführt von Goethe*. [Nach dem Text der Erstausgabe von 1822.] München: Winkler-Verlag, 1964.

Scheible, Johann, ed. *Die fliegenden Blätter des XVI. und XVII. Jahrhunderts*. Stuttgart: J. Scheible, 1850.

Scherer, Wilhelm. *Die Anfänge des deutschen Prosaromans und Jörg Wickram von Colmar*. Strassburg: 1877.

Schmidt, Charles. *Répertoire bibliographique Strasbourgeois, I. Jean Grüninger (1483-1531)*. Strassburg: 1893.

Schmitt, Anneliese, ed. *Ein kurtzweilig lesen von Dil Ulenspiegel. Faksimile des Volksbuches nach der Ausgabe aus dem Jahre 1519. Kommentar der Hrsg. als Beiheft*. Leipzig: Insel-Verlag, 1979.

Schmitz, Günter. *Physiologie des Scherzes*. Hildesheim, New York: Olms, 1972.

Sichtermann, Siegfried H., ed. *Till Eulenspiegel: Vollständige Ausgabe des Textes von Hermann Bote*. 2nd ed. Frankfurt am Main: Insel Verlag, 1981.

Sodmann, Timothy. "Eulenspiegel und seine Illustrationen." *Eulenspiegel-Jahrbuch*, (1980), 3f.

Splittgerber, Walter. *Die französischen Nachahmungen des Eulenspiegel in ihrem Verhältnis unter sich und zum deutschen Volksbuch*. Greifswald: Abel, 1920.

Spriewald, Ingeborg. *Vom "Eulenspiegel" zum "Simplicissimus" zur Genesis des Realismus in den Anfangen der deutschen Prosaerzählung*. Berlin: Akademie-Verlag, 1974.

Stieber, Hans. *Der Eulenspiegel: ein musikalisches Spiel. Vollständinger Klavierauszug mit Text.* Leipzig: Thalia Verlag, 1935.

Stieler, Franz. "Eulenspiegel in Mecklenburg (II)." *Eulenspiegel-Jahrbuch*, (1976), 26f.

Straßner, Erich. *Schwank*. Stuttgart: Metzler, 1968.

Swain, Barbara. *Fools and Folly during the Middle Ages and the Renaissance*. New York: Columbia University Press, 1932.

Thomas, David B., ed. and trans. *The Book of Vagabonds and Beggars with a Vocabulary of their Language and a Preface by Martin Luther (1528)*. London: Penguin Press, 1932.

Thompson, Stith. *The Folktale*. New York: Holt, Rinehart and Winston, 1946.

Thurston, Ada & Curt F. Bühler, compilers. *Check List of Fifteenth-Century Printing in the Pierpont Morgan Library*. New York: Pierpont Morgan Library Publications, 1934.

Urkowitz, Steven. "Good News about 'Bad' Quartos." *"Bad" Shakespeare: Revaluations of the Shakespeare Canon*. Maurice Charney, ed. Rutherford: Fairleigh Dickinson Univ. Press, 1988, 189-206.

Vershofen, Wilhelm. *Till Eulenspiegel. Ein Spiel von Not und Torheit*. Jena: Diederichs, 1919.

Vosseler, Martin. *Till Ulenspiegel. Das deutsche Volksbuch von 1515*. München: Goldman, 1971.

Voulliéme, E. *Die deutschen Drucker des fünfzehnten Jahrhunderts*. Berlin: Reichsdruckerei, 1922.

Walther, Christoph. "Zur Geschichte des Volksbuches vom Eulenspiegel" (1892). *Niederdeutsches Jahrbuch*, vol. 19 (1893), 1-79.

Welsford, Enid. *The Fool: His Social and Literary History*. New York: Farrar & Rinehart, 1936.

Wiswe, Hans. "Sozialgeschichtliches um Till Eulenspiegel" (1971); "Sozialgeschichtliches um Till Eulenspiegel II. Eine Nachlese" (1976). *See* Wunderlich (ed.), *Eulenspiegel-Interpretationen* (below), 175-181.

Wolf, Christa. *Till Eulenspiegel: Erzählung.* [Filmscript] Berlin, Weimar: Aufbau-Verlag, 1973.

Wolf, Oskar Ludwig Bernhard, ed. *Der markische Eulenspiegel; das ist, Seltsame und Kurzweilige Geschichten von Hans Clauert in Trebbin.* Leipzig: O. Wigand, 185-?

Wolfram, Elise. *Das Geheimnis von Till Eulenspiegels Leben.* Leipzig: 1913.

Wunderlich, Werner. *See also* Hermann Bote.

______, ed. *Eulenspiegel-Interpretationen: Der Schalk im Spiegel der Forschung 1807-1977.* München: Wilhelm Fink, 1979.

Zacharias, Alfred. *Till Eulenspiegel erzählt sein Leben. Mit 25 Holtzschnitten des Verfassers.* München: Heimeran, 1950.

TILL EULENSPIEGEL: HIS ADVENTURES

Foreword

In the year 1500 after Christ's birth, as one reckons, I, N., have been asked by various people to collect (for their sake) these accounts and tales and to show how in times gone by a clever, foxy and roguish son of a farmer was born in the Duchy of Brunswick and named Till Eulenspiegel–the sorts of things he dreamed up and did in foreign and German-speaking countries.

For this (my trouble and work) they would have been pretty grateful. I replied that I would be willing to do it, and more, but did not know how to finish anything like it with intelligence and understanding. So I made them a lot of excuses, with an amicable request to let me off from writing about Eulenspiegel (the things he did in various countries, which might have annoyed them), but they showed no willingness to agree with me. So according to my slight understanding, I have committed myself and taken the thing on, with God's help (without which nothing can be done), have started off with diligence, and would like to beg everyone's pardon so my narration puts no one in a bad mood or embarrasses anyone. That would be far from my desire.

My only ambition is to create a happy feeling in hard times, so my readers and listeners may experience good, pleasant entertainment and fun. Also there is in this my rather plain writing no art or elegance, because I am, I'm sorry to say, unfamiliar with written Latin and am a simple layman. My writing will best merit reading (providing that the reading of the usual masses not be interfered with) as the mice bite under the benches, and the hours grow short, and the baked pear tastes good with the new wine.

So I ask everybody: wherever my writing about Eulenspiegel seems either too long or too short, that he improve it. I do not wish to merit mere disapproval.

So much for my foreword. I now present Till Eulenspiegel's birth, along with various fables of Father Amis and Father vom Kalenberg.

1. How Till Eulenspiegel was born, how he was baptized three times in one day, and who his godparents were.

Eulenspiegel was born near a forest called the Elm, in the district of Saxony, in the village of Kneitlingen. His father was named Claus Eulenspiegel and his mother Anna Wibeken. Well, when she had recovered from childbirth, they sent the child to Ampleben, to the village, for baptism, and had it named Till Eulenspiegel – with "Till" after a citizen of Ampleben who became his godfather. Now, Ampleben is the castle that was destroyed as a wicked thieves' castle by Magdeburg, with the help of other principalities, somewhat more than fifty years ago. The church and the village nearby were now in the charge of the worthy Abbot Arnolf Pfaffenmeier of St. Ägidien.

When Eulenspiegel was baptized and they were ready to carry the child back to Kneitlingen, the godmother who was carrying him decided to cross a narrow bridge that lies between Kneitlingen and

Ampleben. Well, they had drunk too many beers after the child's baptism, for the custom there is that one bring the child into the tavern after the baptism and have a good time toasting it (the child's father is supposed to pay for this). Well, the godmother fell into the water and muddied herself and the child so completely that the child almost suffocated. So the other women helped his godmother out with the child, went home to the village, washed the child in a kettle, and made it neat and clean again. Thus was Eulenspiegel baptized three times in one day: once at his baptism, once in that puddle, and once in the kettle with warm water.

2. How all the farmers and their wives complained about the young Eulenspiegel, saying he was a rogue and scoundrel; and how he rode behind his father on a horse, quietly letting the people behind him see his arse.

As soon as Eulenspiegel was old enough to walk and stand, he played lots of games with the young children. Like a monkey, he tumbled about and lay around on pillows and in the grass till he was three years old. Then he began to apply himself to all sorts of mischief, so all the neighbors complained together to Eulenspiegel that his son Till Eulenspiegel was a rascal. Well, the father went to his son and said, "Why are our neighbors saying that you're a rogue?"

Eulenspiegel said, "Dear father, I do absolutely nothing to no one. That I'll easily prove to you. Go mount your own horse, and I'll sit behind you and, keeping quiet, ride with you through the lanes. They'll still lie about me and say what they please. Take note of it."

His father did so, hoisting his son behind him on his horse. Eulenspiegel now lifted his behind with its hole, let all the people look into his arse, and sat back down. So the neighbors and their wives pointed at him, and said, "Fie on you. See what a rogue he is."

So Eulenspiegel said, "Listen, father, you see well enough that I keep quiet and do nothing to anyone. Even so, the people say I'm a rogue."

So the father tried the thing again, seating Eulenspiegel, his dear son, before him on the horse. Eulenspiegel now sat still, but he opened his mouth widely, grinned at the farmers, and stuck out his tongue. This time the people ran over and said, "Look here. He's a little rascal."

His father then said, "You were clearly born in an unlucky hour. You sit still, keep silent and do nothing to anybody. Even so, the people say you're a rascal."

So the father left that place with him, and moved his household into the district of Magdeburg on the Saale – the river – from where Eulenspiegel's mother had come. Well soon afterwards, old Claus Eulenspiegel died, so the mother took care of her son. Well, his mother was poor, and Eulenspiegel had no desire to learn any trade. He grew to be sixteen years old there, amusing himself, and learning lots of ridiculous tricks.

3. How Claus Eulenspiegel moved away from Kneitlingen to the Saale, the river, where his mother was born, where he died; and how his son Till learned to walk the tightrope.

Eulenspiegel's mother lived in a house, and its courtyard led down to the river called the Saale. Well, Eulenspiegel began to walk the tightrope, doing so on the lattice-work of the house, because he did not want his mother to see it. She tolerated no foolishness from him when he played on that rope, and threatened to beat him for it. Once she found him on the rope, got a large club, and tried to shove him off it – so he ran away from her, out through a window, running up to sit on the roof where she could not get at him.

This held him till he got a little older. Then he began performing on the rope again, stretching it across the Saale, from the back of his mother's house to a house opposite. Well, lots of young and old people, observing the rope on which Eulenspiegel was going to perform, came over, eager to see him walk across it, for they were quite curious what sort of rare trick he might demonstrate or what sort of incredible jest he might pull off.

Well, when Eulenspiegel was sitting on his rope, with his performance at its best – for his mother was indoors and unable to do much about it – she crept up secretly anyhow, back in the house, to the lattice-work to which the rope was tied, and sliced the rope in two, so Eulenspiegel, her son, fell into the river, amid much derision, taking quite a bath in the Saale. The farmers also roared with laughter, and the young boys yelled at him, "Heh-heh, have a good bath," and so on. "You've been asking for a bath for quite a while."

This annoyed Eulenspiegel a good deal, so he paid no attention to the water, only to the mocking and screaming of the boys – and considered how he might get even with them and pay them back for this. In the meantime he washed himself off as best he could.

4. How Eulenspiegel relieved the boys of 200 pairs of shoes, over which they fought, making young and old tear their hair over them.

A short time after this, Eulenspiegel decided to avenge the hurt and mockery he had at his ducking. He stretched the rope out from another house, over the Saale, and let the people know he planned to walk the rope. The crowd, young and old, soon collected.

Eulenspiegel then told the boys that each one should give him his left shoe: he planned to show them a fine trick on the rope with their shoes. The boys believed this, thinking it all true. The old men did too.

So the boys started taking off their shoes and giving them to Eulenspiegel. Well, there were almost two equal piles from those boys; that is, twice sixty: half the shoes went to him. So he tied them onto a string, climbing with it onto the rope. When he was on the rope, and had the shoes with him on it, the old men and boys gazed up at him, for they thought he intended to do something extraordinary up there; and the boys became a bit worried, as they wanted their shoes back again.

Well, Eulenspiegel sat on his rope, making his preparations. Then he yelled down from the rope, "Everybody look out, and everybody hunt for his own shoe again." Then he sliced the string in two, tossing all the shoes from the rope to the ground, with one shoe tumbling over the other. The boys and old men rushed right over to them. Well, one found his shoe here, another there. And the one said, "This shoe is mine." The other said, "You're lying. It's mine." So they grabbed one another by the hair and began pummeling each other. One lay underneath, another on top; the one screamed, the other wept, the third laughed. This went on till the old men got into the face-slapping too, pulling each other's hair.

Well, Eulenspiegel was sitting on the rope, laughing and calling down, "Heh-heh! Now look for your shoes, the way I had to finish my bathing yesterday." Then he ran off his rope and left the boys and old men to themselves.

After that – because of the shoes – he dared not approach those boys or the old men but stayed at home with his mother and mended Helmstädt shoes. This made his mother happy enough, and she thought he might still turn out all right. But she did not know that he had now made even more of a fool of himself – so he dared not come out of the house, and so on.

5. How Eulenspiegel's mother tried to convince him to learn a trade – with which she meant to help him.

Well, Eulenspiegel's mother was delighted that her son was so quiet. But she criticized him for not wishing to learn a trade. As he stayed silent, his mother continued to admonish him.

Finally Eulenspiegel said, "Dear mother, anything a man decides on will take care of him all his life."

So his mother said, "I certainly have my doubts about that. I've had no bread in my house for two weeks."

Eulenspiegel said, “That has nothing to do with my statement. But a poor person who has nothing to eat should fast decently for Saint Nicholas, and if he has something, then he'll eat by Saint Martin's Eve. And that's how we'll eat too.”

6. How Eulenspiegel cheated a baker out of a sack of bread at Stassfurt, in the city, and brought it home to his mother.

“Dear God, help me!” thought Eulenspiegel. “How can I satisfy my mother? Where can I possibly find bread for her house?”

Thus he went out of the village where his mother lived, toward the city of Stassfurt. There he noticed a rich baker's establishment, went into the baker's house, and asked whether he would send his master ten shillings' worth of rye and white bread. Eulenspiegel then named the Lord of some place, and went on to say that his master was at Stassfurt, in the same city, naming an inn at which he was staying. The baker was supposed to send a boy with him to the inn, where he would give him the money.

The baker agreed to this.

Now, Eulenspiegel had a sack with a hidden hole, and he let the baker count the bread into this sack. The baker also sent a boy with Eulenspiegel to pick up the money. But when Eulenspiegel had got a crossbow's shot from the baker's house, he let one white loaf drop out of the open hole into the mud. Eulenspiegel at once set down his sack, saying to the boy, "Oh, I couldn't bring this dirty bread to my master. Quick–run home with it and bring me another loaf. I'll wait for you here."

The boy ran back to get another loaf–while Eulenspiegel took off, going to the outer city, to a house. A cart from his village was standing there, on which he placed his sack. He walked on beside it, and so was led to his mother's house.

Well, when the baker's boy returned, Eulenspiegel had vanished with the bread, so the boy raced back to tell the baker. The baker quickly got over to the inn Eulenspiegel had named to him. There he found no one, and realized he had been tricked.

Eulenspiegel returned home, bringing the bread to his mother, and saying, "Look at these! Now, eat them while they last–and fast with Saint Nicholas when they're gone."

7. How Eulenspiegel ate the breakfast bread, or rolls, with other boys, how he was made to overeat, and was beaten into doing so.

Now, there was a custom in the village where Eulenspiegel lived with his mother: whenever a householder slaughtered a pig, his neighbor's children went to his house, there eating a soup or broth called the breakfast bread.

A farmer was living in that district, in that same village, a man who was extremely stingy with his food but who still dared not refuse the children their breakfast bread. So he thought up a scheme to make them sick of breakfast bread–and sliced the fatty rind of the bread into a milk-jug.

When the children arrived, boys and girls, with Eulenspiegel along as well, he let them in and closed the door. Then he poured out his soup, or breakfast bread. Now, there were a lot more of

these pulpy pieces than the children wanted to finish eating. But whenever one walked away from eating and was "full," the householder rushed over with a whip and beat him about the thighs – so everybody had to overeat. This householder was well apprised of Eulenspiegel's trickiness, so he watched him. Whenever he beat one of the others about the thighs, he beat Eulenspiegel even harder. He kept this up till they had been forced to eat all the pulpy pieces and breakfast bread.

Now, this pleased the children as well as grass might a dog, so afterwards none of them had any desire to go to that stingy man's house to eat breakfast bread or butcher's soup anymore.

8. How Eulenspiegel made the stingy householder's chickens play tug-of-war over bait.

The next day, when the man was going out, Eulenspiegel met him.

The man said, "Dear Eulenspiegel, when would you like to come over for some breakfast bread?"

And Eulenspiegel said, "When your chickens play tug-of-war over bait – four to a bit of bread."

But the man said, "Well, if that's your idea, you'll be a long time coming."

Eulenspiegel replied, "But what if I come before it's fatty-soup-time again?" And with that he walked off by himself.

Well, Eulenspiegel kept an eye out till he got his chance and the man's chickens went feeding along the lane. Eulenspiegel had twenty or more strings with him, and tied each, two by two, in the middle. He fastened a bit of bread onto the end of each one, took the strings, and laid them down hidden, with just the bits of bread exposed. Well, the chickens pecked here and there, and gulped down the bits of bread, getting the ends of the strings into their throats. They could not swallow them, though, because another chicken was tugging at the other end. Each one dragged on the next, neither swallowing the string nor able to get it out of his throat, because of the size of the pieces of bread. More than two hundred chickens stood about there, each one choking opposite the other, playing tug-of-war over bait.

9. How Eulenspiegel crawled into a beehive; how two men came by night, intending to steal it; and how he made them tear each other's hair and let the beehive drop.

It once happened that Eulenspiegel went with his mother to the dedication of a church in a village. Well, Eulenspiegel drank till he became drunk, so he went off to look for a place to sleep pleasantly and also be free of trouble from anybody else.

He soon found a pile of honey standing behind the place in the courtyard, and nearby were lying many empty beehives. So he crawled into an empty hive next to the honey, thinking he would sleep a little. But he slept from noon straight through to midnight. Well, his mother thought he had gone home, because she could not find him anywhere.

Now, during that same night two thieves came along, planning to swipe a beehive. "I've always heard the beehive that's heaviest is best." So they lifted the baskets and hives, one after the other, and arrived at the hive in which Eulenspiegel was lying (that was heaviest), and said, "Here's the best beehive." They hoisted it onto their necks and carried it off.

Meanwhile Eulenspiegel awoke and realized what they were about. Well, it was quite dark, so the one man could barely see the other, and Eulenspiegel reached out of the hive and grabbed the first man by the hair, giving him a good yank. At that he became furious with the man behind him, thinking he had pulled him by the hair, and started swearing at him. The man behind him said, "You're dreaming or falling asleep. How could I grab you by the hair? I can hardly hold this beehive in my hands."

Eulenspiegel laughed and thought, "This game'll turn out all right." And he waited until they had gone the length of a field. Then he gave the man behind a good yank on his hair also, making him wince. This man now got just as angry, and said, "I'm walking and carrying enough to break my neck, and you're saying that I'm grabbing you by the hair. But you're grabbing me by the hair, enough to tear my scalp."

The first man said, "You're lying in your throat. How could I grab you by the hair? I can hardly see the road before me. Also, I know you just grabbed me by the hair."

They walked on like this with the beehive, bellowing as if they were about to fight with each other. Not long afterwards, when their quarreling was most violent, Eulenspiegel yanked the first man again, making his head bang against the beehive. This fellow now got so angry that he let the beehive fall and then hit the man in the darkness behind him – in the head with his fists. The man behind also let go of the beehive, and plunged into the hair of the man ahead, and they tumbled over each other. Well, the one lost the other, not seeing where he was – and they lost themselves in the darkness, leaving the beehive lying there.

Well, Eulenspiegel peered out of the basket. Then, seeing it was still dark, he slept again, and stayed lying in there till it became bright day. Then he crawled out of the beehive, but had no idea where he was. So he followed a road till he came to a castle. There he hired himself out as a page-boy.

10. How Eulenspiegel became a page-boy; and how his squire taught him that whenever he found the plant hemp, he should shit on it; so he shitted on mustard, thinking hemp and mustard were the same thing.

Soon afterwards Eulenspiegel approached a country squire at a castle, pretending he was a page-boy. Well, presently he had to ride over open country with his squire. Now, along the paths stood hemp, which is called, in the area of Saxony where Eulenspiegel was at the time, "henep."

So his squire said, as Eulenspiegel was leading his horse for him, "Do you see that plant standing there? That's called 'henep.' "

Eulenspiegel said, "I see it all right."

So his squire said, "Wherever you find it, shit on it. The reason is that with that plant we tie up and take care of those who, without serving a proper Lord, support themselves from the saddle – with the fiber that's spun from those plants."

Eulenspiegel said, "Sure, that's a good thing to do."

The courtier or squire rode here and there with Eulenspiegel, into many cities, and helped to rob, steal, and pilfer, as was his habit. But one day it chanced that they were at home and at rest. Well, when it was getting toward mealtime, Eulenspiegel went into the kitchen. There the cook told the boy, "Go down to the cellar. An earthen jug or pot is standing there, with senep (as in the Saxon speech) in it. Bring that up to me."

Eulenspiegel said, "Yes," but had never in his life seen any senep, or mustard. So when he found the mustard jug in the cellar, he thought to himself, "What does the cook want with this? I suppose he wants to tie me up with it." Then he thought a bit further, "My squire's told me that whenever I find a plant like this I ought to shit on it." So he crouched over the jug, filled it up, and brought it to the cook.

What happened? The cook suspected nothing, quickly prepared the mustard in the little dish, and sent it to the table. The squire and his guest dipped into the mustard – but it had a rather awful taste. The cook was sent for and asked what sort of mustard he had made. The cook tasted the mustard too, spat it out, and said, "This mustard tastes as if it had been shitted on."

Eulenspiegel started laughing. His squire said, "How dare you laugh so casually? Do you imagine we can't taste what it is? If you don't believe it, come and taste this mustard too."

Eulenspiegel said, "I certainly won't eat it. Don't you remember what you told me in open country on the road? – If I see that plant, I'm supposed to shit on it? You take care of thieves that way, by hanging and throttling them? Well, when the cook sent me to the cellar for the senep, I followed your orders."

The squire immediately said, "You worthless scoundrel, this is the absolute end of you! The plant I showed you is called henep or hemp – and the one the cook asked to be brought is called senep or mustard. You've done this out of sheer spite."

And he grabbed a club and tried to smack him. But Eulenspiegel was smart enough: he raced out of the castle and never returned.

11. How Eulenspiegel hired himself out to a priest; and how he ate his roast chickens off the spit.

In the district of Brunswick lies a village, in the Bishopric of Magdeburg, called Büddenstedt. Eulenspiegel arrived at the priest's house there. The priest hired him as a servant. But he did not know him. So he told him he should have happy days and pleasant service with him, eating and drinking the best – as well as his maid – and all he would be asked to do he could do with half-time work.

Eulenspiegel said "Yes" to this (he intended to stick close to its meaning); then he saw that the priest's maid had only one eye.

Well, the priest's maid presently took up two chickens and stuck them on the spit to roast. She told Eulenspiegel to sit down and roast them. Eulenspiegel was agreeable and turned the chickens round. But when they were almost roasted, he thought, "The priest definitely said, when he hired me, that I'd eat and drink as well as he and his maid – and that appears to be nonsense as far as these chickens are concerned. If that's the case, the priest's words won't be true, and I won't get to eat any of these chickens. I ought to be clever enough to make him keep his word." So he snapped one off the spit and ate it without bread.

Well, when it was getting on to mealtime, the priest's maid (who was one-eyed) came over to the fire, meaning to baste the chickens. But she saw just one chicken on the spit, and said to Eulenspiegel, "Well, there were two chickens. Where's the one chicken gone?"

Eulenspiegel said, "Woman, open your other eye too – then you'll see both chickens."

Now, when he poked fun at the woman that way for her one eye, she became extremely angry, and furious, with Eulenspiegel. She ran to the priest and told him how his splendid servant had mocked her for her one eye, how she had put two chickens on the spit, and how when she looked in on him to see how he was roasting them, she had found just one chicken.

The priest went over to the fire in the kitchen and said to Eulenspiegel, "Why're you making fun of my maid? Besides, I see very well that there's just one chicken stuck on the spit, and there were definitely two of them."

Eulenspiegel said, "Yes, there were definitely two of them."

The priest said, "Well, where's the other chicken?"

Eulenspiegel said, "It's stuck there all right. Open both your eyes and you'll see perfectly well that one chicken's stuck on that spit. I said so to your maid, but she got angry."

Well, the priest began to laugh, and he said, "My maid can't open both eyes. She's got just one."

Eulenspiegel said, "You're saying that; I'm not saying it."

The priest said, "Let's forget it. But it's still a fact that one chicken's gone."

Eulenspiegel said, "Yes, one's gone and the other's still stuck there. I've eaten the other, since you promised earlier I was supposed to eat and drink as well as you and your maid. Well, it made me sad that you might be regarded as having lied – that you might be regarded as having eaten both chickens so there'd have been none of it for me. So you'd not be a liar in what you said, I ate one chicken."

Well, the priest accepted that, and said, "My dear servant, that's one roast I didn't get. But from now on, act according to the wishes of my maid, as she sees fit."

Eulenspiegel said, "Yes, dear Father, just as you've told me."

So after that, whatever the maid told Eulenspiegel to do, he half-did. If he were to fetch a bucketful of water, he brought one half-full; and if he were to fetch two logs for the fire, he brought one; were he to give the bull two bundles of hay, he gave it just one – and so on with a lot of things, till she realized that he was doing this to irritate her. She decided to say nothing to him, however, and complained about him to the priest.

So the priest told Eulenspiegel, "Dear servant, my maid's complaining about you. Now, I've absolutely ordered you to do everything she wants."

Eulenspiegel said, "Yes, sir. I've also not done anything other than you've told me to. You told me I could do your business with half-time work, but your maid ought to see well with both eyes. She sees, though, with only one eye, and sees only half. Therefore, I did half-work."

Well, the priest started laughing. But his maid became increasingly irate, and said, "Father, if you plan to keep this fool and rogue as a servant any longer" – she planned to leave him.

So the priest, against his will, had to give Eulenspiegel notice. But he helped the farmers in choir-singing, since the sexton or sacristan of the same village had recently died. Then afterwards, because the farmers could not make do without a sexton, the priest came to an agreement with the farmers to take on Eulenspiegel.

12. How Eulenspiegel became the sexton in the village of Büddenstedt, and how the priest shitted in his church and Eulenspiegel won a barrel of beer.

When Eulenspiegel became a sexton in that village, he could sing out, as was proper for a sacristan. So the priest was now properly supplied with a sacristan.

One day the priest was standing before his altar, dressing himself and preparing to say mass. Eulenspiegel stood behind him, arranging the priest's vestment decently. The priest now let loose so enormous a fart that it thundered through the church.

Eulenspiegel at once said, "Sir, what's this stuff? Is this how you serve Our Lord, with this sort of incense smoke, here before His altar?"

The priest replied, "What're you talking about? This church is mine right enough. I've even got the right to shit in the middle of this church."

Eulenspiegel said, "It will cost either you or me a barrel of beer, if you do it."

"All right," he said. "It's a bet."

So they bet with one another. The priest said, "You think I'm not daring enough?" And he turned round and shitted a really large pile in the church. Whereupon he said, "Look, my dear sacristan, I've won the barrel of beer."

Eulenspiegel said, "No, Father. First we've got to measure accurately whether it's in the middle of the church, as we agreed."

Eulenspiegel measured it. It was far from the middle of the church. So Eulenspiegel won the barrel of beer.

But the maid was outraged. She said, "You won't let that cunning servant go till he brings you into utter disgrace."

13. How Eulenspiegel played a trick during Easter matins that led the priest and his maid to tear the hair of their farmers and go to war with them.

When it was nearly Easter the priest told Eulenspiegel, his sacristan, "It's a custom here that at Easter, during the night, the farmers always put on an Easter play, 'How Our Lord Rises From His Tomb.' " Well, he had to help with it. It was only right that the sacristan arrange and direct it.

Eulenspiegel thought, "How can the play of the Marys possibly be set up with these farmers?" So he told the priest, "Now, there's obviously no farmer here who's educated. You'll have to lend me your maid. She can read and write well."

The priest said, "Yes, yes. Just take whoever can help you with it. Besides, my maid's been in many of these."

His maid was thrilled and wanted to be the angel at the tomb because she knew the lines by heart. Eulenspiegel also looked for a couple of farmers, and found them. Well, he wanted the three of them to play the three Marys, so Eulenspiegel taught one farmer his lines in Latin. The priest was to be Our Lord God, Who was to rise from his tomb. Well, Eulenspiegel approached the tomb with his farmers dressed as the three Marys. At that point, the maid, as the angel at the tomb, spoke her lines in Latin, "Quem queritis?" – "Whom seek ye here?"

The farmer who was the first Mary answered as Eulenspiegel had taught him: "We're looking for a priest's old one-eyed whore."

When she heard this – that she was being mocked for her one eye – she became utterly furious with Eulenspiegel, sprang out of the tomb, and tried to attack him in the face with her fists. But she struck carelessly here, hitting one of the farmers, so one of his eyes swelled up. When the other farmer saw this, he also lunged out, hitting the maid on the head as well, so her wings fell off. When the priest saw that, he dropped his wings, rushed to help his maid, grabbed the hair of one of the farmers, and they dragged one another in front of the tomb. When the other farmers saw what was going on, they ran forward and there ensued a terrific uproar. Well, the priest lay at the bottom with his maid, and the two farmers (the two Marys) also lay underneath – so the farmers had to pull them apart from one another.

But Eulenspiegel had taken note of these events and promptly got out of there. He ran out of the church, walked out of the village, and did not come back.

God knows where they found another sacristan.

14. How Eulenspiegel announced that he planned to fly off the roof at Magdeburg, and dismissed his audience with scathing language.

Soon after Eulenspiegel's experience as a sacristan he arrived in Magdeburg and did lots of clever things. Well, his name became widely known there for the first time, so people knew Eulenspiegel as a name to talk about.

He was now challenged by the best citizens of the city to provide some sort of entertainment. He said he was eager to do so–and that he planned to mount the town hall and fly off the roof. There at once arose such a clamor in the city that young and old gathered at the market place, hoping to see him do it.

Well, Eulenspiegel took up his position on the roof of the town hall, flapping his arms, and acting as if he really meant to take off. The people stood there, with their eyes and mouths open, thinking he was really going to do some soaring. Eulenspiegel then laughed and said, "I believed there was no greater fool or buffoon in the world than I. But I now see clearly enough that this whole city's utterly full of fools. If you'd all told me that you planned to do some flying, I wouldn't have believed it–and you think I'm a fool. How am I supposed to fly? I'm after all neither goose nor bird. After all, I've got no feathers, and without feathers or plumes nobody can fly. So you can see very well it's all been a lie."

Whereupon he turned, ran off the roof, and left the crowd, one part cursing, the other part snickering and saying, "There goes a charlatan. Still, he spoke the truth."

15. How Eulenspiegel pretended to be a doctor, and doctored the doctor of the Bishop of Magdeburg, who was deceived by him.

At Magdeburg lived a Bishop called Bruno, a Count of Querfurt, who heard about Eulenspiegel's pranks and had him summoned to Greuenstein. Well, the Bishop enjoyed Eulenspiegel's tricks and gave him clothes and money. His servants liked him very much and had a lot of fun with him.

Now, the Bishop had a doctor of philosophy staying with him who thought himself quite learned and wise, with the result that the Bishop's royal household heartily disliked him. Well, this professor's attitude was that he disliked having fools around. The professor told the Bishop and his advisors, "One should keep wise people around the Lords of courts, and not retain these clowns, for all sorts of reasons."

The knights and the royal household agreed on this much, that this was not a fair opinion of the doctor's. If somebody disliked clowning, he could easily leave. Nobody had to join in.

The doctor-professor argued against this. "Fools for fools,

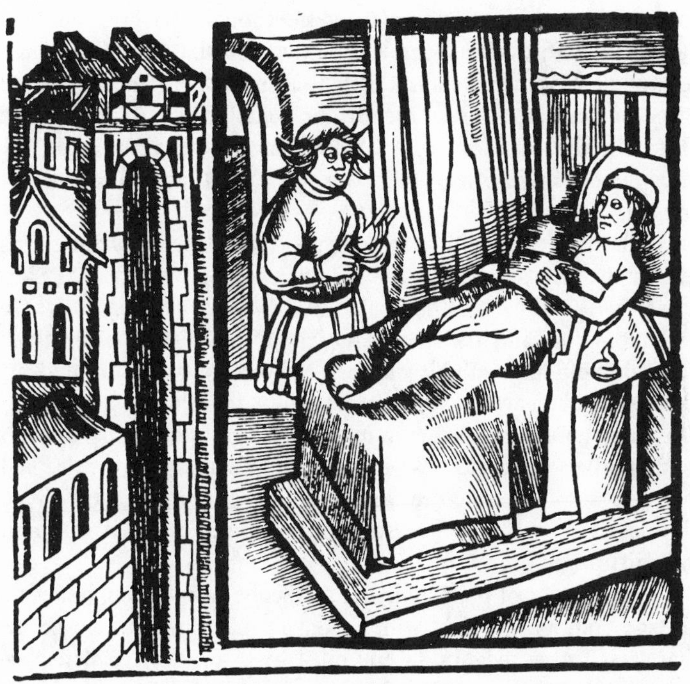

and wise men for wise men. If Princes had wise people around them, wisdom would stretch before them, but because they have fools about, they learn nonsense."

Some immediately said, "Who are the wise? Those who claim they are wise? One easily finds people like that who have been duped by fools. It's appropriate for Lords and Princes to keep all types of people at their courts. For with fools they drive away lots of brooding thoughts, and where Lords are, there fools like to be." So the people of the court approached Eulenspiegel, arranged certain schemes with him, and asked him to dream up an idea (they wanted to help him with it, and the Bishop did too) so the doctor might be repaid for his "wisdom," for the Bishop had listened to it as well.

Eulenspiegel said, "Of course, you Lords and Princes. If you'd like to help me, this doctor shall be taught a lesson."

They agreed on it. Well, Eulenspiegel traveled off over open country for four weeks, giving some thought to how he might handle the professor. Once he had planned the thing through, he returned to Greuenstein and disguised himself, pretending he was a doctor himself, because the Bishop's doctor-professor was often physically ill and took a lot of medicine for what he had. The knights at once informed the professor that a medical doctor had arrived.

The professor did not recognize Eulenspiegel, went to visit him at his inn, and after a bit of conversation, took Eulenspiegel along with him to the palace. Well, they came to an understanding, and the doctor-professor told his physician that if he could help him with his sickness, he would reward him decently. Eulenspiegel answered with the sorts of words that doctors used in those days, and lured the man into spending a night at his house so he might better diagnose his condition. "I would very much like to give you something before you go to sleep, to make you sweat." Through the sweat he was supposed to discover what the man's infirmity might be.

The doctor of philosophy let all this be said to him, believed it all, and climbed into bed with Eulenspiegel. For he believed only that what Eulenspiegel told him must be true. Well, Eulenspiegel gave the doctor a powerful laxative. The doctor thought he was supposed to sweat from this, not realizing it was a powerful laxative.

Eulenspiegel found a hollowed-out stone, deposited a pile of his shit in it, and set the hollowed-out stone, with his excrement, on the bed between the wall and the philosopher. The philosopher lay closest to the wall, with Eulenspiegel lying on the outer side of the bed. Well, the philosopher simply lay here, and turned toward the wall. At that point the excrement in the hollowed-out stone stank right under his eyes, so he had to turn toward Eulenspiegel. Eulenspiegel now released a silent fart, so that he stank horribly. The philosopher turned back again, but at once the filth in the hollowed-out stone attacked the man again, stinkingly. Eulenspiegel kept this up with the philosopher for almost half the night.

Well, at that instant the laxative began to do its work, acting sharply, quickly and forcefully–causing the philosopher to make himself quite filthy and to stink most awesomely. Eulenspiegel now said to him, "What's this, worthy Doctor? Your sweat's been stinking horribly for a long time. What's the matter with you that you sweat such a sweat? It stinks quite foully."

The philosopher lay there thinking, "I smell it all right." Indeed he was so full of the smell that he could scarcely speak.

Eulenspiegel said, "Just lie quietly. I want to get a light, so I can see how bad your condition may be." As Eulenspiegel was pulling himself up, he let another weighty shit fall, and said, "Ah, such pain! I, too, am getting weak. I must have picked this up from your sickness."

The doctor simply lay there, so ill that he could barely raise his head, but he thanked God his physician had left him, so he might get a bit of air. For whenever the doctor had tried to get up during the night, Eulenspiegel had told him he must not move, saying he might first sweat enough.

Eulenspiegel now really got up, left the room, and took off. Meanwhile daylight arrived. The doctor spotted the hollowed-out stone, full of excrement, standing beside the wall, and became so ill that his face was soiled with stink.

Well, the knights and people of the court looked in on the philosopher and wished him a good morning. The philosopher spoke feebly, could not answer well, lying in his room on a bench, on a pillow. So the court people got the Bishop over to the room, and he asked him how things had gone with his physician.

The philosopher said, "I've been hounded by a con man! I assumed he was a doctor of medicine, but he's really a doctor of knavery!" And he told them exactly what had happened to him.

The Bishop and all the people of the court began to laugh, saying, "This happened precisely as you said it would. You said, 'One had better not fool around with fools, because any wise man turns foolish among fools.' But you'll see that one man at least will be made wise through fools. Your physician was Eulenspiegel. You didn't recognize him, and you trusted him. You were tricked by him. But we, who tolerated his foolishness, knew him well. Despite that, we didn't want to warn you – since and because you wanted to seem so wise. Ah, nobody's wise enough to recognize fools too. And if there were no fools, how would the wise be known?"

At that, the doctor fell silent and stopped his griping.

16. How Eulenspiegel made a sick child shit at Peine and was highly praised.

One sometimes shies away from true, proven doctors because they want a small sum of money, but one must often give just as much to tramps.

That's how it went once in the Bishopric of Hildesheim. On that occasion Eulenspiegel traveled there too, and arrived at an inn when the innkeeper was away from home. Now, Eulenspiegel was fabulously famous around there. Well, the innkeeper's wife had a sick child, so Eulenspiegel asked the wife what was wrong with her child and what sort of illness it had.

The innkeeper's wife said, "The child can't make his stool. If only he could make his stool, things would go better for him."

Eulenspiegel said, "There's a solid remedy for that."

The woman said that if he helped her child, she would give him whatever he wanted.

Eulenspiegel said he would take nothing for it. For him this was a craft simple to practice. "Wait a little. It'll soon come on."

Well, the woman had something to do back in the courtyard, and went there. Meanwhile Eulenspiegel shitted a huge pile beside the wall, quickly placed the child's toilet stool over it, and set the child on the stool.

When the woman came back from the courtyard and saw the child sitting on his little stool, she said, "Oh, who managed that?"

Eulenspiegel said, "I managed it. You said your child couldn't get to his stool, so I put him on it."

Then she noticed what lay under the little stool. She said, "Look at this! This must have been hurting my child in his little body. I'll forever be grateful that you've helped my child like this!"

Eulenspiegel said, "This sort of medicine I can practice often, with God's help."

The woman asked him whether he would kindly teach her his skill as well. She would give him whatever he wished. Eulenspiegel said he was about ready to leave, but that when he returned, he would teach it to her. So he saddled his horse, rode toward Rosenthal, turned around, and rode back to Peine, intending to ride through it toward Celle. The naked bastard page-boys were standing there, in front of the castle, and asked Eulenspiegel which road he had come by. Eulenspiegel said, "I'm coming from Coldville," because he saw they did not have much on.

They said, "Listen a minute, if you're coming from Coldville. What does winter have to say to us?"

Eulenspiegel said, "He's got no messages. He'll make his announcements to you in person." And he rode off, leaving the naked boys standing there.

17. How Eulenspiegel got all the patients at a hospital healthy in one day, without medicine.

Once Eulenspiegel arrived at Nuremberg. He posted announcements on the church doors and at the town hall, describing himself as a solid doctor for all sorts of diseases. Well, there were quite a few sick people at the new hospital there, where is preserved the most reverend holy lance of Christ, together with other remarkable objects.

Now, the director of the hospital would have been delighted to get rid of these sick people and would scarcely have begrudged them their health. So he went over to Eulenspiegel, the doctor, and asked him whether, according to the announcements he had posted, he could really help the sick: doing so would pay well. Eulenspiegel said he would certainly make his patients a lot better, if he would set aside two hundred guilders and promise them to him. The director of the hospital promised him the money, providing he helped his patients. So Eulenspiegel swore that if he could not make these sick people healthy, he need not give him a single penny. This pleased the director so well that he immediately gave him twenty guilders.

Well, Eulenspiegel went straight into the hospital, taking two assistants along with him, and asked the patients, each one separately, what was wrong with them. Finally, as he was leaving each patient he made him swear an oath, and said, "What I now reveal to you, you must keep secret and reveal to no one." The patients, with a solemn oath, assured Eulenspiegel of this. He then told each one in private, "If I'm to help you regain your health and get you on your feet, that won't be possible unless I burn one of you into a powder and give it to the others to drink down. That I must do. Therefore, whoever is sickest among you all and cannot walk, I'll burn him into the powder, so I can help the others with him. To get you all up, I'll take the director of the hospital, stand at the hospital door, and shout in a loud voice, 'Whoever isn't sick in there – let him get out here.' Don't be asleep when I do!"

He told this to each one individually – that the last one out would have to pay the reckoning. Everybody listened attentively to these little speeches, and on the appointed day they rushed forward, on their sick and lame legs, as no one wanted to be last. When Eulenspiegel summoned them, according to his promise, they began charging out of the place, including some who had not been out of their beds in ten years. Then, since the hospital was quickly empty, he demanded his payment from the director, telling him he had to hurry off to another town. The director paid him his money, thanking him profusely, and he rode away.

But in three days the sick people came back, groaning with their illnesses. The hospital director asked them, "What's going on here? I got you the greatest master physician, who helped all of you enough to walk out of here by yourselves."

They at once told the director that Eulenspiegel had warned them that whoever was last through the door when he called "time" he planned to burn into a powder. Well, the director of the hospital realized he had been tricked by Eulenspiegel, but he was gone and the director could do nothing about him. So the patients stayed on at the hospital, and the money was lost.

18. How Eulenspiegel purchased bread according to the proverb "One gives bread to him who has it."

Honesty invents bread.

After Eulenspiegel tricked the doctor, he went on to "Half-City"[1] and strolled through the market place. Seeing it was hard winter, he thought, "The winter is hard and the wind blows bitterly as well. You've often heard that 'One gives bread to him who has it.' " So he purchased bread for two shillings, took a table, and went to stand in front of the Cathedral of Saint Stephan, offering his bread for sale. He sustained this foolish illusion till a dog came along, swiped a loaf from his table, and ran into the courtyard with it. Eulenspiegel ran after the dog.

---

1. Halberstadt.

Meanwhile, a sow with ten young piglets arrived, knocking over the table. Well, each of them took a loaf in its mouth and raced off with it. Eulenspiegel started laughing and said, "Now I see well enough the falsity of the proverb 'One gives bread to him who has it.' For it's been swiped from me." He went on, "Oh, Half-City, Half-City, how well you've been named! Your beer and food taste good enough, but your penny-purses are plain pigskin."

And he went back toward Brunswick.

19. How Eulenspiegel apprenticed himself as a baker's boy to a baker – and how he baked owls and long-tailed monkeys.

When Eulenspiegel returned to Brunswick, to the baker's establishment, there was a baker living nearby who beckoned him into his house and asked him what sort of journeyman he was. He said, "I'm a baker's boy."

The baker said, "I've got no boy at present. Would you like to work for me?"

Eulenspiegel said, "Yes."

When he had been with him two days, the baker told him to bake during the evenings because he could not help him till morning. Eulenspiegel said, "Yes, but what'll I bake?"

The baker was a playful man, but he suddenly became irritated. Jesting, he said, "You're a baker's boy and you ask what you're supposed to bake? What does one usually bake? – Owls and long-tailed monkeys!" And with that he went off to bed.

So Eulenspiegel went into the bakery and turned the dough into nothing but owls and long-tailed monkeys, till the bakery was full of them. He baked them.

His boss got up the next morning, planning to help him. But when he came into the baking room, he found, instead of either breakfast bread or wheat bread, only owls and long-tailed monkeys. The fellow at once got extremely angry and said, "Ah! What've you been baking here?"

Eulenspiegel said, "What you told me to bake – owls and long-tailed monkeys."

The baker said, "What'll I do with this foolish stuff? This bread is useless to me. I certainly can't turn it into money." And he grabbed him by the neck and said, "Pay me for my dough."

Eulenspiegel said, "All right. If I pay you for the dough, then the goods that were baked from it ought to be mine."

The baker said, "What do I care about these goods? Owls and long-tailed monkeys can't do my business any good."

So Eulenspiegel paid him for his dough, put the baked owls and long-tailed monkeys into a basket, and trundled them out of the house to the inn "At The Wild Man." Eulenspiegel now reflected, "You've often heard that one can't bring anything so peculiar to Brunswick that one can't make money out of it." Well, it was just the day before Saint Nicholas Eve. So Eulenspiegel took up a position in front of the church with his little business, sold all the owls and long-tailed monkeys, and made a lot more money out of them than he had been forced to give the baker for the dough.

The baker found out about this. It annoyed him, and he ran to Saint Nicholas Church, planning to charge Eulenspiegel for the fire-wood and the costs of baking the things. But Eulenspiegel was already gone, and the baker's trouble went for nothing.

20. How Eulenspiegel sifted flour by moonlight into the courtyard.

Eulenspiegel wandered around the country and came to Uelzen, to the village, where he again became a baker's boy. At home with his boss, the man arranged everything for baking. Eulenspiegel was supposed to sift the flour during the night, to have it ready by morning.

Eulenspiegel said, "Chief, you ought to give me a light, so I can see to do the sifting."

The baker told him, "I'm not giving you any light. To this day I've never given my baker's boys any light. They've had to sift by moonlight. Well, you'll have to do so too."

Eulenspiegel said, "If they've sifted that way. I'll do so too."

The baker went to bed, planning to sleep for several hours. Meanwhile, Eulenspiegel took the sifter, held it out of the window, and sifted the flour into the courtyard, where the moon shone, according to its light. When the baker got up, planning to begin his baking, Eulenspiegel was still standing there sifting. The baker noticed that Eulenspiegel was sifting the flour into the courtyard, which was utterly white with flour. His boss said, "What the devil! What are you doing? Isn't that flour expensive enough, that you're sifting it into that filth?"

Eulenspiegel said, "Come now, Chief, take it easy! It's been done both in and by moonlight – and there isn't much lost, just a handful. I'll quickly scoop that up again. This doesn't hurt the flour one little bit."

The baker said, "While you're busy scooping up the flour – during that time – no dough's being made. It'll take too long to bake."

Eulenspiegel said, "My dear boss, I've got a good idea. We want, after all, to bake as quickly as our neighbor. His dough is lying in his hutch. If you want it, I'll quickly get it – and stick our flour in its place."

His boss looked rather riled and said, "You ought to get yourself to the devil! Oh, get over to the gallows and drag a thief here."

"Yes," he said. So he left for the gallows. The skeleton of a thief was lying there, having fallen down. He lifted it onto his neck, brought it home, and said, "What do you want this for? I've no idea what it's good for."

The baker said, "Didn't you bring anything else!"

Eulenspiegel said, "There was nothing else there."

The baker now became really furious, saying with some heat, "You've insulted my lords' judiciary and robbed their gallows. I'll make a complaint about this to the mayor – you should see how I will."

So the baker left his house for the market place. Eulenspiegel followed him. But the baker was in such a hurry that he did not look back, and so did not notice that Eulenspiegel was following. The bailiff or mayor was standing in the market place. The baker went right up to him and began to deliver his complaint.

But as soon as his boss began his complaining, Eulenspiegel quite nimbly took a place just beside him, opening wide both his eyes. When the baker caught sight of Eulenspiegel, he became so enraged that he forgot what he wanted to complain about, saying furiously to Eulenspiegel, "What do you want?"

Eulenspiegel said, "I don't want anything. But you said I should see how you were going to complain about me to the mayor. If I'm supposed to see it, I've got to open my eyes wide – so I can see it."

The baker told him, "Just get out of my sight! You're a scoundrel."

Eulenspiegel said, "That's what I'm often called. And if I'm sitting in your 'sight,' then I'll have to crawl out of your nostrils when you close your eyes."

The mayor walked away from him, seeing well enough that this was foolishness, leaving them both standing. When Eulenspiegel saw him go, he pushed up against the baker, saying, "When are we going to bake? The sun isn't shining anymore." Then he ran off, and left the baker standing there.

21. How Eulenspiegel always rode on a reddish-gray horse, and was miserable around children.

Eulenspiegel was always cheerful in company. But for as long as he lived, there were three sorts of things he avoided. First, he never rode a gray horse, but always a reddish-gray horse, for the sake of a clownish appearance. Second, he never enjoyed staying wherever there might be children, because people worried more about their needs than his. Third, he disliked staying where there was an old, generous innkeeper. For an old, generous innkeeper did not take proper care of his possessions and was usually a fool; besides, his sort of company could not be found there: in his sort of company there would certainly be money around to be made, and the like.

He also crossed himself every day against healthy food, great good luck, and strong drink. For healthy food was merely weeds, no matter how healthy it might also be. He also crossed himself against nourishing things from the pharmacist's shop: no matter

how healthy they are, they are also a sign of illness. It was the just same with great good luck. For if a stone falls from a roof, or a beam from a house, one might easily say, "Had I been standing there, that stone or beam would have killed me. That was my great good luck." Such good luck he could do without. And the strong drink was water. For while water may drive huge mill wheels with its power, many people of the best company will also drink their deaths from it.

22. How Eulenspiegel hired himself out as a tower bugler to the Count of Anhalt; and how when enemies showed up, he failed to sound his horn; and how, when there were no enemies, he sounded it.

Not long afterwards, Eulenspiegel, approached the Count of Anhalt, to whom he hired himself out as a tower bugler. Now, the

Count had a lot of enemies, so during this time, both in the town and at his castle, he retained many knights and people of his court, and these had to be fed all day. The result was that Eulenspiegel, waiting in the tower, was forgotten and no food was sent up to him.

Well, that very day it happened that the Count's enemies rushed up to the town and, in front of his castle, stole his cows and drove them off. Now, Eulenspiegel was lying in the tower, looking through the window, but he sounded no alarm, either by bugling or shouting. But the noise reached the Count, and he rushed after them with his men.

Some of them looked up to the tower and saw Eulenspiegel lying in the window and laughing. The Count called up to him, "How can you lounge about in the window that way, so completely unaffected?"

Eulenspiegel called down to him, "Before eating, I neither shout nor like shouting."

The Count called up to him, "Aren't you going to sound the alarm for the enemy?"

Eulenspiegel called back, "I don't need to sound the alarm for any enemy. The field's already full, and some have gone off with your cows. If I sound the alarm for more enemies, they'll beat you to death. Get moving, now! Everything's fine."

The Count rushed after his enemies and busied himself with them, but Eulenspiegel and his food were forgotten again.

Well, for a while the Count was content. This was because he also took a quantity of bacon from his enemies, and cut it up for boiling and baking. Up in the tower, Eulenspiegel thought about how he too would like to get hold of some of this loot, and paid careful attention to the hour when it was time to eat. Then he began to shout and sound his horn. "Enemy, ho! Enemy, ho!" The Count ran hastily from the table (on which the food was lying) with his men, laid on harness, took weapons in hand, rushed smartly out through the gate into the field, and searched for the enemy.

In the meantime, Eulenspiegel ran coolly and rapidly down from the tower and headed for the Count's table. He grabbed boiled and baked things from the table – and whatever he pleased – then quickly returned to the tower.

Well, when the knights and footsoldiers got outside, they spotted no enemies. They all agreed, "The tower watchman has done this as a prank." So they returned to the castle gate, and the Count shouted up at Eulenspiegel, "Have you gone foolish and crazy?"

Eulenspiegel said, "Utterly without evil design."

The Count said, "Why did you sound 'Enemy, ho!' that way, when there was nobody there?"

Eulenspiegel said, "Since enemies were lacking, I had to invent some."

The Count at once remarked, "You're scratching yourself with your rogue's nails. When the enemy's around, you don't like sounding the alarm, and when no enemy's there, you sound the alarm for the enemy. This might well be called treason." He dismissed him on the spot, engaged another tower bugler in his place, and Eulenspiegel had to follow them on foot as a footsoldier.

This was pretty irritating to him, and he would have been glad to get out of there altogether, but he certainly could not get out through fair play. So whenever they moved out against the enemy, he delayed in all sorts of ways and was always last through the gate. But when they had finished their business and turned toward home, he was always first inside the gate.

The Count finally asked him how he supposed to understand him: whenever he went out with the Count against the enemy, he was always last, and on going home he was first.

Eulenspiegel said, "You shouldn't be angry about that. While you and your royal household were all eating, I was sitting up in the tower and getting thin. As a result, I've become fairly feeble. If I'm now supposed to be first out against the enemy, I'll have to make up for that time and rush up here, so I'm both the first at the table and last to leave it. Once I get strong again, I'll be the first and last against the enemy."

"So you're now telling me," said the Count, "that you plan to go on with this for the whole length of time you spent sitting up in the tower?"

Eulenspiegel said, "Everybody's right about something, depending on how you take him."

The Count said, "You won't be mine for long," and let him go. Eulenspiegel was happy about this, since he had little enthusiasm for fighting with enemies all day.

23. How Eulenspiegel had his horse shod with gold shoes, for which the King of Denmark had to pay.

So fine an entertainer was Eulenspiegel that his cleverness attracted the attention of a number of princes and lords, and he was widely talked about. He greatly pleased these princes and lords and they offered him clothes, horses, money, and food. Well, he visited the King of Denmark, who liked him a lot and told him that if he could manage some sort of trick, he would have his horse shod for him with the very best horseshoes.

Eulenspiegel asked the King whether he should take him at his word. The King said, "Yes," for he kept his word.

Eulenspiegel rode his horse over to the goldsmith and had his horse shod with gold shoes and silver nails. Then he returned to the King and announced that he would like him to pay for the shoeing. The King said, "Yes," and instructed his accountant to pay for the shoeing. The accountant thought this must be an ordinary horseshoeing, until Eulenspiegel took him to the goldsmith and the goldsmith asked for one hundred Danish marks. The accountant had no intention of paying it, left, and reported the matter to the King. The King had Eulenspiegel summoned and told him, "Eulenspiegel, what an expensive horseshoeing you've gotten! If I had to have all my horses shod like this, I'd soon have to sell both country and people. It wasn't my intention to have the horse shod with gold shoes."

Eulenspiegel remarked, "Gracious Sire, you said they were to be the best horseshoes, and that I ought to take you at your word."

The King said, "You're the most valuable of all the people at my court: you do what I tell you!" And he started laughing–and paid the hundred marks.

Eulenspiegel at once went to have the gold shoes removed and settled with the smith. He had iron shoes put on his horse, and remained with that King to the end of his days.

24. How Eulenspiegel, with a superior trick, humiliated the King of Poland's jester.

In those days His Highness Casimir was King of Poland. Staying with him was an adventurer of unusual humor and clowning who could also play the fiddle well. Eulenspiegel, who was also in Poland, visited the King. The King had heard a great deal about Eulenspiegel, who was very welcome as a guest at his palace. For the King had seen him, heard of his adventures before this, and quite enjoyed him as an entertainer.

Well, Eulenspiegel and the King's fool met, and soon things fell out as they often say: two fools in one house seldom go well together. The King's jester disliked Eulenspiegel, but at the same time did not wish to be thrown out himself. The King noticed this, so he summoned them both to his chamber. He said, "Whichever of you makes the wildest performance – one that the other cannot repeat after him – I'll give that fellow new clothes and twenty guilders. And let's get started right now."

So the two set about their clowning, performing a lot of absurd tricks, with funny faces and peculiar speeches. Whatever the one could think up for the other, and whatever Eulenspiegel did, this same fool repeated as well. The King laughed, along with his knights, and they saw all sorts of bizarre acts.

Eulenspiegel then reflected, "Twenty guilders and a new wardrobe – that would be rather nice. I shall thus do something I would otherwise find unpleasant." For he saw clearly what the King's attitude was – that it was all the same to him who won the prize, and by whatever means.

So Eulenspiegel walked into the middle of the room, lifted his behind, shitted a pile right in the center, took a spoon and split the excrement in half, down the middle. Then he called the other fool over and said, "Fool, get over here and do some lapping up after me now, as I plan to do it before you." And he took up the spoon, scooped half the excrement into it, and ate it. Then he presented the spoon to the clown and said, "Look here, you eat the other half, and after that you produce a pile too, divide it up also, and I'll eat after you."

The King's fool at once said, "No, not a chance! Put your spoon away. Do you want me to be embarrassed for the rest of my life? I certainly won't eat from you, or you from me, like this."

So Eulenspiegel won the championship of clowning, and the King gave him the new clothes and the twenty guilders. Eulenspiegel rode off, taking the King's prize with him.

25. How Eulenspiegel was banished from the Duchy of Lüneburg, and how he cut open his horse and stood in it.

Eulenspiegel practiced his extraordinary buffoonery in the province of Lüneburg at Celle. As a result, the Duke of Lüneburg banished him from the province. If he were found anywhere there, he was to be seized and hanged. But Eulenspiegel did not avoid the province on that account. If his path took him that way, he rode or walked through the district anyhow.

A time soon came when he wanted to ride through Lüneburg. The Duke suddenly appeared, heading toward him, and when Eulenspiegel realized it was the Duke, he thought, "It's the Duke, and if you're careless, they'll catch up with you with their nags and yank you off your horse. Next thing, the angry Duke hangs me from a tree." He rapidly came up with a good idea. He got off his horse, quickly slit open its stomach, shook out its bowels, and took a standing position in its trunk. When the Duke and his knights got closer, they saw Eulenspiegel standing in his horse's stomach.

The Prince came abreast of him and said, "Is that you? What're you doing in this carcass here? Don't you realize that I've banished you from my territory–and that if I find you in it, I'm going to have you hanged from a tree?"

Eulenspiegel simply said, "Gracious Lord and Prince, I haven't done anything so awful that it's worth a hanging."

The Duke said to him, "Get over here to me and explain your innocence.–And what do you mean by this, that you're standing in a horse's carcass?"

Eulenspiegel walked over to him, replying, "Gracious and high-born Prince, I worried about your displeasure and feared terribly for myself, but all my life I've heard that a man is entitled to be left in peace–in his four-poster."

Well, the Duke began to laugh, and said, "Will you stay out of my territory from now on?"

Eulenspiegel said, "Gracious Lord, as your princely Grace wishes."

The Duke rode off, calling back, "Stay as you are."

But Eulenspiegel quickly jumped out of the horse–and to his dead horse he said, "Thanks, my dear horse, that you've helped me out of this and saved my life. And that, in addition, you've made me a respectable man again. Stay where you are. It's better that ravens eat you than that they might have eaten me." And he continued on foot.

26. How Eulenspiegel bought some land from a farmer in the province of Lüneburg, and sat in it, in a tumbrel.

Somewhat later, Eulenspiegel traveled that way again. He went into a village near Celle, and waited for the moment when the Duke might again be riding toward Celle. A farmer was going into a field there. Now, Eulenspiegel had gotten himself another horse and a tumbrel, and drove up to the farmer and asked him whose field it was.

The farmer said, "It's mine, and I've inherited it."

Eulenspiegel next asked how much he would have to pay him for a cartful of earth from his field.

The farmer said, "I'll take a shilling for it."

Eulenspiegel paid him a shilling coin, filled the cart full of earth from the field, crawled into it, and drove up to the castle at Celle on the Aller. When the Duke came riding by, he noticed that Eulenspiegel was sitting in the cart – and sitting in earth up to his shoulders.

The Duke said, "Eulenspiegel, didn't I banish you from my land? – If I found you in it, I intended to have you hanged?"

Eulenspiegel said, "Gracious Lord, I'm not in your land. I'm sitting in my land, which I bought for a shilling. What's more, I bought it from a farmer who told me it was his inheritance."

The Duke said, "Get yourself and your earthy empire out of my earthy empire, and don't come back – or I'll have you hanged, along with horse and cart."

Eulenspiegel quickly leaped out of the cart and jumped onto his horse. He rode out of the district, leaving his cart standing before the castle. And that is why Eulenspiegel's earthy empire is still standing there, in front of the bridge.

27. How Eulenspiegel painted for the Landgrave of Hesse, doing it in white, so whoever was illegitimate could not see it.

Eulenspiegel set amazing things going in the country of Hesse. When he had roamed the country of Saxony through and through, and was almost too well known – so he was no longer quite able to get away with his mischief-making – he moved into the country of Hesse, and arrived near Marburg, at the court of the Landgrave. This Lord asked what he could do. He replied by announcing, "Gracious Lord, I am an artist." This pleased the Landgrave, because he thought Eulenspiegel was a performer and could do alchemy. The Landgrave concerned himself quite deeply with alchemy. The Landgrave asked whether he was an alchemist.

Eulenspiegel said, "No, gracious Lord. I am a painter – one whose equal will not be found in many countries. For my work far exceeds the work of others."

The Landgrave said, "Let's see something."

Eulenspiegel said, "Yes, gracious Lord." Now, he had with him various paintings on canvas and *objets d'art*, which he had bought in Flanders. He pulled these out of his sack and showed them to the Landgrave. The Lord certainly liked them, and said to him, "Dear master-painter, what would you ask for painting over our chamber here – showing the arrival of my wife, the Landgrave of Hesse, how she initiated my friendship with the King of Hungary, and other Princes and Lords, and how long all this has lasted? And we would want to have this thing done as sumptuously as possible."

Eulenspiegel replied, "Gracious Lord, if Your Grace were to let me do it, it would probably cost four hundred guilders."

The Landgrave said, "Master, just let it be well done for us. We plan to pay you well for it."

So Eulenspiegel took the job on, and of course the Landgrave had to give him one hundred guilders right away, so he could buy paints and hire assistants. But when Eulenspiegel, with three assistants, was ready to start, he instructed the Landgrave to allow no one other than his helpers into the room while he was working. That way he would not be disturbed in practicing his art. The Landgrave allowed him this. Eulenspiegel next came to an agreement with his assistants. He ordered them to keep silent and let him do everything. They were not to work. They would receive their pay anyway. Their greatest labor would consist of playing backgammon. His assistants were delighted that they were to earn the same money for doing nothing.

All this went on for about four weeks – till the Landgrave decided to see what master and company might be painting, and whether it would really be as good as the samples. Whereupon he said to Eulenspiegel, "Ah, dear master, we very much wish to examine your work. We request that we be allowed to go into the room with you to view your painting."

Eulenspiegel said, "Yes, gracious Lord. But I've got to tell Your Grace one thing. Whoever enters with Your Grace and views the painting – if he is not of proper and legitimate birth, he won't be able to see my painting."

The Landgrave said, "Master, it must be something fantastic."

As they spoke, they were walking into the room. Eulenspiegel had spread a long linen cloth across the wall where he was supposed to have been painting. Eulenspiegel now drew this back a little, pointed at the wall with a small white stick, and began to speak. "Look, gracious Lord. This man – he was the first Landgrave of Hesse and a pillar of Rome, who afterwards became Kaiser and had as his Princess and Lady mild Justinian's daughter, a Duchess of Bavaria. Look here, gracious Lord. Adolphus was born of him. Adolphus sired William the Black. William sired Ludwig the Pious – and so on, to Your Princely Grace. And indeed I know this much: no one can censure my work, so artistic is it and managed with such beautiful colors."

The Landgrave saw nothing other than the white wall before him and thought to himself, "Maybe I'm supposed to be the son of a whore, but I don't see anything here but a white wall." Nonetheless, he said (wishing to be fair), "Dear master, we are well satisfied – but we aren't sophisticated enough to judge." With that, he left the room.

When the Landgrave approached his Princess, she asked him, "Ah, gracious Lord, what is your master painter painting? You've seen it. How do you like his work? I myself have but little faith in it. He looks like a charlatan."

The Prince said, "Dear Lady, I like his work enormously. You do him an injustice."

"Gracious Lord," she said, "may we not also view it?"

"Yes, with the master's permission."

She had Eulenspiegel brought to her, and requested that she might see the painting too. Eulenspiegel told her what he had told the Prince: whoever was illegitimate would not be able to see his work. Then she, along with eight ladies-in-waiting and a female court jester, went into the room. Eulenspiegel now drew back the cloth, as before, and told the Princess too about the arrival of the Landgrave's wife, one section after the other. But the Princess and the ladies-in-waiting remained silent; no one praised or condemned the painting. Everyone was afraid she might be illegitimate, either on her father's or mother's side. But finally the court jester roused herself and said, "Dear master, maybe I'm to remain a whore's daughter for the rest of my life, but I don't see any painting there."

Eulenspiegel thought quickly. "This isn't good at all. If fools start telling the truth, then I, in truth, must do some traveling." But he tried to laugh it off.

In the meantime the Princess returned to her Lord, and he asked her whether she liked the painting. She answered him, "Gracious Sir, I like as much as Your Grace. But our jester doesn't like it. She says she doesn't see any painting at all. Our ladies-in-waiting say the same–and I am afraid there may be knavery in this business."

The Prince looked into his heart, realizing he had been tricked. Nonetheless, he had Eulenspiegel informed that if he were to pay for this stuff, everyone at court would have to see his work. The Prince said he wished to find out who among his noblemen might be legitimate or illegitimate.

Well, Eulenspiegel went to his assistants and dismissed them. Then he charged the steward another hundred guilders, and got them. Then he left at once. The next day the Prince inquired after his painter–he was gone. Whereupon the Prince, with all the people of his court, went into the room to discover whether anyone could see the painting. But no one could say he saw anything. As they all remained silent, the Landgrave said, "We acknowledge that we have been tricked. Oh, I never wanted to be troubled with Eulenspiegel. He visited us anyhow. We can forget easily enough about the two hundred guilders, though. You can't stop him from being the scoundrel that he is. For that reason he had better stay out of our realm."

But Eulenspiegel was gone from Marburg and had no wish to engage in any more painting.

28. How Eulenspiegel debated with the students at the University of Prague, in Bohemia, emerging victorious.

Eulenspiegel traveled through Bohemia to Prague when he left Marburg. Now, at that time good Christians were still living there – before the days when Wyckliffe brought his heresy from England to Bohemia and it was spread further by John Huss. Well, Eulenspiegel advertised himself as a great scholar there in the answering of great questions – to which any other scholar would be able to offer neither explanation nor reply. He had this written into announcements, and posted them on the church doors and at the lecture halls.

This irritated the rector. The students, professors, and other scholars were annoyed about it, as was the whole university. So they met to find a way by which they could offer Eulenspiegel problems he would be unable to solve. If he did badly, they would be justified in seizing and humiliating him. And it was arranged and agreed among them (and they also concluded and ordained it) that the rector ought to present these questions. So they had Eulenspiegel notified through their porter that he should show up the next day to answer these problems and questions, which would be presented to him in writing before the whole university if he wished to be tested and desired to have his abilities accepted as genuine. Otherwise he would not be accepted at all.

Eulenspiegel, by way of reply, told their porter, "Inform your superiors that I shall do this thing, and that I still hope to come through it a clever fellow – as I have till now."

The next day all the professors and learned men assembled. Eulenspiegel also arrived, bringing with him his innkeeper, several other townspeople, and various good acquaintances, in case of any sudden attack that might come his way from the students. When he entered their meeting, they told him to mount a podium and to answer the questions which would be presented to him.

Well, the first question the rector put to him was that he should state, and prove with true facts, how many currents of water there were in the sea. If he could not solve and answer this question, they would condemn and punish him as an uneducated corruptor of scholarship.

He made a quick answer to this question. "Worthy Lord Rector, tell the rest of the water, which runs from all ends of the sea, to stand still, and I shall measure, prove and report the truth about this matter. For that will be easy to do."

It was impossible for the rector to stop the water from flowing – so he dropped this subject and excused Eulenspiegel from measuring it. But the rector stood there, now looking rather embarrassed, and put his next question. "Tell me, how many days have passed from Adam's time till today?"

Eulenspiegel answered briefly. "Only seven days. And when they've passed, then seven more days commence. This process continues till the end of the world."

The rector presented him with his third question. "Tell me now, how or where is the center of the world located?"

Eulenspiegel answered, "It's right here. I'm standing in exactly the center of the world. And to see whether that's true, have it measured with a string. If I'm off by even a straw's length, I'll admit I'm wrong."

Rather than measuring it, the rector chose to let this question go to Eulenspiegel. Then, with real fury, he offered Eulenspiegel his fourth question. He said, "Tell me, how far is it from the earth to Heaven?"

Eulenspiegel replied, "It's quite nearby. If one speaks or calls from Heaven, one easily hears it down here. Just climb up there. I'll call softly from down here. You'll certainly hear it in Heaven. Of course, if you don't hear me, I'll admit I'm wrong."

The rector had to accept this, and asked his fifth question. "How big is Heaven?"

Eulenspiegel answered immediately. "It's a thousand fathoms wide and a thousand ells[1] high. I can't be wrong about that. If you don't want to believe it, take the sun, moon and all the stars of Heaven, and measure them together. You'll find I'm right, even though the idea doesn't appeal to you."

What could they say? Eulenspiegel was never at a loss for an answer, and they had to admit he was right about everything. But he did not wait long after he had defeated these learned men with quackery. He was afraid they might offer him something to drink to trip him up. So he took off his long academic robe, left, and headed for Erfurt.

29. How Eulenspiegel, at Erfurt, taught an ass to read from an old psalter.

After playing that game in Prague, Eulenspiegel felt a great longing for Erfurt. He was worried that they might still be coming after him. When he got to Erfurt, at which there is a remarkably large and famous university, Eulenspiegel posted his announcements there too. Now, the students of the university had heard a great deal about his jests, and wondered what they ought to set him as a problem, so things would not go for them as they had gone for those who came up against him at Prague, and they would not be humiliated.

---

1. Probably about 250 feet, though the ell, as a unit of measure, varied considerably from place to place.

Well, they decided to offer Eulenspiegel an ass to teach – since there are many asses at Erfurt, both old and young. They sent for Eulenspiegel and told him, "Professor, you've stuck up announcements that you can teach any creature to write and read pretty quickly. Well, the Lords of the University are here and plan to send you a young ass to teach. Are you up to taking it on as well?"

Eulenspiegel said, "Certainly," but added that he would need some time for this particular case, since an ass was a speechless and unintelligent creature. They agreed on twenty years. Eulenspiegel thought, "There are three of us. If the rector of the university dies, I'm free. If I die, who can hold me accountable? If my pupil dies, I'm free anyway." So he took the problem on, and agreed on five hundred old groschen to do it. Of this they paid him some gold in advance.

Well, Eulenspiegel led the ass away with him, and moved into the inn “At The Tower,” where at that time there happened to be a uniquely tolerant innkeeper. He engaged a stall for his pupil alone, and acquired an old psalter. This he placed before the ass, in the manger, inserting oats between each of the pages. The ass was alerted to these, and tossed the pages over with its mouth, to get at the oats, but on finding no more oats, it screamed, “Eee – aa, eee – aa!”

Eulenspiegel took stock of this, went to the rector, and said, “My dear Lord Rector, when would you like to see a bit of what my pupil’s managing to do?”

The rector said “Dear Professor, can he, too, accept instruction?”

Eulenspiegel said, “He’s awfully clumsy with his skills, and it’s very hard for me to teach him. Nonetheless, with a lot of effort and work, I’ve accomplished enough so he recognizes some letters and vowels, and can name them. Would you like to go with me to hear and see this?”

Now, his good pupil had been kept fasting all that time, till three in the afternoon. When Eulenspiegel got there, with the rector and several professors, Eulenspiegel stuck a new book in front of his pupil. As soon as the ass discovered it in the manger, he flipped the pages back and forth, looking for the oats. When the ass did not find any, he began to scream, in a loud voice, “Eee – aa – eee – aa!”

Eulenspiegel at once said, “Observe, dear gentlemen, the two vowels ‘e’ and ‘a.’ These he can do so far. I am hoping he may yet do nicely.”

Well, the rector died pretty soon afterwards. Eulenspiegel thereupon set his pupil free, letting him go where his nature might take him. Then Eulenspiegel got out of there with the money he had kept. He thought, “If you had to make all the asses in Erfurt wise, you’d need quite a few lifetimes.” He had, moreover, no desire to do so, and let the place stay as it was.

30. How Eulenspiegel, at Sangerhausen, in the province of Thüringen, washed pelts for the ladies.

Eulenspiegel arrived in the province of Thüringen, near Nienstetten, at the village there, and asked about accommodations. The innkeeper, a woman, gazed at him and asked him what sort of fellow he was.

Eulenspiegel said, "I'm not a journeyman. Instead I practice telling the truth."

The woman said, "I enjoy accommodating the truth, and I'm especially well disposed to those who tell the truth."

Now, as Eulenspiegel was looking around, he noticed that the lady was squinting, and so he said, "Squint-eyed lady, squint-eyed lady, where shall I sit and where shall I put my staff and sack?"

The innkeeper said, "Ah! May nothing good ever come your way! In all my life nobody's ever mentioned to me that I'm squint-eyed."

Eulenspiegel said, "Dear innkeeper, if I'm always to tell the truth, I can't keep silent about it."

The woman was pleased with this and laughed over it.

As Eulenspiegel was staying there overnight, he struck up a conversation with the innkeeper, and they happened to discuss the fact that he knew how to wash furs. Now, this very much delighted the woman, so she asked him whether he would like to wash pelts. She would tell her neighbors about it, and they would bring all their pelts for him to wash. Eulenspiegel said, "Absolutely." The woman invited all her neighbors, and the women brought all their pelts.

Eulenspiegel said, "You'll need some milk for this."

The women were overjoyed, since they had a yen for clean furs, and brought all the milk they had in their houses. Eulenspiegel then stuck three kettles on the fire, poured milk into them, stuck the pelts in as well, and let them boil and cook. When everything looked ready to him, he told the women, "You'll have to go to the woods and bring me white linden wood from young trees. And strip it, because when you come back I'm going to hoist the pelts out. They'll be soaked enough by then, and I want to wash them through – and for that I'll need the wood."

The women set off for the woods enthusiastically, and their children ran along with them. They took their children by the hands and jumped and sang, "Oh-ho, good new pelts! Oh-ho, good new pelts!"

But Eulenspiegel just hung back laughing, and said, "Ah, wait, your pelts aren't ready yet."

As soon as they were off in the woods, Eulenspiegel dipped their pelts under once more, left the kettles standing with the pelts, got out of the village, and took off. He had no intention of coming back to wash the pelts. Well, the women returned with the linden wood, failed to find Eulenspiegel, and guessed he might be gone. They then tried, each before the next, to get their pelts out of the kettles. But these had been so ruined by the washing that they fell apart. So they left the pelts standing, hoping he might still come back to wash them out.

But he simply thanked God that he had gotten out of there unhurt.

31. How Eulenspiegel wandered around with a death's-head, amazing people with it, and made quite a profit from doing so.

Eulenspiegel made himself notorious in every single country with his malicious tricks. Where he had once been he was no longer welcome. It thus happened that he disguised himself so as not to be recognized. Nonetheless, it finally became clear to him that he could no longer simply trust himself to make a living by idleness – despite his having been a cheery fellow from his youth up and having made money enough through all sorts of clever games. Now that his fame for roguery was spreading through country after country, and his profits were declining, he reflected on what he might undertake – to support himself in idleness anyhow – and got the idea of doing himself up a wandering monk and riding, with relics, through the surrounding districts. So, with a student, he dressed himself to look like a priest, got hold of the skull of a dead man, had it mounted in silver, and went into the country of Pomerania, where priests care more about drinking than praying.

From then on, wherever there might be a dedication of a church in a village, or a wedding, or some other gathering of country people, Eulenspiegel presented himself to the priest as somebody who could pray and preach religion to the farmers, and this so well that they would find themselves utterly entranced. He agreed to give the priest half of whatever he might get in offerings. The uneducated priests agreed to everything – as long as they got some money.

Well, when all the people arrived in church, Eulenspiegel mounted the pulpit, said something from the Old Testament, tossed in the New as well, with Noah's Ark and the Golden Bucket, in which the bread of Heaven lay – and said, moreover, that all this stuff was the greatest holiness. Then at the same time he began to speak of the head of Saint Brendan, who had been a holy man. He had Brendan's head right there – and it had been commanded of him that he use it to collect for the building of a new church, and to do so with purest goodness, never (on pain of death) accepting any offerings from any woman who might be an adulteress.

"And whoever here may be such women, let them stand back. For if they offer me something – those who are guilty of adultery – I won't take it, and they will be revealed in shame unto me! So – know yourselves!"

Then he offered the people the head to be kissed, a smith's head, maybe, that he had stolen from a church graveyard, and gave the farmers and their wives the blessing. After this, both guilty and innocent wives approached the altar with their offerings, rushing so much that they gasped for breath. And he took the offerings, from guilty and innocent alike, refusing none. Well, so firmly did these foolish wives believe in this sly, roguish business that they considered any woman impious who might still be holding back. And those women who had no money offered a gold or silver ring – and each one eyed the next to see if she gave too; and those who had given thought they had confirmed their honor and destroyed their evil reputations. There were also those who offered two or three times, so that everyone could see them do so and leave them out of their malicious gossip. Well, he received the most splendid donations, the likes of which had never been heard of before. And when he had taken up the donations, he commanded, on pain of excommunication, that all those who had given him something never act with deceit, for they were free of it – since if there had been any such deceitful wives there, he could not have accepted any offerings from them. Well, those wives were thoroughly pleased.

As a result, wherever Eulenspiegel went, he preached, and he became rich through doing so. And the people took him for a pious preacher, so well was he able to conceal his knavery.

32. How Eulenspiegel led the city patrol of Nuremberg into following him over a narrow bridge and falling into the water.

Eulenspiegel was inventive in his roguishness. After he had traveled about widely with the head, thoroughly deceiving people, he came to Nuremberg planning to spend the money he had made with his relic. But when he had spent a bit of time there, and had seen all parts of the city, he was unable to repress his true nature. He needed to pull off a clever stunt there as well.

Now, he saw that the city patrol slept, with armor on, in a large chamber under the city hall. Eulenspiegel had gotten to know very well the roads and narrow bridges of Nuremberg–and had especially examined the narrow bridge between the hog market and the "Little House," which is dangerous to cross during the night, as many innocent girls out to get wine have been assaulted there. Well, Eulenspiegel delayed his little prank till everyone had gone to sleep and all was quiet. Then he broke three planks from this very bridge and heaved them into the river (called the Pegnitz). He walked up to the city hall, started cursing, and beat on the plaster with an old knife, till the sparks flew.

When the watchmen heard this, they were soon up and running. As Eulenspiegel heard them coming after him, he raced ahead of the watchmen, took flight toward the hog market, and once there, had them still behind him. He arrived, barely ahead of them, at the place where he had thrown away the three planks, and managed, as best he could, to get across the bridge. But once he made it across, he yelled, "Hey! Hey! What're you waiting for, you weak-hearted scoundrels?" When the watchmen heard this, they raced after him, quite without thinking, as each wanted to be first. As a result, they fell, one after the other, into the Pegnitz. And the passageway across the bridge was so narrow that they started quarreling with each other all along it. So Eulenspiegel called out, "Hey! Hey! Aren't you moving yet? Tomorrow you might run after me some more. You'd have arrived at this bath early enough–tomorrow morning. Even if you hadn't wanted to go hunting half as much, you'd still have got here on time." Well, one man broke his leg, the next his arm, the third received a gash on his head–with the result that none of them got out of there unhurt.

When he had pulled off this bit of mischief, he did not stay at Nuremberg too long and went traveling again. He had, after all, no real wish that he be recognized as the jester in this case. He might be flogged. The people of Nuremberg would probably not take it as a joke.

33. How Eulenspiegel ate for money at Bamberg.

Through cunning, Eulenspiegel once earned money at Bamberg, after he left Nuremberg and felt pretty hungry. He arrived there at the house of a lady innkeeper, whose name was Mrs. Königen. She was a cheerful innkeeper and told him he was welcome there, since she could see by his clothes that he was a rare guest.

When he wanted his morning meal, the woman asked him how he would like to have it, whether he preferred to sit at the table for complete meals, or whether he would like to eat *à la carte*. Eulenspiegel answered that he was a poor fellow. He asked her whether, for the sake of God, she would give him something to eat.

The woman said, "Friend, at the butchers' or the bakers' I get nothing for free. I've got to pay for it. So I've also got to get money for the food."

Eulenspiegel then said, "Ah, woman, I too like to eat for money. For what – or how much – ought I to eat and drink here?"

The woman said, "At the Gentlemen's Table for twenty-four pennies, at the next table there for eighteen[1] pennies, and with my servants for twelve pennies."

Eulenspiegel replied, "Woman, the most money would serve me best." So he sat down at the Gentlemen's Table and soon ate his fill. When he felt good, and had eaten and drunk well, he told the innkeeper that she ought to wind up their business, as he had to be on his way so he would not have too much of a bill.

"My dear guest," said the woman, "give me the meal's price of twenty-four pennies, and go wherever you like. May God speed you."

"No," said Eulenspiegel. "You've got to give me twenty-four pennies, as you said. For you said, at this table one eats a meal for twenty-four pennies. Well, I took that to mean that I should earn money for it – for things have been getting pretty rough for me. I've been eating till the sweat's broken out all over me, and if life and limb depended on it, I couldn't eat any more. So just give me my hard-earned reward."

"Friend," said the woman, "it's true you've eaten enough for three men. But that I'm also supposed to pay you for eating – these two things don't rhyme together at all. All right, this meal is finished and you may as well go. However, I won't give you any money for it. That's lost. And I'll ask no money of you. Just don't come back here again. If I had to feed my guests this way all year round, and raise no more money than from you, I'd soon have to give up house and home."

So Eulenspiegel said goodbye to that place, without earning much in the way of thanks.

---

1. An error? Grüninger has twenty-eight here.

34. How Eulenspiegel traveled to Rome and visited the pope, who took him for a heretic.

Eulenspiegel was dedicated to cunning roguishness.[1] After he had tried all sorts of tricks, he thought of the old saying, "Go to Rome, pious man: come back worthless." So he went off to Rome, to give his mischief a chance there too, and took lodgings with a widow. She could see that Eulenspiegel was a rare fellow, and asked him where he was from. Eulenspiegel said he was from the district of Saxony, was an Easterner, and that he had come to Rome to speak with the pope.

The woman at once said, "Friend you can easily see the pope, but to speak to him, that I doubt. I was born and brought up here,

1. The edition of 1519 has "With thoroughgoing cunning Eulenspiegel equipped himself lavishly," a reference to his apparently elegant appearance in this tale.

and am of the best sort of family, but have never yet been able to exchange one word with him. How could you manage it so fast? I'd easily give a hundred ducats to speak with him."

Eulenspiegel said, "My dear innkeeper, if I get the chance to place you before the pope, so you can speak with him, will you give me the hundred ducats?"

The woman was quick to promise him the hundred ducats, on her honor, if he could arrange it. But she thought it would be impossible for him to manage anything like it, as it would cost him a great deal of trouble and work.

Eulenspiegel said, "My dear innkeeper, if this happens somehow, I'll ask for the hundred ducats."

She said, "Yes." But she thought, "You're still nowhere near the pope."

Eulenspiegel waited. Every four weeks the pope had to read a mass in the chapel called Jerusalem, at Saint John in Lateran. Well, after the pope had finished his mass, Eulenspiegel pushed himself forward in the chapel, as close to the pope as he could. Then as the pope said low mass, Eulenspiegel turned his back on the sacrament. The Cardinals noticed this. And when the pope said the blessing over the communion cup, Eulenspiegel turned his back again. When the mass was over, they told the pope that a peculiar person, a rather distinguished-looking man, had been at mass and had turned his back on the altar during low mass.

The pope said, "It's important to investigate this, as it concerns the Holy Church. For if disbelief were not punished, it would be a sin against God. If the man has in fact done this, it may well be feared that he has fallen into disbelief and is not a good Christian." The pope ordered that Eulenspiegel be brought to him.

The Cardinals immediately approached Eulenspiegel and directed him to appear before the pope, and at the appointed hour Eulenspiegel went to an audience with him. The pope now asked him what sort of man he was. Eulenspiegel said he was a good, Christian man. The pope asked what sort of beliefs he held. Eulenspiegel said he held the same beliefs as his lady-innkeeper, and named her, for she was a woman who was well known there. At that point, the pope summoned the woman. The pope asked the woman about the nature of her beliefs. The woman said she believed in the Christian religion and in what the Holy Christian Church allowed her and forbade her. She held no other beliefs.

Eulenspiegel was standing nearby, and he at once began to bow elaborately, and said, "Most Gracious Father, Thou Servant Among All Servants, I hold the same beliefs as well. I am a good, Christian man."

The pope said, "Why do you turn your back on the altar during the low mass?"

Eulenspiegel said, "Most Holy Father, I am a poor, great sinner and was so glaring in my sins that I wasn't worthy–till I had confessed my sins."

The pope seemed pleased with this, released Eulenspiegel, and went off to his palace. But Eulenspiegel returned to his inn and asked his innkeeper for the hundred ducats. She had to give them to him. Well, Eulenspiegel stayed the same person then as he had been before, and was not much improved by his trip to Rome.

35. How Eulenspiegel cheated the Jews at Frankfurt-on-the-Main out of a thousand guilders, by selling them his excrement as prophet's berries.

No one should mind if the cunning Jew has his eye closed.[1]

When Eulenspiegel got back from Rome, he traveled to Frankfurt-on-the-Main, where it was just fair-time. Eulenspiegel walked here and there and observed the sorts of merchandise everybody had for sale. Then he spotted a young, clever fellow wearing fine clothes, who had a very small shop, with musk from Alexandria, which he sold at a cost far beyond its possible value.

Eulenspiegel thought, "I'm also a lazy, clever scoundrel who doesn't like to work. If I could support myself as easily as this fellow, it would please me very much." So he lay without sleeping all that night, thinking and speculating on business. In the meantime, a flea bit him in the behind. He quickly fumbled about for it, and found several small knots on his behind. He reflected,

---

1. i.e., does not see and gets cheated.

"These must be the little rough sources (which one calls 'Lexander'[1]) from which the musk comes."

When he got up the next day, he bought gray and red taffeta, wrapped the little knots in it, found a seller's bench, bought some spices for it, and took up a position in front of the town hall with his stall. Many people approached him, inspected his curious shop, and asked him the nature of the odd things he had on sale there. For it was an unusual item. It was wrapped, like musk, into a little bundle, and smelled most strangely. But Eulenspiegel gave no one accurate information about his merchandise – until three rich Jews came up to him to inquire about his wares. He told them they were prophet's berries, and that whoever put one of them into his

---

1. There is evidently a pun involved here: on "Alexandria," the source of musk, and the Low German expression for "it licks itself," "leckts selbander."

mouth, and then stuck one in his nose, would speak the truth forever after. The Jews withdrew to consult for a while. Finally one old Jew said, "With this we'll be able to prophesy when our Messiah is to come – something that would be of no small comfort to us Jews."

So they decided they would buy up all these wares, no matter what they might have to pay for them. They at once returned to Eulenspiegel and said, "Merchant, what in a word, would one of these prophet's berries cost?"

Eulenspiegel thought quickly and said, "Indeed, whenever I've got merchandise, Our Lord bestows buyers on me. These delicacies please Jews especially." And he added, "I'll give you one for a hundred guilders – and if you don't wish to pay them, you dogs, take off and leave the junk where it is."

As they did not wish to anger Eulenspiegel, and as they wanted to obtain what he had for sale, they immediately paid him the money, took one of the berries, and quickly went home. Then they had all the Jews, old and young, rung[1] into *schule*. When they met, the oldest Rabbi (named Alpha) stood up and told how, by the grace of God, they had acquired a prophet's berry, which one of them was to put in his mouth to be able to prophesy the coming of the Messiah. In order that salvation and comfort might come to them from it, they ought to prepare themselves with fasting and praying. Then after three days, one Isaac would consume it with great reverence.

And so it happened.

When the man had it in his mouth, Moses asked him, "Well, dear Isaac, how does it taste?"

"Servant of God! We've been cheated by that Goi! This is nothing other than human excrement."

So they all tasted the prophet's berry – until they saw the "tree" on which the berry had grown.

But Eulenspiegel was gone, and he enjoyed himself enormously for as long as the Jews' money lasted.

---

1. Actually, "klopfen," or "knocked," it being the custom then to dispatch someone to Jewish homes to knock on the doors to summon the people to the synagogue.

36. How Eulenspiegel bought chickens at Quedlinburg, and left the farmer's wife one of her own chickens as a pledge for the money.

People were not always as sophisticated as they are now, especially country people.

Eulenspiegel once arrived at Quedlinburg. It was just market-time, and Eulenspiegel had few provisions. For just as he acquired his money, so it left him again, and he wondered how he might acquire provisions. Well, a countrywoman was sitting in the market place, and she had a basketful of good chickens for sale. Eulenspiegel asked what a pair of them would cost.

She answered, "By the pair, two Stevens-shillings."

Eulenspiegel said, "Won't you sell them for less?"

The woman said, "No."

So Eulenspiegel picked up the chickens, with the basket, and walked off toward the castle gate.

The woman ran after him, saying, "Sir – buyer – how am I to understand this? Don't you intend paying me for my chickens?"

Eulenspiegel said, "Yes, with pleasure. I'm the Abbess' scribe."

"I'm not asking about that," said the woman. "If you want to keep the chickens, pay for them. I hope never to have to do with your Abbot or Abbess. My father taught me that I should not buy from or, still less, sell or give credit to those before whom one must bow or raise one's cap. So pay me for the chickens, do you hear?"

Eulenspiegel said, "Woman, you're of little faith. It wouldn't be good if all merchants were as you are. Good comrades would have to go about poorly dressed. But just so you can be sure of your money, take this one chicken as a pledge till I bring you the basket and the money."

The good woman fancied herself well taken care of, and took one of her chickens as a pledge. But she was deceived. For Eulenspiegel – and the chickens and the promised money – did not appear. It went with her as it does with those who are most meticulous in their supervision of what is theirs: they are the first to be cheated.

So Eulenspiegel left that place, and left the woman furious over the single chicken she had taken for her chickens.

37. How the priest of Hoheneggelsen ate one of Eulenspiegel's sausages – something which subsequently did not make him happy.

Eulenspiegel was at Hildesheim, and he bought a good red sausage at the butcher's stall and went on to Hoheneggelsen. He was well known to the priest there, and it was a Sunday morning. When he got there, the priest was saying the early mass, as he wanted to eat pretty soon. Eulenspiegel went into the parsonage, and asked the girl cooking there to roast the red sausage for him.

The girl said, "All right."

Eulenspiegel then went into the church. There, early mass was just finished, and another priest was taking over the high mass, which Eulenspiegel heard to its end.

In the meantime, the priest went home and asked his servant girl, "Isn't there anything cooked, so I can eat a little?"

The girl said, "Nothing's ready, except a red sausage that Eulenspiegel brought. That's cooked. He'd planned to eat it after he got back from church."

The priest said, "Let me have the sausage. I wouldn't mind eating a bit of it."

The girl handed him the sausage.

The priest enjoyed the taste of the sausage so much that he ate it all. And he said to himself, "God bless me, that tasted good. The sausage was good." He said to the girl, "Give Eulenspiegel bacon and cabbage, as he's used to eating. That's much better for him."

Now, when the service was over, Eulenspiegel went back to the parsonage, planning to eat his sausage. The priest greeted him, thanked him for his sausage, told him how good it had tasted, and offered him bacon and cabbage. Eulenspiegel kept quiet, ate what had been cooked there, and left on Monday.

The priest called after Eulenspiegel, "Listen, when you come back, bring two sausages with you – one for you and one for me. I'll pay you back whatever you have to spend for them. Then we'll really enjoy ourselves – till our mouths simply foam."

Eulenspiegel said, "Yes, Father, that's what'll happen. I'll certainly be thinking of you when I get the sausages." He went back to Hildesheim.

Now, it happened, as he hoped it would, that the commercial pig-slaughterers were carrying a sow to their slaughters' burial place. Eulenspiegel asked a slaughterer whether, for money, he would make two red sausages out of his sow, and paid him some silver pennies for them right there. The slaughterer did so, making him two fine red sausages. Eulenspiegel took them, boiled them half through, as was customary with such sausages, and went back to Hoheneggelsen the following Sunday. It happened that the priest was holding early mass. Eulenspiegel went over to the parsonage, brought his sausages to the cook, and told her to roast them for breakfast. The priest was to have one, and he the other. Then he went into the church.

Well, the girl placed the sausages on the fire and roasted them. When the mass was over, the priest noticed Eulenspiegel and immediately left the church for the parsonage, where he said, "Eulenspiegel is here. Did he bring the sausages too?"

She said, "Yes, two sausages, finer than almost any I've ever seen, and they're both just about roasted." She went over and took one out of the hot fire. Now, she was as greedy for the sausages as the priest, so they both sat down to eat together. But as they were eating the sausages so lustily, their mouths began to foam with decayed fat. Another man saw and heard the priest saying to his servant girl, "Oh, my dear girl! How your mouth is foaming!"

But the girl replied, "Oh, dear sir! Your mouth is just the same!"

Just at that moment, Eulenspiegel came in from church. The priest said to him, "Look here, what kind of sausages did you bring? Look how messy my mouth and my servant girl's mouth are!"

Eulenspiegel laughed. "God bless you," he said. "What's happening to you is exactly according to your wishes when you asked me to bring two sausages from which you planned to eat till your mouth simply foamed. But I paid no attention to the kind of foam – as long as vomit didn't follow it. I understand, though. That'll soon come. For these two sausages were made out of a dead sow. As a result, I had to boil them clean with soap. The mess comes from that."

The girl began to gag, and vomited all over the table. The priest did the same. He said, "Get out of my house, you rogue." He grabbed a club to beat him with.

Eulenspiegel said, "This doesn't become a pious man. You told me to bring these two sausages. Well, you've eaten both of them, and now you plan to beat me. First pay me for the sausages. I'll forget about the third one."

The priest became furious and almost crazy with rage and said Eulenspiegel himself ought to have eaten his moldy sausages made from the corpse of a sow, and not have brought this sort of stuff into his house.

Eulenspiegel said, "I certainly haven't made you sick against your wishes. Besides, I wouldn't want these sausages. I might have liked the first one, though. That one you ate against my wishes. Since you've gobbled up the first, good sausage – eat the bad ones too." And he said, "Adieu! Good night!"

38. How Eulenspiegel, with a false confession, talked the priest of Kissenbrück out of his horse.

Eulenspiegel could not keep out of terrible mischief at Kissenbrück, a village in the Asseburg jurisdiction. A priest was living there too, who had a very pretty girl as his maid and a little, pretty, smart horse, both of which the priest liked, the horse as much as the girl.

The Duke of Brunswick was at Kissenbrück just then, and had asked the priest, through other people, to let him have the horse: he would give the priest whatever would satisfy him for it. The priest continually refused the prince, as he had no desire to give up his horse. And the prince was also not entitled simply to have the

horse taken away, since the law there was under his own administration of Brunswick. Well, Eulenspiegel heard about this problem, thought it over, and told the prince, "Gracious Lord, what will you give me if I get that horse away from the priest of Kissenbrück?"

"If you can manage it," said the Duke, "I'll give you the coat I'm wearing." Well, it was a red camlet coat, woven with pearls.

Eulenspiegel accepted this challenge, and rode out of Wolfenbüttel to take lodgings with the priest in the village. Now, Eulenspiegel was well known at the priest's house, for he had often stayed with him before and was welcome there. When he had been at the priest's house for about three days, Eulenspiegel pretended to be ill, complained loudly of pain, and lay down. The priest and his cook, the girl, were unhappy about this, but had no idea what they ought to do about it. Finally Eulenspiegel became so sick that the priest spoke to him, exhorting him to confess and receive God's mercy. Eulenspiegel was quite inclined to do so – as long as the priest would confess him and question him as closely as possible. So the priest told him to consider well the state of his soul, for he had done a lot of crafty things during his lifetime. He had better prove himself true, so God would forgive him his sins.

Eulenspiegel spoke rather pitifully, telling the priest he knew of nothing he had done – aside from one sin, one he dared not confess to him. He would rather he got another priest: he would confess it to him. For Eulenspiegel feared that were he to confess it to the priest, he would become extremely angry. When the priest heard this, he reflected that there must be some secret here, and since he wanted to find out what it was, he told Eulenspiegel, "Eulenspiegel, the road is long. I can't find another priest all that quickly, and if you should die in the meantime, you and I shall bear the blame before Our Lord God, if you now miss your chance. Tell me what it is. Your sin cannot be so awful. I want to absolve you of it. Besides, what good would it do me to get angry? I cannot betray a confession."

Eulenspiegel said, "All right. I'll confess it." It would not be so awful either, but he was sorry that the priest would probably get angry, for the sin concerned him. The priest now ached even more to know what it was, and told him that whether he had stolen something or done him some harm – no matter what it might be – Eulenspiegel should confess it to him. The priest would forgive him and never despise him.

"Ah, dear Father," said Eulenspiegel, "I know that you'll be very angry about it. But I know and fear that soon I must take my leave of this place. So I'll tell it to you, letting God decide whether you become calm or angry. And, dear Father, it's this: I've slept with your servant girl."

The priest asked how often this had happened.

Eulenspiegel said, "Just five times."

The priest thought, "She ought to get five lashes for this." Then he quickly absolved Eulenspiegel, went to his room, and called the girl. He at once asked her whether she had slept with Eulenspiegel.

The girl, his cook, said, no, it was a lie.

But the priest said Eulenspiegel had confessed it to him – and he believed it.

She said, "No."

He said, "Yes."

And he took up a stick and beat her black and blue. Eulenspiegel lay laughing in bed, and thought, "This game ought to turn out well now and have a decent result." And he lay there all day.

During the night he became pretty healthy again. The next day he got up, saying he was getting better, and had to leave for another district, so the priest should figure out how much he had eaten there. The priest did the figuring with him, but was so confused he had no idea what he was doing – so he took money but it was no money, for he was happy enough that Eulenspiegel was leaving. The girl felt the same, since it was because of him that she had been beaten.

When Eulenspiegel was ready to go, he said, "Sir, you should be warned that you have revealed my confession. I plan to go to the Bishop of Halberstadt and expose you."

The priest forgot his sin of malice when he heard that Eulenspiegel intended to bring him difficulties and begged him earnestly to keep silent. It had happened because of rashness. He would give Eulenspiegel twenty guilders as long as he did not sue him.

Eulenspiegel said, "No. I wouldn't take a hundred guilders to keep silent about this. I shall go, and prefer charges, as is proper."

With tearful eyes, the priest called his servant girl, and said she should ask Eulenspiegel to tell her what he should give him: she could give it to him. Finally Eulenspiegel said: if the priest would give him his horse, he would keep silent and the betrayal would remain unknown. Eulenspiegel would, moreover, take nothing but the horse. The priest liked his horse enormously and would rather have given Eulenspiegel all his ready cash than lose his horse. But he gave it up against his will, as necessity forced him to. The priest gave his horse to Eulenspiegel and let him ride off with it.

Eulenspiegel immediately rode to Wolfenbüttel with the priest's horse. Well, he arrived at the moat. The Duke was standing there, on the drawbridge, and saw Eulenspiegel trotting up on the horse. At once the prince took off the coat he had promised Eulenspiegel, went straight over to him, and said, "Look here, my dear Eulenspiegel. Here is the coat I promised you."

Eulenspiegel dismounted, saying, "Gracious Lord, here's your horse." Well, he thanked the Duke profusely, and had to tell him how he had gotten the horse away from the priest. This made the prince laugh, and he was glad about it – and he gave Eulenspiegel another horse in addition to the coat.

But the priest mourned his horse, and beat the girl quite cruelly because of it – so much so that she left him. Thus he lost both.

39. How Eulenspiegel hired himself out to a blacksmith, and how he carried the blacksmith's bellows into his courtyard for him.

Eulenspiegel went over to Rostock, in the district of Mecklenburg, and hired himself out as a blacksmith's assistant. Now, this blacksmith had a favorite saying. Whenever his assistant was supposed to pump hard on the bellows, he said, "Hey! Hey! Follow with the bellows!" Well, Eulenspiegel was standing at the bellows and pumping. And the smith, in a harsh voice, said to Eulenspiegel, "Hey! Hey! Follow with the bellows!" With these words, he went into the courtyard, planning to drain off his water.

Eulenspiegel immediately placed one of the bellows on his shoulder, and followed his boss, saying, "Chief, I'm bringing one bellows here. Where should I stick it? I'll go and get the other one too."

His boss looked around and said, "Dear apprentice, I didn't mean it like that. Go put the bellows back."

Eulenspiegel did so, returning it to its proper place. Now, his boss wondered how he might get even with him for this, and decided to get up at midnight every night for five days, wake up his assistant, and make him work. In fact he woke up both his assistants, and let them do some forging.

Eulenspiegel's fellow assistant questioned him. "What can the boss mean by waking us up so early? He doesn't usually do so."

So Eulenspiegel said, "If you like, I'll ask him."

The boy said, "All right."

Eulenspiegel said, "My dear boss, why're you waking us up so early? It's just midnight."

His boss said, "It's my custom that at the beginning – and for eight days – my boys don't sleep longer than half the night."

Eulenspiegel kept quiet, and his companion dared not speak, till the next night. Then his boss woke them up and Eulenspiegel's companion went to work. But Eulenspiegel took his bed and tied it onto his back. Then, when the iron was hot, he came running down from the garret to the anvil, crashing the bed against the anvil, so the sparks spewed into the bed.

The blacksmith said to him, "Look here! What're you doing? Have you gone crazy? Can't the bed stay where it's supposed to be?"

Eulenspiegel said, "Chief, don't be angry. This is my custom – that during the first weeks I lie on the bed for half the night, and for the second half of the night the bed lies on me."

His boss became furious, ordering him to bring back the bed he had taken. Then he rashly went on, "Now, you maddening fool, get up and out of my house!"

Eulenspiegel said, "Yes." So he climbed up into the garret, putting back the bed he had taken, found a ladder, stuck it against the coping, broke the roof open, went out onto the roof with the ladder, pulled the ladder up after him, set it into the street from the roof, climbed down, and so got away.

The blacksmith heard him making loud noises, and followed him into the garret with his other assistant. There he saw that Eulenspiegel had broken the roof open and climbed out. He now got even more furious and hunted for a skewer, throwing it after him out of the house. But his assistant calmed the blacksmith, saying, "Chief, take it easy! Admit he hasn't done anything other than what you told him to. When you told him to get up and out of the house, he did so, as you now see." The smith let himself be pacified.

What else could he do? Eulenspiegel was gone and his boss had to have the roof mended, and had to be satisfied with that.

His assistant said, "Not much to be gained from a fellow-worker like that one. Whoever doesn't know Eulenspiegel – just let him deal with him, and he'll get to know him."

40. How Eulenspiegel forged a blacksmith's hammer, tongs, and other tools together.

When Eulenspiegel left the blacksmith, it was nearly winter. Well, the winter was cold and froze cruelly. Eulenspiegel fell on hard times because of it, as many workers were going without work. Well, Eulenspiegel had no money to waste, so he wandered on and came to a village where there was another blacksmith, who took him in as an assistant. Eulenspiegel certainly had no great desire to stay on there as a smith's boy, though his hunger and the need of winter forced him to do it, so he thought, "Bear what you can bear, and do what the smith wants till you can stick your finger into the spongy earth of spring again."

The smith had no intention of hiring him just because times were hard. So Eulenspiegel told the smith that if he would give

him any sort of work, he would do whatever he wanted – and eat whatever nobody else wanted. Well, the smith was a wicked man, and he thought, "Take him on for eight days' trial. He won't eat me into poverty that soon."

The next morning they began forging, and the smith drove Eulenspiegel mercilessly, at hammer and bellows, till mealtime, when it was getting on toward noon. Well, the smith had an outhouse in the courtyard. As they were preparing to go to table, he took Eulenspiegel into the courtyard, led him to the outhouse, and said to him, "Look, you say you're willing to eat whatever I want as long as I give you work. Now, nobody'd enjoy what's in here – so you eat it all." He went into the house, ate something, and left Eulenspiegel standing at the outhouse.

Eulenspiegel kept quiet, but he thought, "You've run the wrong way here, and done such things yourself to many people – to the extent that it's now being measured out to you. How do you plan to pay him back for this? For it's got to be paid back, though the winter were twice as harsh."

Eulenspiegel worked for the man until evening. Then the smith gave Eulenspiegel something to eat, for he had gone hungry all day, and besides it stuck in the smith's head that he had shown him to the outhouse. As Eulenspiegel was getting ready to go to bed, the smith said to him, "Get up tomorrow morning. The girl will work the bellows, and you forge whatever you've got, one thing after the other. And cut horseshoe nails till I get up."

Eulenspiegel went to sleep. But when he got up, he thought he would now pay the blacksmith back, even if he had to run through snow up to his knees. He built a fierce fire, took the tongs, melted them in the sand-ladle, and forged them together, doing the same to two hammers, the firing spit, and the poker. Then he took the box in which the horseshoe nails lay, poured the nails out of it, and cut the heads off them, sticking the heads together and the stumps as well. Then, as he heard the smith getting up, he grabbed his leather apron and got out of there.

The smith came into his workshop and saw that the nails and heads had been cut apart and that his hammer, tongs, and other tools had been forged together. He got pretty angry and screamed at the girl to tell him where his assistant had gone. The girl said he had gone out.

The smith said, "He's gone – like a rogue. If I knew where he was, I'd ride after him and give a fine slapping."

The girl said, "He was writing something over the door as he left. It's a face that looks like an owl's."

Now, Eulenspiegel had this custom whenever did some mischief where he was unknown: he took chalk or coal and drew an owl and a mirror over the door, and underneath wrote, in Latin, *Hic fuit*. And this Eulenspiegel had drawn on the smith's door too.

When the smith came out of his house that morning, he found it, as the girl had told him. But because the smith could not read the language, he went over to the priest and asked him to come read the writing over his door. The priest went with the smith to his door, and saw the writing and the picture.

He told the smith, "It simply means 'Eulenspiegel was here.' " In fact the priest had heard a great deal about Eulenspiegel – about the sort of fellow he was – and scolded the smith because he had not let him know, for he would greatly have liked to have seen Eulenspiegel.

The smith instantly got angry with the priest and said, "How could I let you know about it, when I didn't know myself? But I know now that he was definitely at my house. That you can see well enough by my working tools. But that he never comes back, there isn't much against it." He took the coal-brush, whisked off what was above his door, and said, "I don't want any fool's coat of arms over my door."

The priest walked off, leaving the smith standing there. But Eulenspiegel did not appear, and did not return.

41. How Eulenspiegel told something true to a blacksmith, his wife, his assistant, and his servant girl in front of his house.

After he left the smith, Eulenspiegel went to Wismar, on a holy day. He saw a proper wife and her maid standing in front of the smithy there. It was the blacksmith's wife. Well, he took lodgings opposite the smithy, and during the night broke all four horseshoes off his horse, marching up in front of the smithy the next day. That way he was recognized.

When he came up to the smithy, and they realized it was Eulenspiegel, the wife and maid stood at an entrance of the house, as they wanted to hear and see Eulenspiegel's business. Eulenspiegel asked the smith whether he would shoe his horse.

The smith said, "All right." Now, it pleased the smith to be able to converse with Eulenspiegel. After much talk, the smith happened to say to Eulenspiegel that if he could tell him one true thing – something that was really true – he would give his horse one horseshoe.

Eulenspiegel said, "All right:
"If you've got irons and coals
And wind for your bellows' holes –
You can forge well."

The smith said that, by his soul, that was true, and gave him a horseshoe.

His assistant was putting the irons on the horse and felt compelled to say to Eulenspiegel that if he could also tell him something true concerning him, he would give his horse a horseshoe too.

Eulenspiegel said, "All right:
If they want to set about something,
A blacksmith and his boy
Must stand to hard employ."

The boy said, "That's true too," and gave him a horseshoe as well.

The wife and maid saw this, and pressed closer, to be able to speak with Eulenspiegel too, and they told him that if he could say something true to them too, they would give him one horseshoe each.

Eulenspiegel said, "Very well." He said to the wife:
"The wife who stands before her doors
With lots of white in her eye,
If she had the time and were free of chores –

There wouldn't be fish to fry."

The wife said, "By my soul, that's true." And she gave him a horseshoe as well.

Then he told the maid, "When you eat, guard against beef. You won't have to pick your teeth, and your stomach won't bother you."

The maid said, "God protect us, how true that is!" And she gave him an iron horseshoe also.

So Eulenspiegel rode off, with his horse well shod.

42. How Eulenspiegel worked for a shoemaker, and how Eulenspiegel asked him what shapes he should cut. His boss said, "Large and small, like those the swineherd runs past the gate." So Eulenspiegel cut out oxen, cattle, calves, rams, and the like, and ruined the leather.

There was once a shoemaker who much preferred strolling around the market place to working, and he hired Eulenspiegel for cutting. Eulenspiegel asked what sort of shapes he would like, and the shoemaker said, "Cut both large and small–like those the swineherd runs out of town."

Eulenspiegel said, "Sure."

The shoemaker went out, and Eulenspiegel to cutting–and he made pigs, oxen, calves, sheep, goats, rams, and all sorts of beasts out of the leather. In the evening his boss returned, planning to see what his assistant had cut, and he found these animals cut out of his leather. He got angry, saying to Eulenspiegel, "What've you made out of it? How could you cut up my leather so uselessly for me?"

Eulenspiegel said, "My dear boss, I've done it as you wanted it."

His boss said, "You're lying. I didn't mean that you should destroy it. I didn't ask you to do that."

Eulenspiegel said, "Chief, what's the reason for this anger? You told me I should cut large and small out of the leather–like the swineherd runs past the gate. I did so. That's obvious."

His boss said, "I didn't mean it that way. I meant this: they should be large and small shoes, and you should stitch them, one after the other."

Eulenspiegel said "If you'd asked me to do that, I'd gladly have done so. And I'd still be glad to do so."

Well Eulenspiegel and his boss were reconciled, and the shoemaker forgave him that cutting. Even more than that, Eulenspiegel promised him he would do it for him as he told him he wanted it done. So the shoemaker cut out leather for soles, placed it in front of Eulenspiegel, and said, "Now look, stitch the small with the large, one after the other."

Eulenspiegel said, "Sure," and began stitching.

His boss put off going out, as he wanted to watch Eulenspiegel to see how he planned to do it, since he had realized that Eulenspiegel would do exactly what he had told him to do.

Well, Eulenspiegel acted according to his boss's instructions. He took one small shoe and one large, stuck the small into the large, and stitched them together. Well, as his boss was going strolling, he became nervous about what he might be doing. It was then that he saw that Eulenspiegel was stitching one shoe inside the other.

His boss said, "You're my proper assistant. You do everything I tell you to."

Eulenspiegel said, "He who does what he's told doesn't get punished. On the contrary."

His boss said, "Yes, my dear assistant, that's true. My words ran this way–but my meaning certainly didn't. I meant you should make a pair of small shoes, and afterwards a large pair. Or the large first, the small next. You're acting according to the words, not the meaning." He got quite angry, snatched up some leather, and said, "Pay attention a little! Look, here's more leather. Cut the shoes out over a last." Then he thought no more about it, as he had to go out.

His boss was tending to his affairs, and had been out almost an hour, when he realized that he had told his assistant to cut the shoes over a last. He dropped everything and rushed home. Well, during this time Eulenspiegel had been sitting there, and had taken the leather and cut all of it over a single last.

His boss at once said, "Why're you doing the large shoes with the small?"

Eulenspiegel said, "Well, you wanted it that way. I still plan to do everything well. So now, afterwards, I'll cut the large ones."

His boss said, "You can more easily cut small shoes out of large than large out of small. You're using one last, and the other is sitting around unused."

Eulenspiegel said, "True enough, Chief. You told me to cut the shoes out over a last."

His boss said, "I might go on telling you–till I have to run you to the gallows." And he went on to say that Eulenspiegel should pay for the leather he had ruined, since he would now need to buy more leather.

Eulenspiegel said, "The tanner can fix your leather again." Then he stood up, went to the door, turned round in the house, and said, "If I don't come back to this house–at least I've been here." And he left.

43. How Eulenspiegel sprinkled a soup for a farmer, putting filthy-smelling fish oil on it instead of bread and drippings, and thought that was good enough for the farmer.

Eulenspiegel did a great deal of mischief to shoemakers, not just in one place but in many. When he had done this last bit of nonsense, he arrived in Stade. There too he hired himself out to a shoemaker.

On the first day, when he started working, his boss went off to the market and bought a cartload of wood. Well, he agreed to give the farmer a soup as well as money, and brought the farmer, along with the wood, to his house. There he found no one at home (his wife and maid had gone out) but Eulenspiegel, who was alone in the house, stitching shoes. As his boss had to return to the market, he told Eulenspiegel to take whatever he found and make the farmer a soup: he had left him something in the cupboard.

Eulenspiegel said, "All right."

Well, the farmer threw down his wood and came into the house. Eulenspiegel cut pieces of bread into a bowl for him, but found no melted-down fat in the cupboard. So he went to the tank in which the shoemaker's awful-smelling fish oil was kept, and sprinkled the farmer's soup with that. The farmer began eating, and tasted how awful it was, but he was hungry and ate all the soup.

In the meantime, the shoemaker came in and asked the farmer how the soup had tasted. The farmer said, "It tasted very good – and just a little like new shoes." And with that the farmer left the house.

The shoemaker began to laugh and asked Eulenspiegel what he had used to sprinkle the farmer's soup with.

Eulenspiegel said, "You told me to take what I had. Well, I had no fat other than fish fat – as I looked into the cupboard in the kitchen and didn't find any fat. So I took what I had."

The shoemaker said, "Well, that's all right. It's good enough for the farmer."

44. How a bootmaker in Brunswick larded Eulenspiegel's boots, and how Eulenspiegel knocked the windows out of his room.

"Christopher" was the name of a bootmaker at the coal market in Brunswick. Eulenspiegel went over to him, planning to have his boots oiled. When he got to the bootmaker's, he said, "Dear master-bootmaker, would you lard[1] these boots for me, so I can have them back by Monday?"

The bootmaker said, "Very well."

Eulenspiegel left the house and thought no more about it. When he was gone, the apprentice told his boss, "That's Eulenspiegel, who's too mischievous with everybody." – And that if he were to tell him to do "What he told you to do," he would do it and not fail to.

His boss said, "Well, what did he tell me to do?"

---

1. "Lard" was evidently a bit of bootmaker's jargon for "oil."

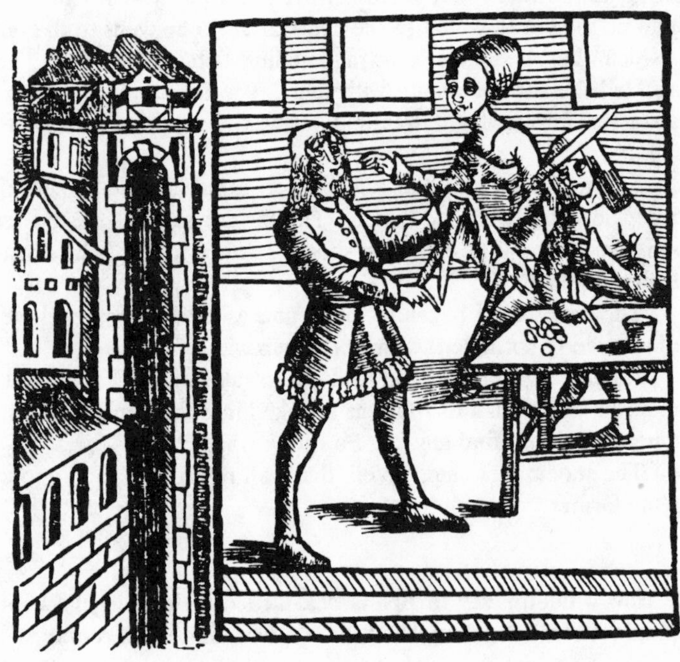

The apprentice said, "He really told you to 'lard' his boots – and he meant to 'oil' them. Now, I wouldn't oil them. I'd lard them, as one bastes a roast."

His boss said, "That we'll do – just as he told us." So he took bacon, cut it up, and larded the boots with a larding-needle – like a roast.

Well, on Monday Eulenspiegel came back, and asked whether they had his boots ready for him. The bootmaker had hung them on the wall, and pointed them out to him, saying, "There they hang."

Eulenspiegel saw that his boots had in fact been larded – and began to laugh, saying, "What a straightforward master-bootmaker you are! You've done it as I told you to. What do you want for this?"

The bootmaker said, "One old shilling."

Eulenspiegel presented the old shilling, took his larded boots, and left the house. Well, the bootmaker and his apprentice watched him go, laughing after him, and they said to one another, "How could that happen to him? Now he's been made a fool of."

In the meantime Eulenspiegel rammed his head and shoulders through the window from the street – for the room was on the ground floor and gave onto the street – and said to the bootmaker, "Dear master-bootmaker, what sort of fat did you use for my boots? Is it sow's fat or boar's fat?"

The bootmaker and his apprentice were puzzled. Finally they realized that Eulenspiegel was lying in the window and knocking the window panes fully half out – with the result that they were falling toward the bootmaker into the room. The bootmaker at once got furious and said, "You tricky liar! If you don't stop, I'll beat you over the head with this stick!"

Eulenspiegel said, "Dear master-bootmaker, don't lose your temper. I'd like to know what sort of fat it was that you larded my boots with. Is it sow's fat or boar's fat?"

The bootmaker went mad with rage, saying he had better leave his windows unbroken.

"If you don't want to tell me what kind of fat it is, I'll have to ask somebody else." And Eulenspiegel jumped back out of the windows.

Well, the bootmaker now got simply furious with his apprentice too, telling him, "You advised me to do this! Now give me advice on how to have my windows fixed!"

The apprentice was silent. His boss became indignant, saying, "Who's made a fool of whom? I've always heard that whoever's bothered by tricksters should cut the traces and let them go. If I'd done so, my windows would still be in one piece."

The apprentice was fired because of this. His boss wanted his windows paid for – since the apprentice had given him the idea to lard the boots.

45. How Eulenspiegel sold a shoemaker of Wismar frozen filth for tallow.

Eulenspiegel once did a lot of damage in leather-cutting to a shoemaker of Wismar, destroying much of his leather and making the good man quite unhappy. Eulenspiegel took stock of this, returned to Wismar, and told the shoemaker to whom he had done the damage that he planned to obtain a huge load of leather and tallow that ought to yield the shoemaker quite a profit, so he might recover his loss.

The shoemaker said, "Well, you're acting fairly, since you've made me a poor man. When you get the goods, let me know."

Then they parted. Well, it was wintertime, and the harnessmakers were cleaning the outhouses. Eulenspiegel went to them and promised them ready money if they would fill twelve barrels for him with the material they were otherwise planning to dispose of in the water. The harnessmakers did so, packing the barrels quite full, so they were four fingers from the top, and left them standing till they had frozen stiff. Eulenspiegel then hauled them away. Well, he caked six barrels over thickly with tallow, beating them tightly shut; smeared six barrels over with cooking fat, beating these all tightly shut; had them brought to his inn, "At the Golden Star," for a Dutch guilder; and sent a messenger to the shoemaker. When the shoemaker arrived, they opened the goods on top, and the shoemaker was quite pleased with them. They settled their purchase, with the shoemaker giving Eulenspiegel twenty-four guilders for the load. He was to give Eulenspiegel twelve guilders at once, the rest in a year. Eulenspiegel took the money and left, as he was worried about what would happen.

The shoemaker received his goods and was as happy as one who has overcome hopeless injury or debt. He summoned help to be able to oil his leather the next day. The shoemaker's boys showed up in strength, thinking they might at least get a good meal, and set about the work, singing loudly, as they usually do. But when they had placed the barrels on the fire and they began to get warm, they regained their natural smell. Everybody said to everybody else, "I think you've been shitting in your pants."

The shoemaker said, "If somebody's stepped in some filth, wash your shoes. It stinks terribly everywhere."

They looked around and found nothing, and began to pour the tallow into a kettle and begin oiling. But the deeper they dug with their oiling the more foully it stank. Finally they realized what it was and left the work standing.

The shoemaker and his helpers ran to look for Eulenspiegel to hold him for the damages, but he had left with the money. He was even supposed to return for the other twelve guilders. So the shoemaker had to take his barrels of tallow to the slaughterers' graveyard, and sustain double his loss.

46. How Eulenspiegel became a brewer's assistant at Einbeck, and how he boiled a dog called Hops, instead of hops.

Once again Eulenspiegel made himself useful in his work.

After people at Einbeck had forgotten about his shitting on the plums,[1] he came back to Einbeck and offered his services to a brewer of beer. It happened that the brewer wanted to go to a wedding, so he told Eulenspiegel to brew beer with his servant girl as best he could. The brewer would return to help him in the evening. Now, above all, Eulenspiegel should work hard and boil the hops well, so the beer would taste strong afterwards and the brewer could sell it. Eulenspiegel said, yes, he would do his best. With that, the brewer and his wife left the house.

Eulenspiegel began his boiling enthusiastically. The servant girl instructed him, as she knew more about it than he did. Well, when the time came for boiling the hops, the girl said, "The boiling

---

1. Possibly a reference to the eighty-seventh story.

of the hops, dear, that you can do very well on your own. Let me go watch the dance for an hour."

Eulenspiegel said, "Sure." But he thought, "If the girl leaves too, you've got a chance for some fun. What sort of joke would you like to play on this brewer?"

Well, the brewer had a large dog called Hops. When the water was very hot, Eulenspiegel took it, threw it into the water, and let it boil through till its skin and hair came off and all the flesh fell off its legs. Well, when the servant girl thought it was time to go home–for the hops must have boiled enough by now–she came back, planning to help Eulenspiegel. She said, "My dear brother, that's enough now. Drain it off."

But when they moved the straining basket and started to dig into it, one shovelful after the other, the girl said, "Did you put hops in here too? I don't notice any yet on my shovel."

Eulenspiegel said, "You'll find it at the bottom."

The girl fished around and lifted the skeleton on her shovel. She began to scream horribly. "God help me, what did you put in here! The devil drink this beer!"

Eulenspiegel said, "I only put into it what our brewer told me to put into it. Why, it's nothing other than Hops, our dog."

At that moment the brewer came home, quite drunk, and said, "What're you doing, my dear children? Are you being good little things?"

The girl said, "I don't know what the devil we're doing. I went to watch the dance for half an hour, and told our new assistant to boil the hops well in the meantime. He boiled our dog. You can see its spine here."

Eulenspiegel said, "Yes, sir. You both told me to do so. Isn't it terrible? I do everything that people tell me to–and never seem to earn much thanks at all. There may be some brewers somewhere who'll be satisfied if their servants do only half what they're told to do."

So Eulenspiegel quit, and left the place–without earning much in the way of appreciation.

47. How Eulenspiegel hired himself out to a tailor and sewed under a tub.

When Eulenspiegel went to Berlin, he hired himself out as a tailor's boy. When he was sitting in the workshop, his boss said, "Boy, when you want to sew, sew well and sew so nobody sees it."

Eulenspiegel said, "Yes," and took the needle, and material with it, crawled under a tub, folded a seam over one knee, and began to sew it there.

The tailor stood watching this, and said to him, "What're you doing? This is strange needlework."

Eulenspiegel said, "Boss, you said I should sew so nobody sees it. Well, nobody sees it."

The tailor said, "No, my dear assistant. Stop and don't sew that way any more. Start sewing so it can be seen."

This went on for maybe three days. Then it happened that they worked till nightfall. The tailor was tired and wanted to go to bed. A gray farmer's coat was lying there, half unsewn, which he tossed to Eulenspiegel, saying "Look, finish the wolf[1] and go to bed too."

Eulenspiegel said, "Yes. You just go ahead. I'll do it properly."

His boss went to bed and thought no more about it. Eulenspiegel took the gray coat and cut it up, making a head like a wolf's out of it, with body and legs, and stretching it over separated sticks, so it quite resembled a wolf. Then he went to bed too.

The next morning his boss got up, woke Eulenspiegel as well, and found the wolf standing in his workroom. His boss was outraged, but he understood well enough what had happened. Eulenspiegel came in just then, and the tailor said, "What the devil did you make out of it?"

He said, "A wolf – as you told me."

The tailor said, "I didn't mean that sort of wolf. I simply called the gray farmer's coat a wolf."

Eulenspiegel said, "My dear boss, that I didn't realize. If I'd known your thoughts ran that way, I'd have preferred making the coat to making the wolf."

Well, the tailor accepted that, since it had happened just once. But after about four days it chanced that his boss felt tired one evening and decided to go to sleep early. It seemed to him, however, that it was still too early for his assistant to go to bed. Now, a coat was lying there that had been finished up to its arms. So Eulenspiegel's boss took the coat and its loose arms, tossed them over to Eulenspiegel, and said, "Cast these arms on the coat, and then go to bed."

Eulenspiegel said, "Yes."

His boss went to bed – and Eulenspiegel hung the coat on a hook and lit two lamps, one on either side of the coat. He took one arm and threw it at the coat, and went to the other side and threw the other at it too; and when the two lamps burned out, he lit two more, casting the arms on the coat straight through the night till morning. His boss now got up and came into the room.

---

1. A slang term for such coats. See Notes on the Tales. The same word play recurs in tale 53.

Eulenspiegel ignored his boss, and kept casting the arms at the coat.

The tailor stood there, looking at this, and said, "What sort of devilish fraud are you engaged in?"

Eulenspiegel said, quite seriously, "This isn't any devilish fraud for me. I've been standing here all night – throwing these crazy arms at this coat, and they won't stay there. It would have been better if you'd told me to go to bed than telling me to 'cast on.' And you knew perfectly well that this was pointless work."

The tailor said, "Is it my fault? Could I know that you would interpret me that way? I didn't mean it that way. I meant that you should sew the arms on the coat."

Eulenspiegel at once said, "The devil reward you for it. If you've a fancy to say something other than what you mean, how is one to rhyme the things together? If I'd known your intentions clearly, I'd have sewed the arms on all right – and gotten a few hours of sleep. Well, you sit and sew all day, and I'll lie down and sleep."

His boss said, "Oh, no, not a chance! I'm not going to keep you on here as a loafer."

Well, they began to quarrel with each other – and so much so that during their quarreling the tailor addressed Eulenspiegel about the lamps: he ought to pay him for those he had used during this business. At that point Eulenspiegel took up his things and walked away.

48. How Eulenspiegel made three tailor's boys fall off a bench – and told people the wind had blown them off it.

Eulenspiegel stayed at an inn near the market place in Bernburg for about fourteen days. Now, hard by the inn lived a tailor who had three boys sitting on a bench and sewing. Whenever Eulenspiegel passed by, they mocked him or threw their remnants at him. Eulenspiegel kept quiet, biding his time. But one day when the market place was full of people, Eulenspiegel had sawn off the supporting posts of the bench the night before, leaving them standing on their foundations.

That morning the apprentices placed the bench on its posts, sat down, and sewed. But when the swineherd began his yelling – that everybody ought to let his pigs be driven out – the tailor's pigs came out of his house, rushed under his window, and began to rub themselves against the benchposts. The result of the rubbing was that the posts were punched out from under the window, and the three boys sitting under the window tumbled into the lane. Eulenspiegel caught sight of them, and as they fell, began calling in a loud voice, "Look, look, the wind's tossing three boys out of this window!" – calling it so stridently that he could be heard all over the market place. Well, the people ran over and laughed and jeered, but the boys were embarrassed, and had no idea how they had fallen from under the window. Finally they noticed that the benchposts had been sawed through – and realized also that Eulenspiegel had done it. They pounded new posts into place, and did not dare make fun of him again.

49. How Eulenspiegel called all the tailors of Saxony together to teach them a skill that would help them and their children.

Eulenspiegel announced a convocation and assembly of the tailors of the Wendish towns and of the district of Saxony–also of those in the districts of Holstein, Pomerania, Stettin, and Mecklenburg; also of Lübeck, Hamburg, Sunt, and Wismar. In his letter he assured them of a grand opportunity–namely, that if they would meet with him (he was in the city of Rostock) he would teach them a tailoring method that would help them and their children forever, for as long as the world lasted.

The tailors in the cities, country towns, and villages wrote one another their views of this idea. They all wrote that they were ready to come to the city at an appointed time and would all assemble there. Each longed more than the next to learn what it might be that Eulenspiegel planned to say, or what sort of method he would teach them, since he had written to them so urgently. Well, they arrived in Rostock at the appointed time–all according to their pledges – with the result that many people wondered what all these tailors were doing there.

When Eulenspiegel heard that the tailors had actually responded to his invitation, he had them draw together in a tight little group. The tailors at once told Eulenspiegel that they had come there and answered him because of his announcement, in which he had alluded to the fact that he could teach them a method that would help them and their children. They asked that he enlighten them, make his method public, and inform them about it. They would reward him well.

Eulenspiegel said, "All right. Let's all meet in a meadow, so each of you can hear me."

They all met on a broad plain. Eulenspiegel climbed up inside a house, peered out of a window, and said, "Honorable men of the craft of tailoring! You should note and understand: if you have a pair of scissors, tape-measure, thread, and a thimble, along with a needle, you've got the right equipment for your profession. Getting hold of this stuff is hardly a difficult proposition for you. In fact, it follows of itself, if you wish to engage in your profession. But here's a method you'll receive from me, and you'll thank me for it. When you've threaded your needle, don't forget to make a knot at the other end, or you'll sew a lot of stitches uselessly, as the thread will have no reason not to slip out of the needle."

Each tailor looked at the next, and they said to one another, "We all knew this skill well enough before – along with everything else he's told us." And they asked him whether he had anything more to say, since they had not planned on traveling ten or twelve miles, and sending messengers to each other, for this nonsense. Tailors had known this method for a long time, for more than a thousand years.

Eulenspiegel responded to this by saying, "There isn't anybody who remembers what happened a thousand years ago." He also said that if his advice did not meet with pleasure and thanks, they might as well take it in displeasure and no thanks – and that the crowd could just go back to where it had come from. The tailors, who had come from so far away, and who really wanted to be instructed by him, at once became pretty angry, but they could not manage to get at him. So the tailors simply dispersed. Some were furious, cursed, and were thoroughly annoyed that they had gone such a great distance for nothing. But those who lived in nearby houses laughed and jeered at the others because they had made such fools of themselves, and said it was their own fault if they believed country rogues and knaves – for they ought to have realized long ago what sort of bird Eulenspiegel was.

50. How Eulenspiegel beat wool on a holy day, because the clothier had forbidden his having Monday off.

When Eulenspiegel arrived in Stendal, he made out that he was a wool-weaver. On Sunday his wool-weaver boss told him, "Dear apprentice, you fellows take your days off on Mondays – but whoever's used to doing that I don't want in my business. A boy's got to work right through the week."

Eulenspiegel said, "Yes, Chief, I like it that way too."

So the next morning Eulenspiegel got up and beat wool,

doing the same on Tuesday, and this quite pleased the wool-weaver. Now, Wednesday was an Apostle's day, which they had to celebrate, but Eulenspiegel acted as though he knew nothing about the holy day. He got up that morning, and started to clean and beat wool – doing it so it could be heard through the whole street. The wool-weaver at once shot out of his bed, saying, "Stop! Stop! This is a holiday."

Eulenspiegel said, "My dear boss, you informed me about no holiday on Sunday. On the contrary, you told me to work the whole week through."

The wool-weaver said, "Dear assistant, I didn't mean it that way. Just stop and don't beat any more. I'll gladly give you whatever you might have earned today."

Eulenspiegel was happy about that, took the day off, and that evening had a conference with his boss. The wool-weaver now told him that he was succeeding quite well with his beating of the wool – only he ought to beat it a little higher.

Eulenspiegel said, "Sure."

He got up early the next morning, stretched the bow over the lath, and placed a ladder against it. Then he climbed up, arranging it so the beater could follow him from the basket, took the wool from the basket (which was standing on the ground) up to the oast and beat the wool so it scattered all over the house. The wool-weaver was lying in bed. He could hear by the beating that Eulenspiegel was not doing it properly. He got up to watch him.

Eulenspiegel said, "Chief, what do you think? Is this high enough?"

His boss said, "Ha! Terrific fellow! If you stood on the roof, you'd be even higher. If you want to beat the wool that way, you could just as well do it sitting down on the roof instead of standing up here on this ladder." With that he left the house for church.

Eulenspiegel took his advice. He took the beater, climbed onto the roof, and beat the wool on the roof. His boss, outside in the lane, caught sight of it. He ran right back, shouting, "What the devil are you doing! Stop! Is beating wool on the roof how it's usually done?"

Eulenspiegel said, "What're you saying now? You just said it would be better on the roof than on the ladder, because that's higher than the rungs of the ladder."

The wool-weaver said, "If you want to beat wool, beat it. If you want to fool around, fool around. Climb off the roof and shit in the wool-basket." With that the wool-weaver went into his house and out into his courtyard. Eulenspiegel at once climbed off the roof, went into the sitting room of the house, and deposited a huge pile of filth in the wool-basket. The wool-weaver came back from the courtyard, saw him shitting in the parlor, and said "Oh, may you never have any happiness! You're behaving like a scoundrel!"

Eulenspiegel said, "Chief, I'm doing nothing but what you told me to. You told me to climb off the roof and shit in the wool-basket. Why are you so angry about it? I'm doing what you told me."

The wool-weaver said, "You'd shit on my head–without being told. Take that excrement and stick it where no one will have it."

Eulenspiegel said, "Yes," and put the excrement on a piece of wood carried it into the dining room.

The wool-weaver said, "Leave that outside! I don't want that in here!"

Eulenspiegel said, "I know perfectly well you don't want it in here. Nobody would want it in here. But I'm doing what you told me."

The wool-weaver got really angry, and ran to the stable, planning to beat Eulenspiegel over the head with a log. But Eulenspiegel left the house, saying, "Can't I earn any gratitude anywhere?"

The wool-weaver then tried to grab the piece of wood on which Eulenspiegel had stuck his shit, but he was in too much of a hurry and made his fingers dirty. He let the filthy thing drop and ran to the well to wash his hands.

In the meantime, Eulenspiegel left.

51. How Eulenspiegel hired himself out to a furrier and shitted in his workroom for him, because one stink is supposed to drive out another.

Eulenspiegel once arrived in Aschersleben. Now, it was deep winter and a bitter time, and he thought, "What'll you take up now, to bring you through the winter?" There was no one who needed an assistant, but a furrier was living there who wanted to hire an apprentice, if one showed up who worked his trade. Eulenspiegel thought, "What'll you do? It's winter, and hard because of it. You've got to bear what you can bear and bear the winter out." So he hired himself out as an apprentice to the furrier.

When he went into the workshop to sew pelts, he was unused to their stink, and said, "Fie, fie! You may be white as chalk, but you stink like filthy garbage."

The furrier said, "You don't like the smell – and still you're sitting here? That it smells is only natural. It's from the wool the sheep has on the outside."

Eulenspiegel kept quiet and thought, "One evil is supposed to drive off another." And he released such a sour fart that both his boss and his wife had to hold their noses.

The furrier said, "What're you doing? If you like making filthy farts, get out of the room into the courtyard and fart as much as you like."

Eulenspiegel said, "For the health of a human being this is much more natural than the stink of sheepskins."

The furrier said, "Whether it's healthy or not, if you want to fart, go into the courtyard."

Eulenspiegel said, "Chief, there it'll be lost. No fart enjoys being out in the cold. They're always where it's warm. To prove it, release a fart. It'll immediately run back to your nose, to the warmth from which it came."

The furrier kept quiet. He knew perfectly well that he was being made the butt of a joke and was certain he would not keep Eulenspiegel for long. Eulenspiegel remained sitting there, and sewed, farted, and breathed out, coughing the hairs out of his mouth. The furrier sat and watched him, keeping quiet till evening, after they had eaten.

Then his boss said to him, "Dear assistant, it seems clear to me that you aren't happy with this trade. I'm convinced you aren't a true furrier's apprentice. That I can see by your attitude. Or you can't have been at it for long, if you aren't used to the work. If you'd merely slept with it for four days, you wouldn't be turning up your nose that way and complaining about it. It wouldn't be offensive to you. Therefore, my dear assistant, if you haven't any wish to stay on here, tomorrow please go wherever your horse takes you."

Eulenspiegel said, "Chief, you're telling the truth when you say I haven't been at this for long. If you'll just let me sleep near the work for four nights, till I'm used to it, then you'll see what I can do."

The furrier was happy with that since he needed Eulenspiegel and he could sew well.

52. How Eulenspiegel slept among pelts for a furrier–dry and damp, as the furrier told him to.

The furrier and his wife went happily to bed. Eulenspiegel took the prepared hides that were hanging on the frames, the dry hides that had been tanned, and the wet ones too. He piled them together on the floor, crawled between them, and slept till morning.

His boss now got up and saw that his hides were gone from their frames. He quickly ran over to his workshop to ask Eulenspiegel whether he knew anything about the hides. But he did not find Eulenspiegel, and saw that his pelts, both dry and damp, were lying in a pile on the floor–all mixed up with one another. He got pretty anxious, and in a tearful voice called his maid and wife.

Well, his shouting roused Eulenspiegel, who peered out of the pelts and said, "My dear boss, what on earth is wrong, that you're shouting so much?"

The furrier was amazed, not realizing that he was in the pile of hides and pelts, and said, "Where are you?"

Eulenspiegel said, "Here I am, in here."

His boss said, "Ah! May nothing good ever come your way! You've taken my pelts off the frames, the dry hides, and the wet ones out of the limewater–and piled them up together here. You're destroying the one with the other for me. What sort of nonsense is this?"

Eulenspiegel said, "Chief, if you're angry about it, and I haven't slept in here more than one night, you'd be much angrier if I slept in here for four nights–as you told me to yesterday evening because I wasn't used to the work."

The furrier said, "You're lying like a knave! I didn't tell you to drag the finished hides across the floor, and the damp ones, and sleep in them." And he looked for a stick to beat him with.

In the meantime, Eulenspiegel hurried downstairs, meaning to run out through the door. The wife and maid were standing at the bottom of the stairs. They tried to stop him. So he screamed wildly, "Let me go for a doctor! The boss has broken his leg!"

They let him go and ran upstairs. But the furrier was coming downstairs, running fiercely after Eulenspiegel, and he stumbled, falling on his wife and maid, and all three piled onto each other.

Well, Eulenspiegel ran out through the door, leaving them in the house together.

53. How Eulenspiegel, in Berlin, made wolves for a furrier, instead of "wolf-pelts."

Swabians are extremely sly people. If they try one sort of thing to make a living, and cannot get by, another must be worse. In reality, they are more fond of the beer mug and of drinking than of working, and for this reason their workshops often stand empty.

A furrier who was a Swabian once lived in Berlin. Now, he was quite skillful in his profession and also careful with his expenditures. As a result, he was also rich and ran a fine

workshop. He had among his clientele the prince of the district, the nobility, and many good people and citizens. Well, it happened that the prince decided to hold a great court that winter, with races and tournaments. He wrote announcements of it to his noblemen and other lords. Since no one wished to be left out, many "wolf-pelts"[1] (or coats) were ordered from the aforementioned furrier just then. Eulenspiegel found out about this, and went to this master-furrier to ask for work.

The furrier, who needed helpers at that time, was happy that he had come, and asked him whether he also knew how to make "wolves." Eulenspiegel said, sure: in the district of Saxony he was by no means the least known for this sort of thing.

---

1. See Chapter 47, in which this term also appears.

The furrier said, "Dear boy, you've come to me at just the right moment. Come on. We'll arrive at a good understanding between ourselves about your wages."

Eulenspiegel said, "Yes, boss. I see that you're honest enough to know very well yourself what they should be, once you see my work. But I don't work with the other workers. I wish to be alone, so I can perform my job according to my wishes and without interference."

So the furrier gave him a little room, offering him many wolf skins that had been scraped and were prepared as pelts, giving him a mass of various pelts, both large and small. Well, Eulenspiegel began to apply himself to the wolf hides, and cut them up, making wolves out of all of them and stuffing them with hay and shaping legs for them with sticks, to make them lifelike. When he had cut up all the hides and made wolves out of them, he said, "Chief, the wolves are all ready. Is there anything else?"

His boss said, "Yes, my dear boy. Sew up as many of them as you can." With that he went up to the room where the wolves, both large and small, were lying on the floor. His boss looked at them and said, "What's this supposed to be? May the plague shake you! What a disaster you've brought on me! I'll have you imprisoned and punished!"

Eulenspiegel said, "Chief, are these supposed to be my wages, then? And I've acted in precise accordance with your own words. You told me to make wolves. If you'd said, 'Make me wolf-coats,' I'd have done that too. And if I'd known I wasn't to earn any more gratitude, I wouldn't have used up so much energy."

So Eulenspiegel took his leave of Berlin, leaving nowhere a good reputation behind him, and went on to Leipzig.

54. How Eulenspiegel, in Leipzig, sold the furriers a live cat sewn into a rabbit skin, in a sack, for a live rabbit.

How quickly Eulenspiegel could invent a fine jest – as he proved to the furriers of Leipzig on Shrove-Tuesday Eve, when they held their feast, or drinking bout, together. Now, it happened that they wanted to eat wild game. Eulenspiegel heard about this and

thought, "The furrier in Berlin gave you nothing for your work. These furriers ought to pay for it."

So he went to his inn, where his innkeeper had a fine, plump cat–which Eulenspiegel stuck under his coat. Then he asked the cook for a rabbit skin: he planned to arrange a smart little jest with it. The cook gave him a skin, into which he sewed the cat. Then he dressed in farmer's clothes and took up a position in front of the town hall, keeping his wild game concealed in his jacket until one of the furriers came by. Eulenspiegel asked him whether he would not like to buy a good hare, and let him look under his jacket. They soon agreed on his giving Eulenspiegel four silver guilders for the hare and six pennies for the old sack in which the hare was kept. The furrier took it off to their guildmaster's house, where they all gathered, with great boisterousness and merriment, and announced that he had bought the finest hare he had seen in a year. One after another, they handled it all over. Then, since they planned to have it on Shrove-Tuesday, they let it run live in an enclosed grass-garden – and got some young dogs, because they wanted to hold a rabbit-hunt.

Well, when the furriers got together, they let the hare loose, with the dogs after it. Since the hare could not run well, it jumped into a tree and cried "Mieow!" – and that it would rather go home again. When the furriers saw this, they shouted fiercely, "You good comrades, come on! Come on! Whoever's made fools of us with this cat – we'll beat him to death!"

This might well have happened. But Eulenspiegel had taken off his clothes and so altered his appearance that they did not recognize him.

55. How Eulenspiegel boiled leather – along with chairs and benches – for a tanner in Brunswick on the Damme.

Shortly after Eulenspiegel left Leipzig, he went on to Brunswick, to a tanner who tanned leather for shoemakers. Well, it was wintertime, so he thought, "You'd better put up with this tanner for the winter." He hired himself out to the tanner.

When he had been with the tanner for eight days, it happened that the tanner was invited out to dinner. That day Eulenspiegel was to tan the leather – completely – by himself.

The tanner told Eulenspiegel, "Boil a full load of leather in the tub."

Eulenspiegel said, "All right. What should I use as wood for this?"

The tanner said, "What sort of question is that? If I haven't got any wood in the woodshed, I've still got lots of chairs and benches with which you can quite finish the leather."

Eulenspiegel said, "Sure." It would be fine.

The tanner went out to his friends'.

Eulenspiegel hung up a kettle, stuck the leather inside it, one hide after the other, and boiled the leather through till it could be pulled apart with one's fingers. Then, when Eulenspiegel had boiled the leather through, he broke up chairs and benches – all of them that were in the house – stuck them under the kettle, and boiled the leather even longer. When this was done, he took the leather out of the kettle, laid it out in a heap, left both house and city, and went on his way.

The tanner sensed nothing wrong, drank all day, and went pleasantly to bed that evening. The next morning the tanner wanted to see how his assistant had done his leather, so he got up and went into the tanning house. Well, he found the leather utterly boiled through, found neither bench nor chair in either house or courtyard, became quite miserable, and went to his room, to his wife, and said, "Woman, something awful has happened. I have a feeling that our new assistant was Eulenspiegel, because he seems to be in the habit of doing everything that he's told. He's gone – and he's chopped all our chairs and benches into the fire and boiled the leather far too much."

His wife began to cry, and said, "Get after him, wild and fast, and bring him back!"

The tanner said, "No, I don't want him back. If only he stays away till I send for him."

56. How Eulenspiegel cheated the wine-tapster at Lübeck, by giving him a jug of water instead of a jug of wine.

Eulenspiegel kept wisely on his guard when he arrived in Lübeck, and conducted himself properly, playing no tricks on anyone, for justice in Lübeck is harsh indeed.

At that time there was a wine-tapster at Lübeck, at the Ratskeller, who was a haughty, proud man. He had managed to convince himself that no one was as clever as he was. He said himself, and made sure it was said about him, that he longed to have a look at the man who could trick him and outsmart him. Well, because of this, a lot of citizens thoroughly disliked him.

When Eulenspiegel heard about this wine-tapster's presumptuousness, he found it impossible to suppress his mischievous nature any longer, and thought, "You've got to find out what he can do." He took two jugs that had been made exactly alike, putting water into the first jug and leaving the other empty. The jug of water he carried hidden under his coat, the empty jug out in the open. Then he went into the wine cellar with the jugs, had a measure of wine poured out for him, and put the jug with the wine under his coat, setting the water jug in its place. He put it on the little shelf, so the wine-tapster did not see it, and said, "Bartender, what does a measure of wine cost?"

"Ten pennies," he said.

Eulenspiegel said, "That's too expensive. I've got just six pennies. May I have it for that much?"

The wine-tapster got angry and said, "Are you trying to set the price of wine for these gentlemen here? This is a fixed price. If you don't like it, just leave your wine in the Gentlemen's Cellar."

Eulenspiegel said, "That's what I wanted to know. I've got these six pennies. If you don't want them, pour the wine back again."

The wine-tapster grabbed the jug in anger, thinking it was wine when it was water, poured it back into the bung-hole, and said, "What sort of fool are you – having wine measured out for you, and you can't pay for it?"

Eulenspiegel took his jug and walked off, saying, "I see rather that you're a fool. There's nobody too wise to be tricked by fools – even if he's a wine-tapster."

With that he left, carrying the jug of wine under his coat, but the empty jug in which the water had been he carried out in the open.

57. How people tried to hang Eulenspiegel at Lübeck; and how, with clever trickery, he got out of there.

Lambrecht, the wine-tapster, listened to the words Eulenspiegel uttered as he left the cellar. Then he went to get a policeman, ran after Eulenspiegel, and caught up with him in the street. The policeman grabbed him, and they found the two jugs with him, the empty jug and the jug with the wine. They pronounced him a thief and led him to prison. Now, some offered it as their judgment that he deserved the gallows for this; and some said it was no more than a subtle jest and thought the wine-tapster should have been

more cautious when he asserted that no one could outsmart him. Eulenspiegel had only done what he did because of the wine-tapster's presumptuousness. But those who disliked Eulenspiegel said it was theft: he must hang for it. Well, sentence was passed on him – death on the gallows.

Now, when the day of judgment arrived, on which Eulenspiegel was to be led out and hanged, there was an uproar through the whole city, with everyone up and out on horse or foot. The Council of Lübeck feared that he might have worked the people up or fixed it so he would not be hanged. Some wanted to see how he would take his end, after his having been so wild a fellow. Others declared he knew the black arts and could escape by them. Most would have rejoiced at his escape.

Now, Eulenspiegel kept still on being led out, saying not a word, with the result that everyone was amazed and thought he was in despair. This went on till they reached the gallows. Then he spoke, calling the whole Council before him, and asking, with great humility, that they grant him one request. He would ask them for neither life nor limb, nor for either money or property, but for something small to be done afterwards – neither continuous mass, nor eternal alms-giving, nor everlasting remembrance – but a different thing that would cause no damage in its accomplishment and that it would be easy for the honorable Council of Lübeck to do – without its costing a penny.

The members of the Council gathered and moved to one side to consult; and they were satisfied that they could grant him his request, since he had already stipulated what he would not ask for. Besides, a number of them very much wanted to know what he intended to request. They told him that whatever he asked for would be done, as long as he did not ask for any of the things he had mentioned earlier. If he agreed, they would grant him his wish.

Eulenspiegel at once said, "I won't ask you for any of the things I mentioned before. But if you plan to keep your word with me with respect to what I ask of you, give me your hands on it."

This they did, all together, swearing by hands and oaths.

Whereupon Eulenspiegel said, "You honorable gentleman of Lübeck, as you've pledged on your honor, I'll make my request of you. And this is it, that after I've been hanged, the wine-tapster come here every morning for three days – the bartender first and the skinner, who'll dig my grave, second – and that before they eat, they kiss me with their mouths on my arse."

Well, they vomited and said this was hardly a civilized request.

Eulenspiegel said, "I consider the esteemed Council of Lübeck honest enough to keep its word with me – that it has pledged me by their hands and sworn oaths."

They all went off to consult about this – with the result that, by permission and for other appropriate reasons, it was decided that they would let him go. Well, Eulenspiegel went on from there to Helmstädt, and was never again seen in Lübeck.

58. How Eulenspiegel had a giant purse made at Helmstädt.

Eulenspiegel arranged still another jest, with a purse. A pursemaker was living at Helmstädt. Eulenspiegel visited him, asking whether the pursemaker would like to make him a large, pretty purse.

The pursemaker said, "Of course. How big should it be?"

Eulenspiegel said that he would like to have it made big enough, for those were times in which one carried large purses that were big and roomy. The pursemaker made Eulenspiegel a big purse. When he came for it and saw the purse, he said, "This purse isn't big enough. It's a mere purselet. If you'll make me one that's big enough, I'll pay you nicely."

The pursemaker made him a purse out of an entire cowhide, making it so big that one might easily have put a yearling calf into it – a purse that one had to drag along.

When Eulenspiegel came for it this time, he was still not happy with the purse and said the purse was still not big enough. If the pursemaker really wanted to make him a purse, he should make one big enough for him: he would give him two guilders for it. The pursemaker took the two guilders and made him a purse for which he used three oxhides. Three men would have had trouble carrying it on a bier. You could have poured a bushel of corn into it.

When Eulenspiegel came back, he said, "Chief, this purse is big enough, but the big purse I had in mind isn't this purse. So I don't want it either–it's still too small. If you can make me a purse big enough so I can take one penny out of it and two more are still left inside it–so I'd never be without money and never have to grovel for a living–I'd buy it from you and pay up. These purses you've made me are empty. They're useless to me. I've got to have full purses. Otherwise I can't go out among people."

And he left, leaving his purses with the pursemaker, and said, "You keep them in case of a good sale." Eulenspiegel also left him the two guilders, although the pursemaker had easily cut him ten guilders' worth of leather.

59. How Eulenspiegel cheated a butcher of Erfurt out of roast.

Eulenspiegel could not suppress his clownish nature when he arrived at Erfurt, where he soon became well known among both citizens and students.[1] Once he went to the butchers' stalls because meat was on sale. A butcher immediately told him that he ought to get something to take home with him.

Eulenspiegel said, "What should I take with me?"

The butcher said, "A roast."

Eulenspiegel said, "All right." He grabbed a roast by one end and left with it.

The butcher ran after him, saying, "Not like this! You've got to pay for the roast."

Eulenspiegel said, "You said nothing to me about paying. You spoke instead about whether I wouldn't like to take something with me." The man had pointed out the roast so he might take it

1. For Eulenspiegel's experience with the students of Erfurt, see Chapter 29.

home with him. This Eulenspiegel could prove with his neighbors, who were standing nearby.

The other butchers came over and – out of malice – said yes, that was true. The other butchers disliked him, for whenever customers approached them and tried to buy something, this butcher called them over to him and lured them away. So they declared absolutely that Eulenspiegel should keep the roast. While this butcher argued with them, Eulenspiegel stuck the roast under his coat and went off with it – leaving them to settle things among themselves as best they could.

60. How Eulenspiegel cheated a butcher of Erfurt out of another roast.

Eight days later, Eulenspiegel returned to the butchers' stalls. The same butcher now solicited Eulenspiegel again, with flattering words, "Come on over and get a roast."

Eulenspiegel said, "Yes," and tried to touch the roast, but the butcher was quick and grabbed it tightly.

Eulenspiegel said, "Just leave the roast lying there. I fully intend to pay for it."

The butcher laid the roast on his counter.

Eulenspiegel went on, "If I tell you a word that will be in your interest, will the roast be mine?"

The butcher said, "Well, you may tell me such words as will be useless to me . . . but you may also tell me words that could indeed be in my interest, and then you might take the roast."

Eulenspiegel said, "I don't plan to touch your roast unless my words please you." And he went on, "I'll say this: 'Come on, Mr. Moneybags, and pay the people!' How do you like that? Don't you like it?"

The butcher said, "These words quite please me – and certainly are to my liking."

Eulenspiegel said to those who were standing around them, "Dear friends, you've heard him. Well, the roast is mine."

Eulenspiegel took the roast and walked off with it, saying sarcastically to the butcher, "Well, I've got another roast – as you promised me."

The butcher stood there, not knowing what he could possibly say to this. Twice he had been tricked, and made to feel the shame of his fellow butchers' ridicule as they stood around him and laughed at him.

61. How Eulenspiegel became a carpenter's boy in Dresden, and failed to win much praise.

Eulenspiegel soon cleared out of the district of Hessen for Dresden, near the Bohemian Forest on the Elbe. There he took on the role of carpenter's boy. A cabinet-maker hired him. The cabinet-maker needed an apprentice, as his own apprentice had given up the trade and gone traveling.

Now, a wedding was being held in the city, to which the cabinet-maker was invited. He told Eulenspiegel, "Dear boy, I've got to go to the wedding and won't be back during the day. Do well and work hard and install the four planks on that table, in the glue, as tightly as possible."

Eulenspiegel said, "Yes. Which planks belong together?"

The carpenter placed them on top of one another for him – those that belonged together – and went off to the wedding with his wife. Eulenspiegel, the trusty helper who always aimed at doing his work more absurdly than properly, started off and bored through the finely milled table planks or counter planks, which his boss had stacked there for him, in three or four places. Then he piled them into plank blocks, wedged them together, boiled glue in a large kettle, stuck the planks in, carried them up inside the

house, and shoved them out of the window, so the glue could dry in the sun. Then he took time off.

That evening his boss came home, having had a lot to drink, and asked Eulenspiegel how he had worked that day.

Eulenspiegel said, "Chief, I've stuck the four table planks together as tightly possible in the glue – and had a decent time off as well."

This quite pleased his boss, and he said to his wife, "This is a fine assistant. Treat him well. I'd like to keep him a long time." They went off to bed.

But the next morning his boss told Eulenspiegel to bring him the table he had finished. Eulenspiegel came along, dragging his work in from the work-floor. When his boss saw that the rogue had ruined his planks, he said, "Look here, my apprentice, have you ever been taught carpentry?"

Eulenspiegel answered: why was he asking this?

"I'm asking it because you've ruined these fine planks for me."

Eulenspiegel said, "My dear boss, I've done it as you told me to. If it's ruined, that's your fault."

The carpenter got angry, saying, "You damned fool! I'll throw you out of my workshop for this! I've no use for your sort of work!"

Eulenspiegel took his leave of that place and did not earn much thanks – despite his having done all he was told to do.

62. How Eulenspiegel became an optician, and found no demand for his services in any country.

The electors were angry and contentious among themselves, with the result that there was no Roman Kaiser or King. Well, it came about that the Count of Supplenburg was chosen as Roman King by the mass of electors, but there were a number among them who fancied themselves able to take over the empire by force. So this newly elected King had to camp near Frankfurt for six months to see whether anybody might try to overthrow him. Since he had assembled a very large crowd, on horse and foot, Eulenspiegel speculated on what it might be possible for him to do there: "Lots of foreign Lords are arriving, who won't think of me as lacking in talent. If I can manage to join their retinue, I'll do well." He set out for the place.

The Lords of all countries were going there. Thus it happened that the Bishop of Trier and his company found Eulenspiegel in the Wetterau near Friedburg, on the road to Frankfurt. As he was oddly dressed, the Bishop asked him what sort of fellow he was.

Eulenspiegel replied, "Gracious One, I am an optician and come from Brabant. There is nothing to do there, so I'm wandering in search of work. But there seems to be absolutely no demand for our skills."

The Bishop said, "I should think your craft would be thriving, better with each day–the reason being that each day the people become more sickly and lose their vision. As a result, a lot of eyeglasses are certainly needed."

Eulenspiegel answered the Bishop, "Yes, gracious Lord, Your Grace speaks the truth. But there's one thing that's ruining our craft."

The Bishop said, "What is it?"

Eulenspiegel said, "If only I might tell Your Grace without your getting angry!"

"No." said the Bishop. "I'm used to such things from you and your kind. Just speak freely."

"Gracious Lord, it is ruinous to the craft of spectacle-making–so much so that one may well fear that it may vanish–that you and other great Lords, Popes, Cardinals, Bishops, Kaisers, Kings, Princes, Councilors, Governors, Justices of cities and countries (God save us!) presently just wink at what is right–and this, presently, because of gifts of money. But in ancient times, one finds it written, Lords and Princes, as many as there were of them then, were in the habit of reading and studying after justice, so that injustice might be decently avoided. To do so, they needed lots of eyeglasses, so in those days our craft did well. Moreover, popes studied a lot more then than now, so eyeglasses are disappearing. Of course, they are now so well educated from the books they buy that they know their pages by heart – so they don't open their books more than once in four weeks. For this reason our craft lies in ruins, and I'm running from one country to the next and finding work nowhere. This evil condition has spread so widely that farmers in the country are concerned and are keeping an eye on it."

The Bishop understood this text without any further explanation, and told Eulenspiegel, "Follow us to Frankfurt. We shall offer you our festive regalia and clothes."

This Eulenspiegel did. He remained with the Lords till the Count was confirmed as Kaiser. Then he traveled with the Kaiser back to Saxony.

63. How Eulenspiegel hired himself out as a cook and houseboy to a merchant in Hildesheim, and behaved quite mischievously.

On the right, in the street that one takes out of the hay-market in Hildesheim, there lived a rich merchant. Once he went walking in front of his house, intending to go into his garden. On the way, in a green field, he came across Eulenspiegel, who was lying down. The merchant greeted Eulenspiegel, asked him what sort of fellow he was, and what his trade might be. Eulenspiegel answered him with concealed roguishness and cunning: he was a cook's apprentice and was out of work.

The merchant quickly said, "If you can be trusted, I'll take you on myself – and give you new clothes and a nice piece of change. I've got a wife who complains all day long about cooking, and I'd very much like to earn her gratitude."

Eulenspiegel promised him enormous loyalty and honesty. So the merchant hired him, asking him his name.

"Sir, my name is Barto-lo-me-us."

The merchant said, "That's a long name. It can't easily be said. You'll be called 'Crazy.' "

Eulenspiegel said, "Of course, my dear Squire. It's all the same to me what I'm called."

"Well, well," said the merchant, "you're the boy for me. Come on, come on. Come into my garden with me. We're going to take some herbs home with us, and young chickens as well. I've invited guests for next Sunday, whom I'd like to treat nicely."

Eulenspiegel went into the garden with him and cut rosemary, with which he was to stuff the chickens in Swiss style – and others with onions, eggs, and other herbs. Then they went home together. When his wife saw her guest's odd clothes, she asked the master of the house what sort of fellow this was and what her husband planned to do with him – or whether her husband was just worried that their bread might be molding.

The merchant said, "Woman, be content. He's to be your very own servant. He's a cook."

His wife said, "Yes, dear husband, he looks as if he ought to be able to cook fine things."

"Just be happy," said her husband. "Tomorrow you'll see very well what he can do." And he called Eulenspiegel: "Crazy!"

Eulenspiegel answered: "Squire!"

"Get a sack and follow me to the butcher's. I want to get meat and a roast."

Eulenspiegel followed him. His Squire bought meat and a roast there, and said to him, "Crazy, put the roast to one side tomorrow to let it cool and brown slowly, so it doesn't burn. Put the other meat beside it, so it'll be hot for eating."

Eulenspiegel said yes, got up early, and put the food on the fire. But he put the roast on a spit and placed it between two barrels of Einbeck beer in the cellar, so it would stay cool and not burn. As the merchant had invited the City Secretary and other guests for dinner, he came to find out whether his guests had arrived and whether the food was ready–and asked his new servant.

Eulenspiegel answered, "Everything's ready but the roast."

"Where's the roast?" said the merchant.

"It's lying in the cellar, between two barrels. I knew of no cooler place in the house where I could put it, according to your instructions."

"But is it ready?" said the merchant.

"No," said Eulenspiegel. "I didn't know when you wanted to have it."

While this was going on, the guests arrived. The merchant told them about his new servant and how he put the roast in the cellar. Well, they laughed and made a good joke of it. But the wife was unhappy for her guests' sake, and told the merchant he ought to let the boy go: she could no longer bear him in the house; she could see he was a rogue.

The merchant said, "Dear wife, just keep calm. I'd like to use him for a trip to the City of Goslar. When I get back, I'll have him take off." He could barely persuade his wife to be satisfied with this.

When they had eaten and drunk and there had been good cheer all evening, the merchant said, "Crazy, get the carriage ready, and grease it. Tomorrow we're going to Goslar. There's a priest living there, called Father Heinrich Hamenstede. The man is here and will travel back with us."

Eulenspiegel said yes, and asked what sort of grease he ought to use. The merchant threw him a shilling and said, "Go buy wagon grease and have my wife mix old fat under it.

Eulenspiegel did precisely that, and when everyone was asleep, he greased the carriage inside and out, and especially where one was supposed to sit. The merchant got up early the next morning, with the priest, and told Eulenspiegel to hitch up the horses. He did so. They seated themselves and drove off. At once the priest began to heave about, and said, "What, by the gallows, is so fatty here? I'd like to stop, so this carriage stops throwing me around and making my hands so filthy everywhere."

They ordered Eulenspiegel to stop and told him they were both being smeared with grease, front and back. They also began to get angry with him. In the meantime a farmer came by, driving to market with a load of straw. They bought several bundles from him, wiped off the carriage, and seated themselves inside once more.

The merchant now said angrily to Eulenspiegel, "You damned fool! May nothing good ever come your way! Drive to beat the gallows!"

Eulenspiegel did so. When he arrived under the gallows, he stopped short and unhitched the horses.

The merchant said, "What're you trying to do – or what do you mean by this – you fool!"

Eulenspiegel said, "You told me to drive under the gallows. Here we are. I thought we wanted to rest here."

At this, the merchant saw by looking out of the carriage that they were stopped under the gallows. What could they do? They began to laugh at the joke, and the merchant said, "Hitch up, you fool, and drive straight on and don't look to either side!"

Eulenspiegel now unhitched the coupling pins from the traveling carriage. When he had driven an acre's length further, the carriage separated, and the rear portion of it, with the roof, remained standing still. But Eulenspiegel went on by himself. They shouted after him, and had to run till their tongues hung out of their mouths before they caught up with him. The merchant tried to beat him to death. The priest helped, as best he could.

Well, they completed their journey and returned home. His wife asked how it had gone.

"Strangely enough," said the merchant, "but at least we're back." With that he called Eulenspiegel and said, "Fellow, stay here tonight. Eat and drink what you like. But tomorrow clear out of my house. I won't have you here any more. You're a tricky fool – wherever you come from."

Eulenspiegel said, "Dear God, I do everything I'm told – and still earn no gratitude. But if you're not pleased with my service, I'll clear out of your house, and leave tomorrow, according to your words."

"Yes, do that," said the merchant.

The next day the merchant got up and told Eulenspiegel, "Eat and drink yourself full and get yourself out of here. I'm going to church. Don't let yourself be found here again."

Eulenspiegel kept quiet. As soon as the merchant was out of the house, he began clearing out – chairs, tables, benches. Whatever he could carry and haul he dragged into the lane – copper and pewter pots and candles. The neighbors started wondering what was going on there, with all these things being lugged into the street.

The merchant found out about it. He came puffing up to Eulenspiegel and said, "You trusty servant – what're you doing here! Do I still find you here?"

"Of course, Squire. I wanted first to obey your words – since you told me to clear out the house, and then leave." He went on, "Grab here with your hands. This load is too heavy for me. I can't manage it alone."

"Leave it lying!" said the merchant. "And go to the devil! These things cost too much to be thrown into filth like this!"

"Dear Lord God," said Eulenspiegel, "isn't it a great wonder? I do everything I'm told – and still earn gratitude nowhere! I'm not deceived – I was born in an unlucky hour."

Well, Eulenspiegel took his leave of that place, letting the merchant take back what he had cleared out. The merchant's neighbors laughed at him, to his face and behind his back.

64. How Eulenspiegel became a horse-dealer in Paris, and removed the tail from a Frenchman's horse.

Eulenspiegel played an amusing trick on a horse-dealer at the lake at Wismar. A horse-dealer always stopped by there who refused to buy any horse unless, during the bargaining, he pulled the horse by its tail. He did this even to horses that he did not buy, as he thought he could find out by pulling his own sign whether the horse would live long. His sign was this. If a horse had a long tail, he pulled it by the tail: if the long hair on its tail was curly, he did not buy it, since he believed that it did not have long to live. If the hair on the tail was straight, he bought it, and was convinced that it would live long and had a hardy constitution. Well, this had become so common an idea at Wismar that everyone swore by it.[1]

---

1. As this tale has to do neither with Paris nor with a Frenchman, it many be assumed that some sort of editorial error has taken place here.

Eulenspiegel found out about this, and at once thought, "You ought to play some trick on him, be it what it may, to set these people free of this superstition." Well, Eulenspiegel was now able to help himself with black magic. He got hold of a horse, practiced black magic on it according to his purposes, and rode to the market with it. There he asked such a high price for the horse that everybody refused to buy it from him, until the very merchant arrived who pulled horses by their tails. Eulenspiegel asked a good price of this fellow for his horse.

The merchant could see very well that the horse was a fine one, and fine for its money. He went over to it, planning to pull hard on its tail. Now, Eulenspiegel had so arranged things that as soon as he pulled on the horse's tail it came off in his hand, while the horse appeared to have lost its tail.

The merchant stood there, getting more and more worried. But Eulenspiegel started shouting, "Curses on this villain! Look, dear fellow citizens, how he's insulted and ruined my horse!"

The citizens rushed right over and saw that the merchant had the horse's tail in his hand and that the horse no longer had a tail. Well, the merchant felt terrified. But the citizens intervened and arranged that the merchant paid Eulenspiegel ten guilders, and that Eulenspiegel kept his horse. So Eulenspiegel rode off on his horse, and replaced its tail.

But after that experience, the merchant never again pulled a horse by the tail.

65. How Eulenspiegel played a huge joke on a pipemaker at Lüneburg.

At Lüneburg lived a pipemaker who had been a country tramp and had been run out of the country with other lazy logs. He was sitting at his beer. Well, Eulenspiegel arrived at these festivities and found much company there. So the pipemaker invited Eulenspiegel to dinner – but with this purpose, to make a fool of him – and told him, "Come by tomorrow at noon and eat with me, if you can."

Eulenspiegel said yes, not understanding his words right away, and went along the next day, planning to go to dinner at the

pipemaker's. When he came up to his door, the door was bolted above and below and all the windows were closed. Eulenspiegel walked back and forth before the house two or three times, till it was after midday, but the house remained shut. He realized that he had been tricked. He left the place and kept quiet till the next day.

Eulenspiegel now came up to the pipemaker in the market place and said to him, "See here, my worthy fellow, are you in the habit of doing things like this – of inviting people for dinner, then going out yourself and shutting the doors above and below?"

The pipemaker said, "Didn't you hear how I invited you? I said, 'Come by tomorrow at noon and eat something with me – if you can.' Well, you found the doors locked, so you couldn't come by."

Eulenspiegel said, "Thanks very much. I didn't realize that. I'm learning something new every day."

The pipemaker laughed and said, "I don't want to annoy you. Go there now. My door's open. You'll find cooked and baked things on the fire. Go on ahead. I'll come after you. You may eat by yourself. I don't want any guests but you."

Eulenspiegel thought, "That'll be fine." So he went at once to the pipemaker's house, and found everything as the pipemaker had said. The maid was turning the roast, and his wife was moving about arranging things. So Eulenspiegel went into the house and told the wife that she and her maid were to leave immediately. The master of the house had just been presented with a large fish, a sturgeon, which they were to help him carry home. Eulenspiegel would turn the roast in the meantime.

The woman said, "Of course, dear Eulenspiegel. I'll go with the girl and be back in a flash."

Eulenspiegel said, "Go, quickly!"

The woman and her maid hurried off toward the market. But the pipemaker met them on the way and asked them why they were in such a rush. She said Eulenspiegel had come to the house and told them that he had been presented with a huge sturgeon which they were to help him carry home.

The pipemaker got angry, saying to his wife, "Couldn't you have stayed at home? He hasn't done this for no reason. There's some trick here."

Now, in the meantime Eulenspiegel had bolted the door, above and below, so when the pipemaker, together with his wife and maid, arrived at the house, they found the door locked.

He said to his wife, "Now you see the sort of sturgeon you were supposed to get."

They knocked on the door.

Eulenspiegel came to the door and said, "Stop this knocking. I'm not letting anyone in. The master of the house ordered and definitely said I was to be in here alone. He wants no guests but me. Go away and come back after dinner."

The pipemaker said, "That's true. I said that. But I didn't mean it. Well, let him eat. I'll play another trick on him for this." And he went, with wife and maid, to a neighbor's house to wait till Eulenspiegel was finished.

Well, Eulenspiegel prepared the food thoroughly, sat down at the table, stuffed himself, and put what was left back on the fire, taking his good time about it. Then he opened the door and left it open.

The pipemaker now came in and said, "Fine people don't do the sorts of things you've done, Eulenspiegel."

But Eulenspiegel said, "Should I have done with another what I was supposed to do by myself? If I'm invited to dinner, and the master of the house wants nobody but me – and I let in more guests – the fellow certainly won't be happy." With these words he left the house.

The pipemaker gazed at him: "I'll pay you back for this, rogue that you are."

Eulenspiegel said, "Whoever can do so best is master."

Well, the pipemaker went that very hour to the horse-slaughterer and told him, "There's a good man at the inn, Eulenspiegel by name, whose horse has died." The slaughterer ought to pick it up. The pipemaker showed him the house. The horse-slaughterer recognized the pipemaker at once, and said, yes, he would do it. So he drove his slaughterer's cart up to the inn the pipemaker had shown him and asked for Eulenspiegel. Eulenspiegel came to the door and asked what he wanted. The horse-slaughterer said the pipemaker had come to him and told him that Eulenspiegel's horse had died, that he ought to pick it up: but was he indeed Eulenspiegel and was this true? Eulenspiegel turned around, pulled down his pants, and stuck up his arse. "Look here, and tell this to the pipemaker: if Eulenspiegel hasn't been sitting in this alleyway, then I don't know what street he's sitting in."

The slaughterer was furious, drove his slaughterer's cart to the pipemaker's house, left the cart standing there, and complained to the pipemaker so strongly that the pipemaker had to give the horse-slaughterer ten guilders.

Eulenspiegel saddled his horse and rode out of town.

66. How Eulenspiegel was tricked by an old farmer's wife and lost his purse.

A long time ago, at Gerdau in the district of Lüneburg, there lived an old couple who had been married to each other for about fifty

years, and who had grown children whom they had well provided for and established. Now, there was an extremely greedy priest living in the parish at that time, a man who particularly liked being wherever people might be feasting or carousing. This priest arranged things among his parishioners as follows–that every farmer had to invite him to dinner at least once a year and take care of him and his maid for one or two days, and feed them very well indeed. But for many years the two old people had had no wake, baptism or banquet that the priest might have turned into a wild party. This annoyed him, so he thought of a scheme to force the farmer to offer him a feast. He sent him a messenger to ask him how long he and his wife had been established in the state of matrimony.

The farmer answered, "Dear Father, it's been so long that I've forgotten."

The priest responded, "This could be a dangerous situation for your holy soul. If you've been together fifty years, the vows of matrimony expire, like a monk's in a cloister. So talk to your wife, come back to me, and let me know the facts, so I may recommend help for your blessed soul, as I am required to do for you and all my parish children."

The farmer did so and discussed it with his wife, but was unable to give the priest an accurate reckoning of the years of his marriage. Full of worry, they returned to the priest, so he might offer them sound counsel in the matter of their unworthiness.

The priest said, "Because you do not know the exact number of years, and out of concern for your souls, I shall, next Sunday, unite you anew–so in case you are not in a state of matrimony you shall arrive in it. Slaughter a fine ox for the event, and sheep and pigs. Invite your children and good friends to your banquet. And enjoy yourselves, because I'll be there too."

"Ah, dear Father, just be there. For us this won't be a matter of just a pile of chickens. That we have lived so long with one another–and now for the first time may be out of wedlock–that would not be good." With that they went home to make their preparations.

The priest invited various prelates and priests with whom he was acquainted to the affair. Among these was the Prior of Ebsdorf, who always had a decent horse or two and also greatly enjoyed eating. Eulenspiegel had been staying with him for some time. The Prior said to him, "Take my young stallion and come along. You'll be welcome."

Eulenspiegel did so. When they arrived there–and were eating and drinking and growing merry–the old woman, who was supposed to be the bride, was sitting on the table, as brides are supposed to do. But as she was tired and felt weak, she was allowed to go outside. She went behind the house, to the River Gerdau, and dangled her feet in the water. At the same time, the Prior and Eulenspiegel came by, riding home to Ebsdorf. Well, Eulenspiegel honored the bride with some fine jumping of the young stallion, but did so a bit too much, with the result that his belt-purse, which was carried on one's side in those days, fell off. When the good woman saw it fall, she got up, took the purse, and went back to the river, sitting down over the purse. When

Eulenspiegel had ridden an acre's length further, he missed his purse for the first time, and raced back to the Gerdau to ask the good old farmer's wife whether she had not picked up or found an old, rough purse.

The old woman said, "Yes, friend. For my wedding I picked up a rough purse indeed. I still have it and am sitting on it. Is that the one?"

"Ha," said Eulenspiegel. "If you've had it since your wedding it must be quite a rusty purse by now. I've no need of your old purse."

Thus was Eulenspiegel – roguish and cunning as he was – nonetheless tricked by an old farmer's wife and forced into losing his purse. The woman of Gerdau still have that same rough bride's-purse. I believe that the old widows there are even holding it for safekeeping. Whoever is interested ought to ask about it.

67. How Eulenspiegel tricked a farmer at Ueltzen out of some green fabric from London by making him believe it was blue.

Eulenspiegel always preferred eating cooked and baked things, so he was ever alert to where he might get them. Once he went to the fair at Ueltzen, as a lot of Wends and other country people were coming to it. He strolled here and there, observing everywhere what there was to do. Among other things, he saw that a country fellow was purchasing a green fabric from London and planning to go home with it. Eulenspiegel thought, in the end, that he might enjoy tricking this farmer out of that fabric. He asked about the village where the farmer lived, picked up a Scottish priest and a tramp, and went out of the city with them to the road by which the farmer had to travel. He then laid his plans for how they would handle him, so the farmer with the green fabric would be persuaded it was blue. Each of them was to station himself an acre's length away from the other on the road leading out of the city.

When the farmer came out of the city with his fabric, meaning to bring it home, Eulenspiegel asked him where he had bought that fine, blue material. The farmer replied that it was green, not blue. Eulenspiegel said it was blue. He would bet twenty guilders on

it – and the first person to come up to them, who knew green from blue, would tell them so well enough, so they could be clear about it. Eulenspiegel then gave a signal to the first fellow to come over.

The farmer said, "Friend, we two have just bet twenty pennies on the color of this fabric. Tell the truth, whether it's green or blue. As you say it, that's how we'll let it be."

The first fellow lifted it and said, "It's a fine blue fabric."

The farmer said, "No! You're both rogues – and probably set this up with each other to trick me."

Eulenspiegel now said, "Just a minute. To let you see I'm right, I'll let this first test pass, and let the matter be settled by this pious priest who's just coming over. What he says will either make or break me." The farmer agreed.

When the priest came up to them, Eulenspiegel said, "Father, just tell the truth – what's the color of this fabric?"

The priest said, "Friends, that you can see well enough yourselves."

The farmer said, "Yes, Father, that's true. But these two are trying to convince me of something I know must be a lie."

The priest said, "Why should I bother with this quarrel of yours? What do I care whether it's black or white?"

"Ah, dear Father," said the farmer, "settle it for us. I beg you to do so."

"If you really want it that way," said the priest. "Well, I can't say anything other than – the fabric is blue."

"Do you hear that?" said Eulenspiegel. "The fabric is mine."

The farmer said, "Indeed, Father, if you weren't an ordained priest, I'd think you were lying and that all three of you were rogues. But as you're a priest, I have to believe it."

So he gave Eulenspiegel and his companions the fabric, with which they clothed themselves against winter, while the farmer had to go about in his torn coat.

68. How Eulenspiegel shitted in the baths at Hanover, believing that the place was a House of Cleansing.

The bathkeeper at the baths in Hanover, near the Lein Gate, did not like having his place called a "Bathhouse" but a "House of Cleansing." Eulenspiegel found out about this, and when he got to Hanover, went to these baths, undressed, and said, as he stepped into the bathing room, "God bless you, sir, and your house servants, and everyone whom I find in this clean house."

The bathkeeper was pleased with this remark, told him he was welcome, and said, "Dear guest, you're speaking the truth. This is a clean house and also a house of cleansing – and not a bathhouse. For dust is in the sun, and is also in earth, ashes, and sand."[1]

Eulenspiegel said, "That this is a house of cleansing is obvious, for we come into it unclean and come out of it clean."

---

1. This sentence has no intelligible meaning. Something has perhaps been omitted; see also Notes on the Tales.

With these words, Eulenspiegel deposited a great pile of shit in the water trough in the middle of the bathing room, creating a stink through the whole place.

The bathkeeper said, "It seems clear to me that your words aren't quite appropriate to your deeds. Your words pleased me well enough, but your deeds don't please me in the least. Your words were fine, but your deeds stink horribly. Is this how one behaves in a house of cleansing?"

Eulenspiegel said, "Isn't this a house of cleansing? I needed cleansing more inside than outside – otherwise I wouldn't have come in here."

The bathkeeper said, "One usually does your sort of cleansing in the lavatory. This is a house of cleansing-by-sweating – and you're turning it into a shithouse."

Eulenspiegel said, "Doesn't this filth come from the human body? If one wants to cleanse oneself, one must cleanse oneself inside as well as outside."

The bathkeeper got pretty angry and said, "One cleanses oneself of this sort of stuff in the shithouse, and the horse-slaughterer takes it out to the slaughterer's burial place. But I'm not in the habit of washing and scouring it." With these words, the bathkeeper ordered Eulenspiegel out of the baths.

Eulenspiegel said, "Mr. Keeper, let me bathe for my money. You'd like having a lot of money, and I'd like a good bath."

The bathkeeper said Eulenspiegel should simply get out of his place; he had no interest in Eulenspiegel's money. If Eulenspiegel refused to leave, he would show him the door at once.

Eulenspiegel reflected, "This would be dirty fighting–naked with razors." He started out through the door, and said, "How nicely I've bathed for a bit of filth." He then left and got dressed in a room in which the bathkeeper and his employees usually took their meals.

The bathkeeper tried to trap him in there and frighten him by pretending to hold him prisoner and threatening him. While this was going on, Eulenspiegel realized that he had not cleansed himself quite enough in the bathing room. He spotted a folding table, opened it, shitted a pile on it, and folded it up again. Well, the bathkeeper soon let him out, and they settled their quarrel.

Eulenspiegel at once told him, "Dear Keeper of the Baths, in this room I cleansed myself thoroughly for the first time. You'll be thinking about me a great deal before noon. I'm leaving this place."

69. How Eulenspiegel bought milk from the countrywomen in Bremen, and mixed it all together.

Eulenspiegel did strange and amusing things in Bremen. Once he went to the market there and observed that the farmers' wives brought a lot of milk to sell. He waited for a market-day when a good deal of milk was being delivered, acquired a large vat, set it up in the market place, purchased all the milk that was brought for selling, and had it all poured into the vat. Now, for each woman he

marked a ring around the vat – the first had this much, the next had that much, and so on. He told the women to wait till he had collected all their milk. Only then would he pay each woman separately.

The women sat in a circle in the market place, and Eulenspiegel kept buying milk till no more women were arriving with it, and the vat was nearly full.

Eulenspiegel now turned to them, making a joke of the thing, and said, "I haven't any money just at present. Whoever doesn't want to wait fourteen days may take her milk out of the vat." With that, he left.

The women created an uproar and riot. One had this much, the next that much, the third the same, and so on – till they began beating and smashing one another over the head with their pails, little casks and bottles, and pouring milk into their eyes and over their clothes and on the ground, and it looked as though it had rained milk.

The farmers, and everybody who stood there watching, laughed at the absurdity – that women would go to market like this – and Eulenspiegel was praised a good deal for his roguishness.

70. How Eulenspiegel gave twelve blind men twelve guiders – how they took them, how they spent them, and how in the end they lived miserably because of them.

Since Eulenspiegel was always wandering from one district to the next, the time came when he arrived in Hannover again and engaged in many curious exploits. Once he went riding an acre's length on the road by the gate and ran into twelve blind men.

When Eulenspiegel drew abreast of them, he said, "You blind men – where are you coming from?"

The blind men stopped. They could hear very well that he was mounted on a horse. They thought he must be a high-ranking personage, doffed their hats and caps, and said, "Dear Squire, we've been to the city. A rich man died there, for whom a funeral was held, and alms were given out. But it was horribly cold."

Eulenspiegel told the blind men, "It's cold indeed. I'm only afraid you may freeze to death. Look, here are twelve guilders for you. Go on back to the city, to the inn from which I've just come" – and he told them which house it was – "and spend these twelve guilders, for my sake, till winter is over and you can go on your way again before frost-time."

The blind men stood there, bowing and thanking him profusely. The first blind man thought the second had the money, the second thought the third had the money, the third thought the fourth had the money, and so on, till the last thought the first had it. Well, they went back into the city to the inn that Eulenspiegel had told them about. When they got to the inn, the blind men all said that a good man had ridden up behind them, and given them, by the grace of God, twelve guilders which they were supposed to spend, for his sake, till winter was over. The innkeeper was eager for their money and took them in for the twelve guilders. He did not reflect that he ought to have asked them which blind man had the twelve guilders. He said, "Yes, my dear brothers, I'll treat you nicely." He slaughtered and chopped and cooked for the blind men, and let them eat, till it seemed to him that they had used up the twelve guilders. At that point he said, "Dear brothers, if we do a reckoning, the twelve guilders are just about spent."

The blind men agreed, and each asked the next which of them had the twelve guilders, so they might pay the innkeeper. The first did not have the guilders; the second did not have them either; the third likewise did not; the fourth the same; and the last had the twelve guilders no more than the first. The blind men said so, and scratched their heads. They had been tricked.

So had the innkeeper. He sat down to think. "If you lose them now, your food won't be paid for. But if you keep them on, they'll stuff themselves and eat even more – and still leave you with nothing – till you've got twice your loss." He led them out to his pigsty, locked them in, and offered them a bed of straw and hay.

Eulenspiegel started thinking that the blind men must have

used up that money by now, so he disguised himself and rode into the city, to the very same inn. When he reached the courtyard, planning to tie up his horse in the stable, he saw the blind men lying in the pigsty. He went straight into the house and said to the innkeeper, "Mr. Innkeeper, what reason can you have for keeping poor blind men in your pigsty? Haven't you got any sympathy for them? They must be eating stuff there that's doing harm to life and limb."

The innkeeper said, "I wish they were where all rivers meet[1] – and I had my food paid for." And he told Eulenspiegel everything about how he and the blind men had been tricked.

Eulenspiegel said, "What, Mr. Innkeeper, can't they offer any security?"

The innkeeper thought, "Oh, if I just had some!" And he said, "Friend, if I could get some definite security, I'd take it and let those unhappy blind men go."

Eulenspiegel said, "Fair enough. I'll ask around in the city, and see whether I can find you a pledge."

Eulenspiegel next visited a priest and said, "My dear Lord Priest, how would you like to perform a genuinely friendly deed? My innkeeper was possessed of the evil spirit last night. He desperately wants you to exorcise it for him."

The priest said, "Of course. But he'll have to wait patiently for one or two days. One can't be in too much of a hurry about these things."

Eulenspiegel quickly said to him, "I'll get his wife, so you can tell her that yourself."

The priest said, "Yes, just have her come."

Eulenspiegel went back to the innkeeper and said, "I've found you a pledge. The man's your priest, who will promise it to you and give you what you want. Just let your wife go along with me to him. He'll tell her all about it."

The innkeeper was agreeable – in fact delighted – and sent his wife with him to the priest.

Eulenspiegel started right in. "Dear Father, here's his wife.

---

1. i.e., in the sea. See Lappenberg, p. 271.

Just tell her yourself what you told me and what you promised me."

The priest said, "Certainly. My dear woman, just wait one or two days, and I'll help him with this."

The woman said, "All right." She went home with Eulenspiegel and told her husband what she had heard. The innkeeper was thrilled, let the blind men go, and sent her off. Eulenspiegel now made his own travel arrangements and sneaked out of there.

On the third day the wife went back and asked the priest for the twelve guilders the blind men had spent.

The priest said, "Dear woman, is that what your husband told you to do?"

The woman said, "Yes."

The priest said, "I was told that your husband was possessed by the evil spirit. Bring him to me, so I can help free him of it, with God's help."

The wife said, "Charlatans, who are liars, act this way when they're supposed to pay up. You'll find out right away whether my husband has been captured by an evil spirit." And she ran home and told her husband what the priest had said.

The innkeeper prepared himself – with pikes and halberds – and raced over to the priest's house. The priest saw him coming, and called on his neighbors for help. He crossed himself and said, "Come help me, my dear neighbors! Just see! This man is possessed of the evil spirit!"

The innkeeper said, "Priest! Think about your promise – and pay me!"

The priest simply stood there, crossing himself.

The innkeeper attempted to attack the priest. His neighbors got between them, but were able to separate them only with enormous efforts. Then, as long as that innkeeper and the priest lived, the innkeeper demanded payment for his expenses. The priest, however, said that he owed the innkeeper nothing – rather that the innkeeper was possessed of the evil spirit. The priest wished only to free him of it. This state of affairs dragged on for as long as they both lived.

71. How Eulenspiegel, in Bremen, basted his roast from his behind, so nobody wanted to eat it.

After Eulenspiegel played that joke[1] in Bremen, he became quite well known there. It went like this in the city of Bremen: all the citizens enjoyed having him around and wanted him to play all sorts of pranks. As a result Eulenspiegel spent a long time in that city.

An association existed there at that time. It included citizens and other inhabitants, such as merchants. They had an agreement among themselves that each of them in succession would prepare a feast, with a roast, cheese, and bread. Whoever failed to attend, without a good excuse, would have to pay the host for the whole meal, at prevailing Bremen-market prices. Eulenspiegel came to

---

1. Cf. other Bremen stories, such as Chapter 69. See also the commentary on the various orderings of the tales, in the Introduction.

one of their meetings. They welcomed him as a fun-maker, and he was allowed to join their organization.

As the question of hosting the feast went around, it fell to Eulenspiegel as well. He invited his fellow members to his inn, purchased a roast, and stuck it on the fire. As the hour of the feast approached, the invited members gathered in the market place and discussed among themselves whether they ought to go along to Eulenspiegel's to eat. Each asked the next whether anybody knew if he had cooked something. They did not want to go there for nothing. Well, they came to an agreement that they would go there together: better that everybody discover the trick than one person alone.

When they all arrived at Eulenspiegel's inn, he took a piece of butter, stuck it into the groove of his behind, turned his arse backwards to the fire, over the roast, and basted the roast like that, with the butter from his groove. As his guests arrived at the door, stopped, and tried to see whether he had cooked anything, they saw him standing there like that, near the fire, and basting the roast.

They said things like this: "The devil be his guest! I certainly won't eat that roast."

But Eulenspiegel demanded payment from them for the food – which they all cheerfully offered as long as they did not have to eat it.

72. How Eulenspiegel sowed stones in a city in Saxony; and how, when he was asked about it, he said he was sowing rogues.

Soon after that, Eulenspiegel came to a city on the Weser. There he took careful note of the people's business, and what their commercial transactions were like, till he was familiar with all their ways and how affairs were handled there.

Since he had fourteen inns available to him, what he lacked in one place he found in the next, and soon came to hear and see nothing that he did not already know about. But the people tired of him, and he likewise tired of them. So he collected little stones near the river, walked back and forth through the lanes near the city hall, and sowed his "seeds" to left and right.

Foreign merchants came up to him and asked him what he was sowing.

Eulenspiegel said, "I'm sowing rogues."

These merchants said, "There's no need for you to sow them here. There are more than enough of them here already."

Eulenspiegel said, "That's true. But they're living in the houses. They ought to be run out of town."

They said, "Why don't you also sow honest people?"

Eulenspiegel said, "Honest people? They wouldn't grow here."

These words attracted the attention of the city council. Eulenspiegel was sent for and ordered to collect his "seeds" and leave the city. He did so – and arrived, ten miles from there, in another city, planning to sow his seeds in Ditmarschen. But reports about him had preceded him to that particular city. If he wanted to enter it, he had to promise to travel through it, with his "seeds," without eating or drinking. Since nothing else seemed possible, he rented a little boat, planning to have his "seeds" and belongings lifted into it. As his sack was being lifted, it tore open in the middle, and he left both "seeds" and sack behind.

Well, Eulenspiegel ran off. He is still supposed to return.

73. How Eulenspiegel hired himself out to a barber in Hamburg, and entered his shop through his windows.

On one occasion Eulenspiegel went to Hamburg and went into the hops market. As he was standing there looking around, a beard-shearer came by who asked him where he was from.

Eulenspiegel said, "I come from here and there."

The barber asked him, "What sort of craft are you apprenticed to?"

Eulenspiegel said, "Well, in a word, I'm a barber."

The barber hired him.

Now, this barber lived at the hops market, just across from where they were standing. His house had high windows that faced the street, where his shop was located. The barber told Eulenspiegel, "See that house over there? Where those high windows are? Go in there, and I'll be along after you in a minute."

Eulenspiegel said yes, went straight through the high windows into the house, and said, "God, Almighty God, bless this craft."

The beard-shearer's wife was sitting in the shop and spinning. She got frightened and said, "Good Heavens! Is the devil himself after you? How come you're climbing in through the windows? Isn't the door wide enough?"

Eulenspiegel said, "Dear woman, don't be angry with me. Your husband told me to do this, and hired me as an apprentice."

The woman said, "It's a trusty servant indeed who does his boss real damage."

Eulenspiegel said, "Dear woman, shouldn't a servant do what his boss has told him to do?"

At this point his new boss came in and heard and saw the argument Eulenspiegel had started. His boss said, "Boy, why couldn't you have come in through the door and left my windows in one piece? Why on earth did you break into my house through the windows?"

Eulenspiegel said, "My dear boss, you told me to go in where the high windows were. You were to come along after me in a minute. Well, I did what you told me – but you didn't really come along after me, although you told me to go first."

His boss said nothing, as he needed him, and thought, "If I want to recoup my loss here, I'd better accept what he's done – and deduct it from his wages."

His boss let Eulenspiegel work for about three days. The barber then told Eulenspiegel to sharpen the shearing knives.

Eulenspiegel said, "Yes, gladly."

His boss added, "Make them even on the back, like the blade."

Eulenspiegel said yes, and started sharpening the shearing knives, making the reverse edges like the blades. His boss came over to see what he was doing, and saw that he was sharpening the knives, reverse edges and blades alike, and that he was also about to sharpen the knives he had lying on the grindstone.

The barber at once said, "What're you doing! This is getting to be awful."

Eulenspiegel said, "How's it getting to be awful? I'm not hurting you, since I'm doing what you told me to."

His boss got pretty angry and said, "I'm telling you that you're an awful, damned fool! Stop! Just leave off all this sharpening! And go back where you came from!"

Eulenspiegel said yes, went into the shop, and jumped back out through the windows – where he had come from. The beard-shearer now got even angrier, and raced after him with the bailiff to catch him to make him pay for the windows he had broken.

But Eulenspiegel was quick. He boarded a ship and got out of the country.

74. How a woman who had snot hanging out of her nose invited Eulenspiegel for a meal.

It once chanced that a court was to be held, and Eulenspiegel wanted to ride to it. But his horse was lame, so he went on foot.

Now, it was quite hot and he began to get hungry, and there was a small village on the way. There was no inn at the small village, but it was high noon, so he went on into the village anyway, as he was well known there. He came into a house where a woman was sitting and making cheese. She had a lump of whey in her hands. Since she was bending over the whey, neither of her hands was free – and a huge piece of snot was hanging out of her nose. Eulenspiegel wished her good day, and saw the snot. She noticed it, but could not wipe her nose with her arms. Neither could she suck the snot back in.

She told him, "Dear Eulenspiegel, go sit down and wait. I'm going to give you good, fresh butter."

But Eulenspiegel turned and started back out through the door.

The woman called after him, "Wait and eat something first."

Eulenspiegel said, "Dear woman, after that falls off." He went across to another house, thinking, "You wouldn't like that butter. Whoever's got a little dough doesn't need to throw eggs into it. It'll get fatty enough from her snot."

75. How Eulenspiegel got to eat a white jam by himself, by letting a lump fall into it, out of his nose.

Eulenspiegel played quite a trick on a farmer's wife, so he could eat her white jam all by himself. He came into a house and was hungry. Well, he found the wife alone, sitting by the fire and cooling a white jam. It looked so tasty and good to him that he ached to eat it, so he asked the woman whether she would simply give him her white jam.

The woman said, "Yes, my dear Eulenspiegel, gladly. If I could do without it myself, I'd give it to you to eat all by yourself."

Eulenspiegel said, "My dear woman, that may indeed occur, precisely according to your words."

The woman set all the white jam down before him, putting the bowl of white jam on the table, with bread as well. Eulenspiegel was hungry, and began to eat, but the woman came

over, planning to eat with him, as farmers usually do.

Eulenspiegel reflected, "If she joins in too, there won't be anything here before long." So he coughed up a big ball of phlegm and threw it into the bowl of white jam.

The woman got angry and said, "Shame on you! Now, you rogue, you'll have to eat that white jam by yourself!"

Eulenspiegel said, "My dear woman, your first words were thus: you would like to do without it yourself, and I could then eat the white jam by myself. Just now, though, you were coming over to eat with me – and you'd have eaten this bowlful of white jam in three gulps."

The woman said, "May nothing good ever come your way! If you won't allow me to have my own food, how would you ever allow me to have yours?"

Eulenspiegel said, "Woman, I'm simply acting according to your words."

So he ate up all the white jam, washed out his mouth, and left.

76. How Eulenspiegel shitted inside a house and blew the stink through a wall to a host who disliked him.

Eulenspiegel traveled fast and arrived at Nuremberg and stayed there for fourteen days. A pious man lived next door to the inn where Eulenspiegel was staying–a man who was rich and liked going to church and had little use for musicians. If musicians were about, or showed up wherever he was, he left. This man also had a custom, that once a year he invited his neighbors to dinner, and treated them handsomely, with food, wine, and the best sorts of drinks. If the neighbors whom he usually invited had a stranger staying with them–business people, two or three–he always invited them too and welcomed them. Well, the time came around when everybody was offering invitations. Eulenspiegel was staying at the inn next door to the man's house. Well, the man offered an invitation to his neighbors, as was his custom, and to the guests they had, who were strangers, but he did not invite Eulenspiegel, who looked like a clown and musician, like the sorts of people whom he was not in the habit of inviting.

Now, when the neighbors went to dinner at the house of this pious man, along with the respectable strangers whom he had also invited and who were staying with them, Eulenspiegel's innkeeper (with whom he was staying) went along too, taking his own guests who had also been invited to dinner. His innkeeper told Eulenspiegel that the rich man had taken him for a clown and so had not invited him.

Eulenspiegel had to accept that, but he thought, "If I'm a clown, I ought to show him some clowning." Of course, it annoyed him that the man had treated him with contempt.

Well, it was just after Saint Martin's Day, when parties like this usually took place. The host sat in a well appointed room with his guests, where he served them their meal. Now, the room was hard by the wall of Eulenspiegel's inn. When they were seated and truly enjoying themselves, Eulenspiegel bored a hole through the wall into the room in which the guests were sitting, took a bellows, produced quite a pile of his excrement, and blew on it with the bellows, into the hole he had bored into the room. Now, this created a stink so awful that nobody had any desire to remain in that room. Everybody looked at the person next to him. The first thought the second must be making the stink, the second thought the third was doing so. Well, Eulenspiegel did not stop working his bellows till the guests had to get up and could no longer remain there amid the stink. They searched under the benches. They looked in every corner, to no avail. Nobody knew where it was coming from, and everybody went home.

Eulenspiegel's innkeeper now came by – and was so sick with the stink that he brought up everything he had in his stomach. He told Eulenspiegel how badly the room had stunk of human filth.

Eulenspiegel began to laugh, saying, "If that fellow didn't want to invite me to dinner, and be generous to me with his food, at least I've been more generous and true with him than he was with me. I've been generous to him with my food anyhow. If I'd been there, the place wouldn't have stunk so badly." And within the hour he paid his innkeeper and rode off. He was a bit worried about what might happen.

Well, his innkeeper listened carefully to what he said – that he knew something about the smell – but the innkeeper still could not understand how Eulenspiegel could have managed it. It all puzzled him greatly. With Eulenspiegel out of the city, the innkeeper went looking about the house and found the bellows, quite coated with shit, and found the hole as well that Eulenspiegel had bored through the wall of the neighbor's house. The innkeeper found them within the hour, brought his neighbor over, and told him about it – how Eulenspiegel had done it and what he had said.

The rich man said, "Dear neighbor, nobody's improved by rogues and musicians. That's why I never want them in my house. If this nonsense emerged from your house, I can't do anything about it. I knew your guest was a clown. I could read it by his appearance. Better that this happened in your house than in mine. He might have done worse things to me."

Eulenspiegel's innkeeper said, "Dear host, you've noticed something all right, and that's the way it is. You've got to set up two lights for a clown.[1] And that's something I'll certainly have to do, since I've got to take in all kinds of people. I've got to take in clowns, along with the best people, if one comes along."

With that they parted. Eulenspiegel was gone, and he did not come back.

77. How Eulenspiegel, at Eisleben, frightened an innkeeper with a wolf he had promised to catch.

At Eisleben lived an innkeeper who was arrogant, considered himself clever, and fancied himself an important householder.

Well, during the days of winter, after a great snow had fallen, Eulenspiegel arrived at his inn. Three merchants also came along

---

1. i.e., so you can spot him.

from Saxony, traveling toward Nuremberg. They got to the inn in dead of night.

Well, the innkeeper was quite sharp-tongued and short in welcoming these three merchants. He said, "By the devil, where are you coming from?" – because they had taken so long to get there and had arrived at his inn so late.

The merchants said, "Mr. Innkeeper, you really shouldn't be put out with us. We had quite an adventure along the way. A wolf gave us a lot of trouble. He attacked us in the snow on the moor. We had to fight him off. That's what kept us so long."

When the innkeeper heard this, he simply sneered at them and said it was a complete disgrace that they had allowed a wolf to delay them. If he were alone and two wolves met him on the moor, he would simply pummel them and drive them off – they certainly could not frighten him. But these merchants, had been three in number, and had let themselves be terrified by a single wolf. His taunting lasted all evening, till the innkeeper showed them to their beds, and Eulenspiegel sat nearby, listening to him.

When they went up to bed, the merchants and Eulenspiegel were placed in one room. The merchants immediately began to discuss how they might get even with the innkeeper for what he had done.

Eulenspiegel quickly said, "Dear friends, it's clear to me that the innkeeper's a pompous boaster. If you'll listen to me, I'll pay him back so he'll never say a word to you about that wolf again."

This delighted the merchants, and they promised him money and provisions.

Eulenspiegel now told them to keep on with their business trip, and on their way back, to stop off at the inn again. He would also be there, and then they would get even with the innkeeper. So it happened. The merchants got ready for their journey, paid their bill, paid Eulenspiegel's as well, and rode off.

But the innkeeper called sarcastically after them, "You merchants, watch out that you don't run into a wolf on the meadow!"

The merchants said, "Mr. Innkeeper, thank you for warning us. If wolves eat us, we won't be back. If wolves eat you, we won't find you here again." With that, they rode off.

Eulenspiegel now rode into the Harz Mountains to set traps for wolves. God gave him the good luck to catch one. He killed it and let it freeze stiff against the time when the merchants returned to the inn at Eisleben. Then he placed the wolf in a sack, and met the three merchants there, as they had agreed. But Eulenspiegel had brought his dead wolf without anybody's knowing about it.

During dinner that evening, the innkeeper kept teasing the merchants about the wolf. They said that so indeed it had gone with them and that wolf. Now, if it happened that the innkeeper met two wolves on the meadow, would he really be able to beat off one of them while he killed the other? The innkeeper boasted hugely that he would cut both wolves to pieces – and this sort of talk went on all evening, till they went to bed.

Well, Eulenspiegel kept quiet till he approached the merchants in their room. At that point Eulenspiegel said, "Good friends, keep quiet and watch. What I'm going to do you're going to like too. Keep a light burning for me."

Well, when the innkeeper and all his servants were in bed, Eulenspiegel crept softly out of their room. He took the dead wolf, which was frozen stiff, lugged it to the hearth, and planted it on sticks so it stood up properly. Then he pried open its mouth, and inserted two children's shoes into it. He now returned to the merchants in their room and yelled, "Mr. Innkeeper!" The innkeeper, who was not yet asleep, heard this and called back, asking what they wanted – whether a wolf was maybe nipping at them.

They replied, "Ah, dear innkeeper, just send your maid or boy to bring us something to drink! We can't stand this thirst!"

The innkeeper got angry, saying, "That's the Saxon way, all right. They drink day and night." He called out to his maid to get up and bring them something to drink in their room.

The maid got up and went to the fire, planning to light a lamp. She looked up – and looked the wolf right in the mouth. She was terrified, dropped the lamp and ran into the courtyard, imagining only that the wolf had already devoured the children.

Eulenspiegel and the merchants again called for something to drink. The innkeeper thought his maid must be asleep, so he called his servant boy. The boy got up and also tried to light a lamp. He too saw the wolf standing there. He at once thought it must have eaten the maid whole. He let the lamp fall and ran into the cellar.

Eulenspiegel and the merchants took note of these developments, and Eulenspiegel said, "Keep quiet now. This game's about to get interesting." Eulenspiegel and the merchants then called out for the third time: where were the maid and boy? – They weren't bringing anything to drink. The innkeeper had better come himself, and bring a light. They could not leave their room.

The innkeeper thought only that his boy must also have fallen asleep. He got up, thoroughly irate, and said, "The devil serve these Saxons their drinks!" He too lit a lamp at the fire. But when he saw the wolf standing in front of him on the hearth, and saw the little shoes in its mouth, he began to scream. He shouted, "Murder! Save me, dear friends!" He raced to the merchants' room, shrieking, "Dear friends, come help me! A terrible animal is standing at the fire – and it's eaten my children, my maid, and my boy!"

The merchants were all too ready to accompany him. Eulenspiegel was also. They all went to the fire with the innkeeper. The boy emerged from the cellar. The maid came in from the garden. The innkeeper's wife brought his children out of their rooms. They were in fact all very alive. Eulenspiegel now walked over and poked the wolf with his foot. It lay there and lifted not a paw.

Eulenspiegel said, "This is a dead wolf. Were you doing all that screaming over this? What sort of weak character are you? Can a dead wolf really attack you in your own house, and chase you and all your servants into corners? And it isn't so long since you were going to kill two live wolves out in open country. But you've only got words where some have courage."

The innkeeper listened to him, realizing he had been tricked. He went back to his room, to bed, feeling ashamed of his vain words and that a dead wolf had so humiliated him and all his servants. The merchants laughed. Then they paid what they and Eulenspiegel had spent and rode off.

But after that the innkeeper no longer talked so much about his bravery.

78. How Eulenspiegel shitted on an innkeeper's table in Cologne, telling him he would come and find it.

Just after that, Eulenspiegel arrived at an inn in Cologne. He kept to himself for two or three days, and so went unrecognized. During those days, however, he noticed that his innkeeper was a cheat.

He now thought, "Guests don't have it so good where their innkeeper's a cheat. You'd better look for another hotel."

That evening his innkeeper revealed to Eulenspiegel that he already had another hotel. The innkeeper showed the other guests to bed, but not him.

Eulenspiegel at once said, "What's this, Mr. Innkeeper? I pay as much for my food as those whom you've shown to their beds – and I'm supposed to sleep on this bench?"

The innkeeper said, "Look, here are a couple of sheets for

you." Whereupon he loosed a fart, with another on top of it, adding, "Look, here's a pillow." Then he loosed a third fart, and really began to stink, saying, "See? There's a whole bed for you. Get by somehow till morning, and then pile these together for me again."

Eulenspiegel kept quiet, but he thought, "See? Of course you see. You've got to pay this cheat back with a trick." But he stretched out on the bench for the night.

Well, the innkeeper had an elegant folding dinner-table. Eulenspiegel opened it, shitted into it, and folded it up again. The next morning he got up early, went to the innkeeper's door, and called out, "Mr. Innkeeper, I thank you for my overnight stay," and with that let fall a huge shit, calling in to him, "Those are the bead feathers. The pillows, sheets and blankets I've put together in a pile."

The innkeeper said, "Mr. Guest, that's just fine. I'll look for the pile when I get up."

Eulenspiegel said, "Just look around. You'll find it." With that, he left the house.

The innkeeper was to have quite a few guests for lunch, and he said, "My guests shall eat at my pretty table." But when he opened the table, he found himself attacked by a terrific stink. He discovered Eulenspiegel's excrement, and said, "He pays according to one's labor all right: a fart paid for with a shit." Then he had Eulenspiegel invited back, planning to test him further. Eulenspiegel came straight back, and they settled their fooling, so that from then on Eulenspiegel got into a good bed.

79. How Eulenspiegel paid the innkeeper with the sound of his money.

Eulenspiegel stayed quite a while at that inn in Cologne. Then it happened that the food was brought to the fire very late, so it was high noon before lunch was ready. Eulenspiegel felt annoyed that he had to go hungry so long. Well, the innkeeper could see that this bothered him, so he told Eulenspiegel that whoever could not wait till the food was ready could just eat whatever he had. Eulenspiegel went off to one end of the table to eat a roll, and then went to sit by the hearth, where he basted the roast till it was ready. Well, when the clock struck twelve, the table was laid, the food was served, and the innkeeper and his guests took their places – but Eulenspiegel stayed in the kitchen.

The innkeeper said, "What's this? Don't you want to sit at the table?"

"No," said Eulenspiegel. "I don't want to eat. I got full from the smell of your roast."

The innkeeper said nothing, and ate with his guests. When the meal was over, they paid the innkeeper. Then one left, another stayed behind, but Eulenspiegel remained sitting by the fire. The innkeeper came over with his tally board. He was irritated, and told Eulenspiegel to pay him two Cologne white-pennies for the meal.

Eulenspiegel said, "Mr. Innkeeper, are you the sort of fellow who takes money from someone who hasn't eaten his food?"

The innkeeper said acidly that he had better just pay the money. Even if Eulenspiegel had eaten nothing, he had still gotten full from the smell. He had been sitting near the roast and that was the same as if he had sat at the table and eaten the roast. The innkeeper would count that as a meal.

Eulenspiegel took out a Cologne white-penny and threw it onto the bench. "Mr. Innkeeper, do you hear that sound?"

The innkeeper said, "I hear the sound all right."

Eulenspiegel was fast with his penny and flipped it back into his purse. He said, "The sound of that penny helps you exactly as much as the smell of your roast helped my stomach."

The innkeeper was not a little peeved, as he wanted the white-penny, but Eulenspiegel refused to hand it over, and even threatened to bring the matter to court. The innkeeper gave in. He had no desire to go to court. He was afraid that Eulenspiegel might pay him back as he had with the folding table. The innkeeper let him go.

Well, Eulenspiegel left that place – letting the innkeeper honor his own bill – and left the Rhine. He then traveled back to the district of Saxony.

80. How Eulenspiegel took his leave of Rostock.

After playing that trick, Eulenspiegel rode quickly out of Rostock,[1] and came to an inn in a country town.

There was little to eat in the house. There was nothing but poverty there, and the innkeeper had many children–whom Eulenspiegel did not enjoy being around.[2] Well, Eulenspiegel tied up his horse in the stable, went into the house, and walked over to the fire. But he found a cold hearth and a bare house. He saw at once that there was nothing but poverty in the place.

---

1. This tale ought perhaps to follow other chapters having to do with Rostock, such as 39 or 49. See Notes on the Tales.

2. See Chapter 21.

He said, "Mr. Innkeeper, you've got terrible neighbors."

The innkeeper said, "Yes, Mr. Guest, so I do. They steal everything I've got in the house."

Eulenspiegel began to laugh, thinking, "The innkeeper here is like a guest." He wanted to stay there, despite the children, whom he did not like because he saw that they went to do their business behind the door of the house, one child after the other.

Eulenspiegel told the innkeeper, "Your children certainly have filthy habits! Don't you have some place other than behind your front door for them to do their business?"

The innkeeper said, "Mr. Guest, why let it bother you? It doesn't bother me. I'm leaving tomorrow."

Eulenspiegel kept quiet. Later, when he felt the need, he shitted a huge filthy pile into the fireplace.

Well, the innkeeper came in while Eulenspiegel was about his business and said, "The plague on you! Shitting in the fireplace? Isn't the courtyard big enough?"

Eulenspiegel said, "Mr. Innkeeper, why let it bother you? It doesn't bother me. I'm leaving today." And he mounted his horse and rode out through the door.

The innkeeper called after him to stop and clean his shit out of the hearth.

Eulenspiegel said, "Whoever's last sweeps out the house. That way my shit and your shit can be cleaned out together."

81. How Eulenspiegel killed a dog, paying an innkeeper with its skin, because the dog had eaten with him.

It once happened that Eulenspiegel went to stay at a house in a village, and found the innkeeper's wife alone. She had a shaggy little dog that she loved a lot, and that was always lying in her lap when it had nothing to do.

Eulenspiegel sat by the fire and drank beer from a jug. The woman had accustomed her dog to getting a bowlful of beer whenever she was drinking, so the dog could drink too. Well, while Eulenspiegel sat and drank, the dog got up, rubbed itself against Eulenspiegel, and jumped right onto his neck.

The innkeeper sat watching this and said, "Oh, give him a bit to drink in the bowl. That's what he wants."

Eulenspiegel said, "Certainly."

The innkeeper went about her work, and Eulenspiegel drank and gave the dog some to drink in the bowl, sticking in a bit of meat too. Well, the dog became quite full, lay down by the fire, and stretched out there.

Eulenspiegel now told the woman, "Let's figure out how much I owe you." He went on, "Dear innkeeper, if a guest ate your food, drank your beer, and had no money, would you maybe give the guest credit?"

It did not occur to the woman that he meant her dog, and she thought, "He must mean himself." She said, "Mr. Guest, there's no credit here. People either pay with money or provide collateral of some sort."

Eulenspiegel, "Then for my part, I'm happy. Anybody else takes care of his own bill."

The innkeeper went out. As soon as he could manage it, Eulenspiegel took her dog under his coat into the stable. There he skinned it, stuck the skin under his coat, and went back into the house, to the fire.

Eulenspiegel called the woman over to him and said, "Let's settle up."

The innkeeper totaled what he had spent, but Eulenspiegel paid for only half his meal. She asked who was supposed to pay for the other half. He had, after all, drunk his beer by himself.

Eulenspiegel said, "No, I didn't drink it by myself. I had a guest who drank with me and who had no money–but he offered excellent collateral. He's going to pay the other half."

The woman said, "What guest? What sort of collateral have you got?"

Eulenspiegel said, "It's his very best coat, which he was wearing." He pulled out the dog's coat, saying, "Here, dear innkeeper. This is the coat of the guest who drank with me."

The woman was horrified. She realized at once that it was her dog's skin, got totally enraged, and said, "Oh, that nothing good ever comes your way! How could you skin my dog!" She flew into a tantrum.

Eulenspiegel said, "Innkeeper, the fault's entirely your own. Rage all you like. You told me yourself to take care of your dog, and I said, 'The guest has no money.' You didn't want to give him credit. You wanted money or collateral. Well, he had no money, and the beer had to be paid for. Obviously, he had to leave his coat as collateral. Accept it, please, for the beer he drank."

The innkeeper became even crazier with rage, telling him to walk straight out of her house and never come back.

Eulenspiegel said, "I'm not going to walk out of your house. I'm going to ride out of it." He saddled his horse, rode out through the door, and said, "Innkeeper, keep that as collateral till I get your money. I'm planning to come back, uninvited. If it then happens that I don't drink anything at your house, I won't have to pay for any beer."

82. How Eulenspiegel convinced the same innkeeper that Eulenspiegel was lying on the wheel.

Now listen a bit to what Eulenspiegel did near Strassfurt.

There is a village nearby, and he took lodgings there. He dressed himself differently, went to his inn, and noticed there was a wheel standing in the house. He stretched out on it and wished the lady-innkeeper good day. Then he asked her whether she had ever heard of Till Eulenspiegel. She said that what she had heard about that scoundrel she would not like to hear repeated.

Eulenspiegel said, "Woman, what's he done to you to turn you so against him? Because wherever he goes he doesn't leave without some sort of trick."

She said, "I found that out, all right. He was here and skinned my dog. Then he offered me its skin for the beer he drank."

Eulenspiegel said, "Woman, that wasn't nice."

The woman said, "He'll have his own surprises, I'm sure."

He said, "Woman, that's happening already. In fact, he's stretched on the wheel."[1]

The innkeeper said, "God be praised for that."

Eulenspiegel said, "I'm him! Adieu! I'm leaving!"

83. How Eulenspiegel seated a lady-innkeeper in hot ashes on her bare arse.

Nasty, angry gossip brings nasty rewards.

---

1. The medieval punishment of strapping prisoners to a revolving wheel was commonly reserved for serious criminals, such as arsonists, thieves, and highwaymen; mere murderers were simply stabbed to death with a sword. See Notes on the Tales.

When Eulenspiegel left Rome[1], he arrived at a village with a large inn. The innkeeper was not at home. Well, Eulenspiegel asked his wife whether she had ever met Eulenspiegel.

The woman said, "No, I don't know him. But I've heard this much about him, that he's a perfect scoundrel."

Eulenspiegel said, "Dear innkeeper, why do you say he's a scoundrel when you don't even know him?"

The woman said, "What difference does it make that I don't know him? There's nothing ever said against the idea. People say he's a wicked fellow."

Eulenspiegel said, "Dear woman, has he ever done anything wicked to you? You've just heard gossip that he's a scoundrel."

The woman said, "I'm just telling you what I've heard from the people who come and go here."

Eulenspiegel kept quiet. But the next morning he got up early, raked aside the hot ashes, went straight up to her bed, lifted the lady-innkeeper right out of her sleep, set her bare arse into the hot ashes, and quite scorched her arse. He said, "How's that, woman? Now you've got the right to say that Eulenspiegel's a scoundrel. You've encountered him now and even seen him. You'll remember him by this."

The woman started screaming with pain. But Eulenspiegel left the house, and laughed, saying, "That's how to finish one's trip to Rome."

84. How Eulenspiegel shitted in his bed and convinced his innkeeper that a priest had done it.

Eulenspiegel played a wicked trick at Frankfurt-on-the-Oder. He went there with a priest. They both stayed at the same inn. That evening the innkeeper's wife treated them handsomely, offering them fish and venison.

When they were ready to sit down at the table, the woman seated the priest near the head of it. She also served the priest the

---

1. See Chapter 34, which this tale ought perhaps to follow.

best of what was in the serving-bowl, saying, "Father, eat this for my sake."

Eulenspiegel sat far down the table, looking the innkeeper and his wife firmly in the eye, but no one served him anything or asked him to eat. He had to pay just as much anyway, though.

When the meal was over and it was time to go to bed, Eulenspiegel and the priest were placed in a single room, and each found a fine bed ready for him to sleep on. Well, the next morning the priest was up early. He said his prayers, paid the innkeeper, and traveled on. Eulenspiegel remained lying there till it was about to strike nine. Then he shitted in the bed in which the priest had slept.

The innkeeper's wife soon asked her house-boy whether the priest or other guest was up yet, or whether they had already reckoned up and paid.

The boy said, "Yes. The priest was up early. He prayed, paid, and left. But I haven't seen the other fellow today."

The woman was worried that Eulenspiegel might be ill, so she went into his room and asked him whether he did not want to get up.

He said, "Yes, Mrs. Innkeeper. I wasn't feeling terribly well – till now."

In the meantime the woman tried to take the sheets off the priest's bed. As she opened it, she discovered a huge pile of excrement lying right in the middle of it.

"God save me!" she said. "What's this here!"

"Yes, Mrs. Innkeeper, that doesn't surprise me a bit," said Eulenspiegel. "Because last night that priest was served everything good and the very best that was brought to the table. There wasn't anything said all evening except, 'Father, eat this.' It surprises me that so much of what the priest ate stayed in him – that he didn't shit all over the room too."

The woman was furious with the innocent priest and said that if he came back, he would be sent packing. But Eulenspiegel – that honest boy – she would gladly let stay on with her.

85. How a Dutchman ate Eulenspiegel's baked apple, into which he had put saffron, off his plate.

Eulenspiegel paid back a Dutchman, fairly and cleanly. It happened that merchants from Holland were once staying at an inn in Antwerp. Eulenspiegel, who was also staying there, felt a bit ill, so he did not order any meat, but just cooked boiled eggs for himself.

When the guests were sitting at the table, Eulenspiegel sat down at the table too, bringing his soft-boiled eggs with him. One of the Dutchmen took Eulenspiegel for a farmer and said, "What's this, farmer? Don't you like the innkeeper's food? Do you have to have eggs cooked for you?" And with that he took both eggs, broke them open, poured them out, one after the other, placed the shells in front of Eulenspiegel, and said, "There – lick the barrel. The yolk's gone." The other guests laughed. Eulenspiegel laughed with them.

That evening Eulenspiegel bought a fine apple, which he hollowed out and filled with flies or gnats. Then he baked the apple slowly, peeled it, and sprinkled it on the outside with ginger. When everybody was sitting at the table that evening, Eulenspiegel brought his baked apple out on a plate and then turned away, as if he were reaching for more. As he turned his back, the Dutchman snatched his baked apple right off his plate, and gulped it down. Within an hour the Dutchman began to vomit, bringing up everything he had in his stomach and feeling so violently ill that the innkeeper and other guests thought he must have poisoned himself with the apple.

Eulenspiegel said, "This is actually no poisoning at all. It's a cleansing of his stomach. A cleansed stomach receives its food easily. If he'd told me he was so eager to gulp down my apple, I'd have warned him. There weren't any gnats in my soft-boiled eggs, but there were plenty in my baked apple. He'll have to vomit them up again."

With that the Dutchman came to himself and no longer felt quite so worried. But he said to Eulenspiegel, "Eat and bake all you like! I wouldn't eat with you again, even if you had fieldfares!"

86. How Eulenspiegel made a woman break all her pots at the market in Bremen.

After Eulenspiegel played that trick, he went back to Bremen, to the Bishop[1] there. The Bishop had a lot of fun with Eulenspiegel, and liked him too, since he was always engaged in some roguish adventure which both made the Bishop laugh and led him to maintain Eulenspiegel's horse free of charge.

Eulenspiegel then suddenly acted as if he had wearied of clowning and preferred going to church. The Bishop scoffed at him for this, but he refused to be dissuaded, and went off praying, till in the end the Bishop got pretty annoyed with him.

Well, Eulenspiegel secretly made an arrangement with a woman, a potter's wife, who sat selling pots in the market place.

---

1. See Chapter 69 for a related story.

He bought up all her pots, and agreed with her on something she was to do when he waved or gave a signal.

Eulenspiegel then went home to the Bishop and pretended that he had just been to church. The Bishop began to jeer at him again, till finally Eulenspiegel said, "Gracious Lord, come to the market place with me. There's a potter's wife there who sells clay pots. I'll make a bet with you. I won't speak to her or wink at her – and without saying a word I'll make her get up, grab a stick, and smash those clay pots to pieces."

The Bishop said, "That I'd like to see." But first he offered to bet him thirty guilders that the woman would never do it. They shook hands on it, and the Bishop went to the market place with Eulenspiegel.

Eulenspiegel pointed the woman out to him, and they went across to the city hall. Eulenspiegel stayed close to the Bishop, but made signs to the woman, with words and gestures, as if he wanted her to do something. Finally he gave the woman the sign they had agreed on. She at once got up, took a stick, and smashed her clay pots to pieces. Everybody in the market place laughed.

When the Bishop got home again, he took Eulenspiegel aside. He asked Eulenspiegel to tell him how he had made the woman break her own pots. Only then would the Bishop give Eulenspiegel the thirty guilders he had lost on their bet.

Eulenspiegel said, "Of course, Gracious Lord, with pleasure." He told the Bishop how he had first paid for the pots and afterwards set it up with the woman. He had not used black magic after all. When Eulenspiegel told him everything, the Bishop laughed and gave him the thirty guilders. But Eulenspiegel had to promise to tell nobody about it: the Bishop would get him a fat ox if he kept his word. Eulenspiegel said, sure, he would be happy to keep quiet about the matter. Then he got his things together, and went traveling.

With Eulenspiegel gone, the Bishop called a meeting of his knights and servants. He told them he knew the trick by which he too could make the woman break all her pots. His knights and servants had no particular interest in seeing pots smashed, but they did want to learn the trick of the thing.

The Bishop said, "If each of you gives me a good, fat ox for my kitchen, I'll teach the trick to all of you."

It was just autumn, when oxen are fattest. Each of them thought, "You can risk a few oxen to learn this trick – that can't do any harm." So each knight and servant sent the Bishop a fat ox. They delivered them all together, and the Bishop received sixteen oxen. Well, each ox was worth four guilders, so the thirty guilders the Bishop had given Eulenspiegel were paid back twice over.

As the oxen were standing there, Eulenspiegel came riding by and said, "Half this loot belongs to me."

The Bishop told Eulenspiegel, "Stick to what you've promised me. I'll treat you as I promised you. Just let the Lords of the country earn their keep too." And the Bishop gave him a fat ox. Eulenspiegel took it and thanked the Bishop.

The Bishop then collected his servants, drew himself up, and told them to listen to him. He would tell them all about the trick. He now told them everything – how Eulenspiegel had set it up in advance with the woman, and how he had paid for the pots. As the Bishop told them about it, his servants sat there feeling utterly betrayed, but not one dared say a word to the others. One fellow scratched his head, the next scratched the nape of his neck. They all felt miserable, as they were bitter about losing their oxen. In the end they had to accept things as they were, and they consoled themselves with the idea that the Bishop was after all a noble lord. If they had been forced to give him the oxen, well, the oxen were still around, and it had all been just a joke. Actually, they felt less annoyed about the oxen themselves than about having been such fools as to give away their oxen to learn this trick – which was pure nonsense – and that Eulenspiegel had gotten one ox.

87. How a farmer taking plums to the market in Einbeck gave Eulenspiegel a ride in his cart, and how Eulenspiegel shitted on them.

The Most Serene and High-Born princes of Brunswick once held racing, jousting, and tilting matches with many foreign Princes, lords, knights, and servants, and their tenants as well, in the city of Einbeck.

Now, this happened during the summer, when plums and other fruits were getting ripe. Well, an honest, simple peasant was living at Oldenburg near Einbeck, who had an orchard of plum trees. He had a cartful of his plums picked, planning to drive it to Einbeck. Lots of people were arriving there, and he thought he could get rid of his plums better now than at other times.

When he got near the city, he came across Eulenspiegel, who was lying there in the shade, under a green tree. Well, Eulenspiegel had drunk so much at the lords' court that he could neither eat nor drink any more – and looked more dead than alive. As the honest man was driving by, Eulenspiegel called out as feebly as he could, "Ah, good friend. Look, I've been lying here sick like this and without any help for three days and nights. If I lie here this way for one more day, I'm sure I'll die of hunger and thirst. For the sake of God, give me a lift into the city."

The good man said, "Ah, good friend. I'd be happy to do so, but I've got plums in my cart. If I put you on top of them you'll ruin them."

Eulenspiegel said, "Take me along. I'll manage in the front of the cart."

The man was old. He strained life and limb in getting the rogue (who made himself as heavy as possible) into his cart. Then, on account of his ailing passenger, he drove more slowly.

When Eulenspiegel had been traveling a while, he pulled the straw off the plums, secretly lifted his behind, shitted on the poor man's plums, and pulled the straw back over them. When the farmer reached the city, Eulenspiegel cried, "Stop! Stop! Help me out of the cart! I've got to stay outside here, at the gate."

The good man helped the evil rogue out of his cart and drove to the market by the shortest route possible. When he got there, he unhitched his horse and rode it to his inn. In the meantime, many citizens were coming into the market place. Among them was one who was always first whenever something was brought for selling but who rarely bought anything. This fellow now came over, pulled the straw half off, and made his hands shitty. At that moment, the farmer returned from his inn. Eulenspiegel had changed his clothes and arrived there too, by another way. He said to the farmer, "What've you brought to sell?"

"Plums," said the farmer.

Eulenspiegel said, "You've brought them like a rogue! These plums are shitty! You ought to be banned from the whole country with these plums!"

The man looked at him more closely, realized who he was, and said, "There was a sick man lying outside the city – a man who looked just like this man standing here, except he had different clothes on. I drove him – for the sake of God – up to the gate. And that very rogue did this disgraceful thing to me."

Eulenspiegel said, "That rogue definitely deserves a beating."

Well, the honest man had to drive his plums off to the slaughterers' graveyard, and was unable to sell them anywhere.

88. How Eulenspiegel counted the monks into vespers at Marienthal.

Now, the time came when Eulenspiegel had run around through every country. He was old and fed up and began to feel worried about dying. So he thought he might commit himself to a cloister, in his poverty, end his days well, and serve God for the rest of his life, because of his sins. If God took charge of him, he might not be lost.

With this in mind, he went to the Abbot of Marienthal and asked him whether he would take him in as a brother: he would leave the cloister his entire estate. Knaves were acceptable to the Abbot too, and he said, "You're still strong. I'll be happy to take you in, as you've asked. But you'll have to do something and have a job. As you can see, my brothers and I all have things to do, and each of us is assigned something."

Eulenspiegel said, "Yes, Father, that's fine."

"All right then! Now – God knows – you don't like working. You'll be our porter. That way you can continue your easy life and have nothing to worry about – just getting food and beer from the cellar and opening and closing the gate."

Eulenspiegel said, "Worthy Lord, may God reward you for thinking so well of me, an old, sick man. I'll do everything you tell me and not do anything you forbid me."

The Abbot said, "Look, here's the key. You mustn't let everyone in. Let every third or fourth person in. For if lots of people are let in, they'll eat the cloister into poverty."

Eulenspiegel said, "Worthy Lord, I'll handle it properly."

Well, of all who arrived there, whether they belonged to the cloister or not, Eulenspiegel always admitted only every fourth person, and no more. Complaints about this reached the Abbot, who said to Eulenspiegel, "You're a perfect scoundrel! Can't you let in those who are surrendered to the cloister and belong here?"

"Father," said Eulenspiegel, "I've been letting in every fourth person and no more, as you told me. I've simply obeyed your orders."

"You've done it like a rogue," said the Abbot, who would have been delighted to get rid of him. He appointed a different gatekeeper, as it was clear to him that Eulenspiegel had no intention of giving up his old tricks. The Abbot now assigned him another job, saying, "Look, you're to count the monks into vespers at night – and if you miss even one, you can just go on your way."

Eulenspiegel said, "Father, that's a tough job for me to handle. But if that's how it's got to be, I'll have to do it as best I can."

And that night he ripped a number of steps out of the staircase.

Now, the Prior was a God-fearing old monk who was always first in coming to mass. He came quietly enough to the staircase, but as he tried to walk downstairs, he fell through and broke a leg. Well, he screamed horribly, so the other brothers ran out to see what was the matter with him – and they fell down the stairs, one after the other.

Eulenspiegel immediately said to the Abbot, "Worthy Lord, have I done my duty? I've counted all the monks." Eulenspiegel handed the Abbot the tally board, on which he had notched the monks off as they fell, one after the other.

The Abbot said, "You've counted them like a damned rogue! Get out of my cloister and go to the devil where you please!"

So Eulenspiegel headed for Mölln. There he fell seriously ill, and a short time afterwards, he died.

89. How Eulenspiegel fell ill at Mölln, how he shitted in the pharmacist's medical book, how he was brought to "The Holy Ghost," and how he said a sweet word to his mother.

Eulenspiegel became weak and quite ill as he went from Marienthal to Mölln. There he stayed with a pharmacist to get medicine. Now, the pharmacist was rather malicious and tricky, so he gave Eulenspiegel a strong laxative. When morning came, the laxative began to work, and Eulenspiegel got up to relieve himself. But the house was locked up everywhere. He was full of worry and need, so he went into the pharmacy, shitted into one of the books, and said, "The medicine came from here. It ought to be returned here. That way the pharmacist doesn't lose anything. I can't pay for it anyway."

When the pharmacist found out about this, he got furious with Eulenspiegel and no longer wanted him in his house. He had Eulenspiegel brought to the hospital (called The Holy Ghost). Eulenspiegel told the people who were taking him there, "I've struggled hard and always prayed to God to let the Holy Ghost come into me. So now He sends me the opposite – that I come into the Holy Ghost. So He stays outside of me, and I enter Him."

The people laughed at his words and left him there. Indeed, a man dies as he has lived.

It became known to his mother that he was ill. She got ready in a hurry and came to see him, thinking to get some money from him, for she was an old, poor woman. When she arrived at his bedside, she began to wail, and said, "My dear son, where are you sick?"

Eulenspiegel said, "Dear mother, here between the bed-box and the wall."

"Ah, dear son, say a sweet word to me."

Eulenspiegel said, "Dear mother, 'honey'–that's a sweet word."

His mother said, "Ah, dear son, give me some sweet advice to remember you by."

Eulenspiegel said, "Yes, dear mother. When you want to do your business, turn your arse away from the wind. Then the stink won't get into your nose."

His mother said, "Dear son, give me some of your belongings."

Eulenspiegel said, "Dear mother, one should give to him who has nothing and take from him who has something. My possessions are hidden–where, nobody knows. If you find something that's mine, you may take it, for of my goods I leave you all that's crooked and straight."

In the meantime Eulenspiegel was getting very ill, so the people urged him to confess and take communion. Eulenspiegel did so, for he knew very well that he would never get out of his sick bed.

90. How Eulenspiegel was told to repent of his sins–so he repented of three sorts of tricks he had not played.

Eulenspiegel had better feel repentance and sorrow for his sins during his illness. Then he could receive Holy Communion and die more sweetly–or so an old beguine told him.

Eulenspiegel replied, "It won't happen that I'll die sweetly, for death is bitter. Also, why should I confess in secret what I've done during my life? Lots of countries and people know what I've done. The man I've treated well will speak well of me, and the man to whom I've done something awful won't keep quiet because I'm repentant. I'm repentant about only three sorts of things, and I'm sorry that I didn't, and couldn't, do them."

The beguine said, "Dear God, just be happy if it's something terrible you didn't do, and just be sorry for your sins."

Eulenspiegel said, "All I'm sorry for are those three things I didn't do – and never got to do."

The beguine said, "What are these things? Are they good or bad?"

Eulenspiegel said, "There are just three things. The first is this. In the days of my youth, whenever I saw a man walking in the street, whose coat showed because it hung down below his cloak, I followed him, thinking his coat might trip him, because I wanted to lift it up. But whenever I got up to somebody like that, I saw that his coat was fashionably meant to be that long – so I got angry and would gladly have snipped his coat off, as much of it as hung out below his cloak. And I'm just sorry I never got to do that. The second thing is that whenever I saw somebody sitting or walking, who was picking his teeth with a knife, that I couldn't stick the knife through his throat. That makes me sorry too. The third thing is that I can't stitch up the arses of all the old women who are past their prime. That makes me sorry as well, since they're of no use to anybody on earth and just make the ground shitty where fruit grows."

The beguine said, "Oh, God save us! What're you saying! I hear you all right. If you were strong and had the power, you'd sew up my hole for me too – for I'm a woman of easily sixty."

Eulenspiegel said, "I'm sorry that hasn't been done."

The beguine then said, "Well, the devil protect you!" And she walked away from him and left him lying there.

Eulenspiegel said, "There's no beguine who's really devout when she's angry. Then she's more spiteful than the devil."

91. How Eulenspiegel prepared his legacy–in which the priest covered his hands with shit.

Be careful, all you religious and worldly people, that you do not dirty your hands on legacies, as happened with Eulenspiegel's legacy.

A priest was brought to Eulenspiegel to confess him. When the priest came to him, the priest thought, "He's been an extraordinary person, so he must have gotten a lot of money together. It can't be otherwise. He must have a remarkable amount of money. You ought to be able to tease it out of him now, at his final end. Maybe there'll be some for you, too."

Well, when Eulenspiegel began to confess to the priest and they began to talk, the priest said to him, in the middle of other things, "Eulenspiegel, my dear son, reflect on your soul's holiness here at your end. You've been an amazing fellow and have committed many sins for which you should be sorry. But if you have a bit of money–I would give it to honor God and poor priests, such as I am. Thus would I advise you, for that money was strangely come by. And should you decide to do such a thing–to show me your money and entrust it to me–I shall certainly arrange that you arrive in God's grace. And should you wish to give me some too, I would thank you all the days of my life and read vigils and masses for you."

Eulenspiegel said, "Yes, my dear fellow, I'll think of you all right. Just come back this afternoon. I'll put a piece of silver right into your hands. That way you'll be sure of it."

The priest was delighted, and came running back that afternoon. Well, while he was gone, Eulenspiegel got a jug, filled it half-full with human excrement, and strewed a bit of money on top, so the money covered the excrement.

When the priest returned, he said, "My dear Eulenspiegel, here I am. If you would like to give me something now, as you promised, I am ready to receive it."

Eulenspiegel said, "Yes, dear Father. If you'll just grab modestly, and not be greedy, I'll let you make a grab into this jug. That way you'll remember me."

The priest said, "I'll do as you wish, taking as little as I can."

Eulenspiegel opened the jug, saying "Look, dear Father, the jug's rather full of money. Just reach in and pull out a handful. But don't reach too far."

The priest said, "To be sure." But he became pretty eager – driven by greed – and plunged right into the jug, thinking he would pull out a good handful, and shoving his hand deep inside. He now discovered something damp and soft under the money. He pulled his hand out again. His knuckles were covered with excrement. The priest said, "Ah, what a terrible rogue you are! If you can trick me now, at your very end, when you're lying on your death-bed, those you tricked in the days of your youth have every right to complain."

Eulenspiegel said, "Dear Father, I warned you not to dig too deep. If your greed betrayed you and you ignored my warning, it's not my fault."

The priest said, "You're a rogue to end all rogues! If you could talk yourself out of the gallows at Lübeck, you'll be able to answer me all right." He walked away, leaving Eulenspiegel lying there.

Eulenspiegel called after him to wait and take his money. The priest refused to listen.

92. How Eulenspiegel divided his possessions into three parts – one for his friends, one for the Council of Mölln, and one for the priest there.

As Eulenspiegel became more seriously ill, he made his last will and testament, dividing his possessions into three parts – one for his friends, one for the Council of Mölln, and one for the priest there – but with this stipulation: that when God finally took him and he went his way to death, that his corpse be buried in hallowed ground and his soul dispatched with vigils and masses according to Christian practice and custom. Then, after four weeks, they might together unlock the fine chest, well secured with expensive locks, that he showed them – if it was still locked – and divide among themselves what was in it and come to an agreement about his property.

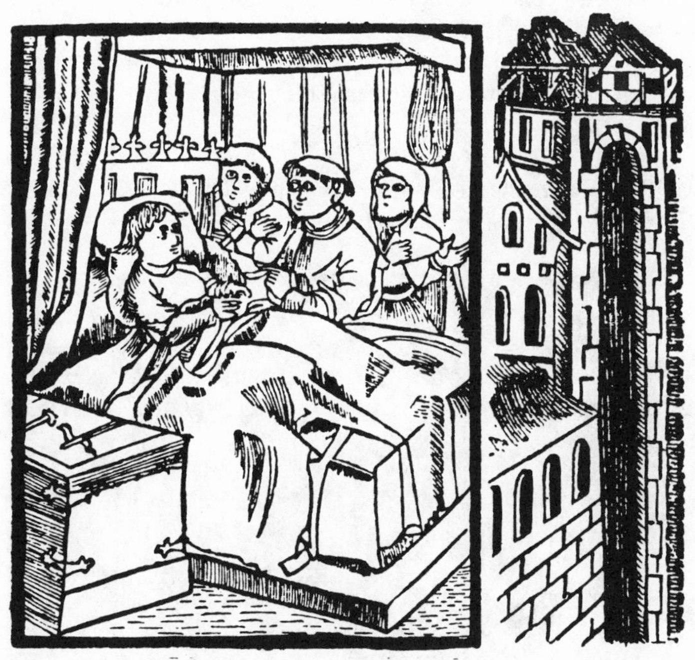

All three parties took this cheerfully, and Eulenspiegel died. When everything had been done according to his will, and the four weeks had slipped by, the Council, the parish priest, and Eulenspiegel's friends came over and opened the chest to divide the treasure he had left. But when it was opened they found nothing in it but stones. Everybody looked at everybody else, and they began to get angry. The priest suspected that since the Council had been taking care of the chest, they had secretly removed the treasure and locked the chest up again. The Council thought his friends had taken the treasure during his illness and filled the chest with stones. His friends thought the priest must secretly have carried off the treasure when everybody left to let him confess Eulenspiegel. Well, they parted unpleasantly.

The priest and the Council now decided to dig Eulenspiegel up again. But when they began to dig, the grave stank so badly that no one could remain there. So they filled in the grave a second time.

Well, Eulenspiegel stayed buried, and in his memory a stone was placed on his grave, which can still be seen in that spot.

93. How Eulenspiegel died and how pigs knocked over his bier during the vigils, so he took a tumble.

After Eulenspiegel had given up the ghost, people came to the hospital to mourn him. Well, they placed him on a bier made of wooden planks. The priests arrived to sing vigils and started singing.

The hospital sow now trotted in with her piglets, walked under the bier, and began to rub herself against it so Eulenspiegel fell off. The women and priests rushed over to chase the sow and piglets outside – but the sow got angry and refused to let herself be moved. In fact the sow and piglets tore madly through the hospital, leaping and racing over the priests, over the beguines, over the sick, over the healthy, and over the coffin in which Eulenspiegel was lying – causing the old beguines to scream and yell so much that the priests gave up their vigils and ran outside, letting the others finally chase the sow and piglets away.

The beguines now set about placing the tree of the dead[1] back on the bier. But it got placed incorrectly, with Eulenspiegel's belly facing the ground while his behind was turned upwards. Well, when the priests left, the beguines said they would bury him. The priests were happy to let them do so, but they would not come back. So the beguines picked up Eulenspiegel and carried him the wrong way around, lying on his belly because the tree was turned over, to the churchyard. There they set him down beside his grave.

The priests now came back anyway and considered what advice they ought to give on how to bury him – he could not simply lie down in his grave, like other Christians. Then they noticed that the tree was turned over and that he was lying on his belly. Well, they began to laugh and said, "He's showing us himself that he wants to lie upside down. Well, that's how we'll do it."

94. How Eulenspiegel was buried, as he wanted to be buried not by religious or lay people but by beguines.

Things went oddly at Eulenspiegel's burial. When everybody had gathered in the churchyard, around the tree of the dead in which Eulenspiegel was lying, and they set it on two ropes and tried to lower it into his grave, the rope at his feet snapped and the tree shot into the grave, leaving Eulenspiegel standing upright in his coffin.

Everybody who was standing there quickly agreed, "Let him stand. As he was odd while he lived, he ought to be odd in death too."

---

1. This was an actual tree trunk, which had been dug out and to which the body was firmly strapped, that served as the coffin. See Notes on the Tales.

So they filled in the grave and left him standing up. They placed a stone over the grave, and on half of it carved an owl, with a mirror which the owl held in its claws. Over that they carved on the stone:

Don't move this stone: let that be clear –
Eulenspiegel's buried here.
Anno domini MCCCL.

95. How Eulenspiegel's epitaph and inscription were carved over his grave at Lüneburg.

EPITAPH

Don't move this stone: let that be clear –
Eulenspiegel's buried here.

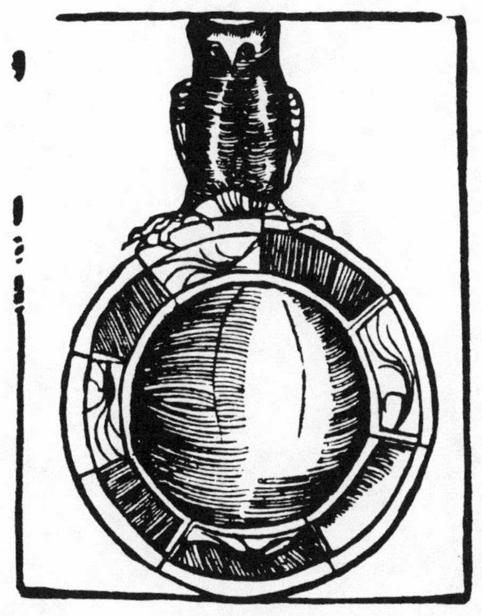

Printed by Johannes Grüninger in the
free city of Strassburg, on Saint
Adolph's Day, in the year
MCCCCCXV.[1]

---

1. The 1519 edition has "in the imperial city of Strassburg on St. Margaret's Day." For a discussion of the reference to Lüneburg in the title here, see Notes on the Tales.

NOTES ON THE TALES

Title page. The edition of 1515 reads *Ein kurzweilig lesen von Dyl/Ulenspiegel gebore uß dem land zu Brunßwick. Wie er sein leben volbracht hatt. xcvi seiner geschichten*. The edition of 1519 has *Dil* instead of *Dyl*, and *hat* instead of *hatt*. A literal translation would read *An amusing story of Dyl* (or *Dil*) *Eulenspiegel*, though the idea of the book as a compilation, collection, or even vintage of tales is implicit in the use of the word *lesen* here. (The rest of the subtitle reads *born in the country of Brunswick. How he spent his life. 96 of his tales.*) The earliest complete editions of the tales use the Low German "Ulenspiegel." The first appearance of the High German "Eulenspiegel" occurs in Weygrand Han's edition (1557, 1563), published in Frankfurt (Schröder, 20; Sichtermann, 253). The familiarity, fame, and widespread use of "Eulenspiegel," even before Han's publication of it, together with its universality today, argue its use in the present translation. Further discussion of Eulenspiegel's name and its possible meanings is to be found in the Introduction and in the note on tale 1, below. Grüninger's assertion that the book presents 96 tales is incorrect; there are in fact 95. The error may result from a miscounting of the tales after tale 41; the next tale is numbered 43, with this confusion running through the rest of the book.

Foreword. The author's, or compiler's, Foreword presents a number of knotty problems, having to do with the date of composition, the author's references to himself, and the literary conventions present here. These are discussed in the Introduction (Sources and Influence). The word "countries" is to be understood as including various principalities in what is today Germany, as well as Poland, Denmark, and Italy (Rome, specifically), where Eulenspiegel's adventures also take place. The references to the tales of Pfaffe Amis and Pfaffe vom Kalenberg are considered in the Introduction (Sources and Influence).

1. The Elm (or Melbe, in the 1515 edition; the Melme, in the 1519 edition) is a forest in Saxony, extending from Ampleben to Schöppenstedt (Lappenberg, 223; Lindow, 9). Kneitlingen, Eulenspiegel's birthplace, is spelled Knetlingen in the 1515 edition, which frequently retains Low German forms (Lindow, 9). This village was described, in 1654, as still containing the house in which Eulenspiegel was born (Lappenberg, 223). The several references in this tale to Eulenspiegel's parents, their names, and the name of his godfather are historically inconclusive. Most likely, they form part of the author's technique, one common enough among many authors, that allows him to lend authenticity to his hero's exploits by mentioning names recognizable to his audience. Thus a Frau Ulenspiegel, referred to in court documents of around 1355 as living in Brunswick, is not necessarily Eulenspiegel's mother (Lindow, 10); the family name "Ulenspegel," while recorded in Brunswick in 1335, 1337, and 1355, is connected only much later–and then perhaps falsely–with the qualities of the hero (Lindow, 10; see also the more detailed account of Eulenspiegel's name in the Introduction, Artistic Achievement); and Uetzen, the name of Eulenspiegel's godfather, which is mentioned only in the 1519 edition, and which shows up as an old family name in Ampleben in 1360, is nowhere connected with a "Till von Uetzen" (Lindow, 10). The destruction of the castle at Ampleben, noted in this tale, is recorded as having occurred in 1425, during a skirmish between Brunswickers and the robber-baron Herwig von Uetzen (Lindow, 10; Lappenberg, 225). An Abbot Arnold Papenmeyer, from Brunswick and Altwick, perhaps alluded to in this tale, was in fact alive in 1500, the year in which N. claims to have done his writing (Lappenberg, 226); in the 1519 edition he is described as the Abbot of Saint Ägidien. The custom of toasting an infant after baptism, with "Kindelbier," was common in the fourteenth century (Lindow, 10). What was uncommon, and indeed unknown, is Eulenspiegel's triple baptism. At a minimum, it suggests his life to come, with its jests and absurdities. The end of Eulenspiegel's life (see tales 93 and 94) presents a similar topsyturvydom.

2. Various editors (Lindow, 13; Sichtermann, 257) argue that the last part of this tale, in which Eulenspiegel's father is described as moving his household to the principality of Magdeburg, properly belongs at the beginning of the tale that follows. The editions of 1515 and 1519 present this section as it appears here.

3. The possible influence of this episode on Friedrich Nietzsche's *Also sprach Zarathustra* (1883) should certainly be considered. In Zarathustra's well known encounter with a tightrope walker (Pt. I, 3-8), he watches as a jester suddenly joins the professional acrobat on his rope, high above assembled townspeople. The jester, who is also walking the rope, leaps over the professional rope-walker, terrifying him. He loses his balance and falls into the crowd. He dies in Zarathustra's arms. Zarathustra carries his body off to the gravediggers. On the way, he is accosted by a man who rebukes him and describes him as one who "talked like a jester" (Kaufmann trans., 133).

4. The reference to Helmstedt shoes ("helmstetesche Schuch") here has not been satisfactorily explained. Lindow (17) sees in this phrase a now lost slangish reference to senseless and pointless activity of some sort.

5. Eulenspiegel's aphoristic statement here that "anything a man decides on will take care of him all his life" ("wozu sich einer begibt, daz wurt ihm sein Lebtag gnug") seems to find an echo in Hermann Bote's *Köker* (ca. 1520): "Wo sik ein jederman to hol, des wart eme sin levedage genoch." It thus forms part of the "evidence" that Bote may be the author of the Eulenspiegel stories. This issue is dealt with in the Introduction (Date and Authorship). See also Lindow, 19. The Saint Nicholas referred to here is Pope Nicholas I (d. 867), whose death-day falls on November 13; Saint Martin's Day, honoring Bishop Martin of Tours (316/7-397), falls on November 11 (Sichtermann, 260). Pope Nicholas (not to be confused with Nicholas, the patron-saint of scholars, who was Bishop of Myra in Lycia and who died in 326) was devoted to fasting. Bishop Martin was known for his philanthropy, this extending even to his dividing his coat among the poor. Eulenspiegel's idea, therefore, is that one should fast with the fasting and eat with the generous. See also Lappenberg, 230.

6. The theme of this tale – the deception of a baker – also appears in Johannes Pauli's *Schimpf und Ernst* (561; edition of 1522) (Lindow, 21).

7. The breakfast bread (*weckbrot*) mentioned here is actually, as can be seen, not a bread at all but a soup, or the breakfast itself. The modern German *Abendbrot*, literally "evening bread," but actually "supper," is comparable. The statement that the malicious householder sliced "the fatty rind of the bread into a milk jug" is confusing (as bread has no fatty rind), and is perhaps meant to suggest that he had mixed pig-fat (or some other fat) in with the bread.

8. Compare with Wilhelm Busch's *Max und Moritz*, ch. 1.

9. Lindow (27) observes that this tale appears in the poem *Salomon und Markolf* (1479; W. Hartmann ed., Halle, 1934, lines 1197f), and believes that its presence there is perhaps the result of its having been taken from an earlier edition of Eulenspiegel's adventures.

10. That Eulenspiegel hires himself out as a page-boy at a castle here seems to hark back to an earlier, definitely medieval stage in the development of the Eulenspiegel legend, and perhaps in the composition of the tales; the same may be said of the word play on "henep" and "senep," which is apparently a residue of a Low German play on these words ("Hennep" and "Sennep") (see Lindow, 30; Sichtermann, 262-63).

11. Büddenstedt is in Brunswick, between Schöningen and Helmstädt. The idea that the priest here comes to an agreement with the farmers to take Eulenspiegel on as a sacristan reflects a common North German custom in place well before the Reformation (Lindow, 36).

13. Easter passion plays, such as the one described here, commonly, and throughout Europe, mingled various Latin phrases, or tropes, with the vernacular of the audience. From the tenth century, such plays included a *Visitatio Sepulchri*, performed after

Matins on Easter Sunday and allowed a greater dramatic freedom precisely because it was formally separated from the mass. A "sepulchre," or some sort of structure (the meaning apparently varied from place to place; but see the woodcut accompanying this tale for one conception), was put up near the altar or in the transept. The drama at its simplest involved a question asked by the angel at the tomb of Christ, and a response by the three Marys as they visited the tomb on Easter morning. This part was in Latin. The angel asked, "Quem quaeritis, mulieres?" (Whom are you seeking, women?) To this they replied, "Jesum Nazarenum, crucifixum." The angel then informed them of Christ's resurrection, and they, and presumably the audience, rejoiced. (The 1515 edition spells "quaeritis" as shown.) The satire in this tale is clearly directed at the farmers' inability to understand the Latin, and perhaps at their ignorance more generally. (For a solid account of the development of this dramatic form, see W.T.H. Jackson, *The Literature of the Middle Ages*, "9. The Drama," Columbia Univ. Press, New York, 1960, 279-81.)

15. The Bruno of this tale is probably Burchard III, Archbishop of Magdeburg from 1307 to 1325. His predilection for fools, jesters, and entertainers is documented by his contemporaries (Lappenberg, 235-37; Lindow, 44). While Eulenspiegel plays the part of a medical doctor in this tale, the Bishop's "doctor" is probably a learned man who had received a degree of some sort. He is in any case no physician.

16. Peine, between Brunswick and Hannover, dates from at least 1130. The "naked bastard page-boys" present a puzzle. In the earliest editions of the tales one finds "Bankressen," which may refer to the illegitimate children of the local nobility. Lindow (50) prefers a substitute term, "Bankriese," or "miserably dressed castle-watchmen out of uniform"; or "Bankerte," which would refer to some similar form of castle low-life. Lindow also suggests "Bankrese," which in its plural would mean "lazy rascals lying about on benches, or on a bench." Sichtermann (118, n4) observes that "Bankerte" can in fact mean "bastards." "Coldville," from "Koldingen," not far from Hannover, reflects the Low German word play on "kold."

17. A hospital fitting exactly the description of the hospital in this tale was established at Nuremberg in 1331 (Lappenberg, 238; Lindow, 52).

18. "Half-City" is Halberstadt, with the word play intended. Eulenspiegel's aphoristic reference is to Matthew 12, 13: "For whoever hath, to him shall be given, and he shall have more abundance: but whosoever hath not, from him shall be taken away even that he hath."

19. The first sentence of the 1515 edition of this tale speaks of a "weaver" as living nearby; the 1519 edition corrects this to "baker." Walther (52) speaks of a house in Brunswick called "At the Wild Man." Saint Nicholas Eve is December 5. Saint Nicholas is the patron saint of school children and sailors.

20. The Uelzen of this tale is a town south of Lüneburg (Lappenberg, 240; Lindow, 60).

21. Lindow (64) believes that the rather witty reflections on food, fate, and drink found here are more properly those of a court jester than a *Schalk* of Eulenspiegel's ilk. This chapter, which in fact presents neither prank nor adventure, must therefore be an alien addition to a now "lost" and earlier compilation of Eulenspiegel's tales. In fact, however, many chapters offer quite similar "witty" reflections, while others show Eulenspiegel playing the part of a court jester (cf., for instance, 23, 24, 25, and 38). On the enigma of the "foolishness" of Eulenspiegel's reddish-gray horse, no clear facts are forthcoming. One possibility is that the pranksterish quality of the horse derived from its mottled appearance. Motley was of course a traditional and conventional part of the costume of professional medieval and Renaissance jesters and buffoons. Enid Welsford (339) provides interesting comments on the subject of fools' clothing.

22. The "Count of Anhalt" mentioned here is most likely Bernhard II of Anhalt, who acquired the title "Prince of Anhalt" in 1318 (Lappenberg, 241; Lindow 65). Bernhard II was a descendant of the Bernburgers. A tower, still referred to as "Eulenspiegel's," and thought to be over eleven hundred years old, still stands in Bernburg. An Eulenspiegel memorial was erected there in 1959 (Sichtermann, 283).

23. The 1519 edition describes Eulenspiegel here as a "Hofman," or "Gaukler" (Honegger, 23, n4), an entertainer who traveled from court to court. The 1515 edition, whose terminology is a bit curious in this as in other places, terms him a "koufman," or (in this instance) an entrepreneur. Lappenberg (242) wishes to identify the Danish king here as Christopher II, who died in 1332.

24. If there is any historical basis to this tale, the king involved may have been Casimir III (1330-1370) (Lappenberg, 243; Lindow, 71).

25. Celle was founded by Otto of Lüneburg in 1292 (Lindow, 73).

26. Johann Christoph Sachse, described by Goethe as the German Gil Blas, reported (in 1822) the existence of an "Eulenspiegel stone," or memorial of some sort, near Lüneburg, commemorating Eulenspiegel's adventure here.

27. This tale makes an oblique reference to Flanders as an important center of Renaissance painting in the fifteenth and sixteenth centuries (Eulenspiegel has apparently purchased various paintings there). The Landgrave's personal concern with alchemy is described in the 1519 edition, but not in that of 1515. As it is the Landgrave's gullibility that is being satirized, this new emphasis makes sense. Satirical treatments of quack alchemists are fairly frequent in late medieval and Renaissance literature (cf. Chaucer's "The Canon's Yeoman's Tale" and Ben Jonson's *The Alchemist*), in which gullibility is likewise an issue. The Landgrave's gullible devotion to alchemy is here skillfully interwoven with two quite ancient folk-tale motifs whose use, in this adventure of Eulenspiegel's, is also to satirize gullibility. These are the motif of the invisible object as a test of legitimacy (cf., Hans Christian Anderson's "The Emperor's New Clothes") and the magical object as a test of nobility (as, for instance, in the sword test which must be passed by a future king, such as King Arthur, before he can be accepted as a rightful or proper king: only the rightful and proper king will be able to draw the sword from the stone). Beliefs in such possibilities are plainly one target of Eulenspiegel's manipulations here. Lappenberg (224) suggests that the Landgrave's wife may be the Elizabeth who was the wife of Ludwig VI, Count of Thüringen, and the daughter of Andreas II, King of Hungary. She died in 1227. Lindow (79) notes that the ancestral line indicated by Eulenspiegel as he describes his "painting" is a complete invention. Female fools, or jesters, such as the one referred to in this tale, make infrequent appearances in German literature straight into the eighteenth century; for the most part they are presented as mentally incompetent (Lindow, 80; see also the discussion of fools, jesters, and professional clowns in the Introduction, Artistic Achievement).

28. The University of Prague, mentioned here, was founded by Emperor Karl IV in 1348 as the first German university (quite a few universities, in Italy, France, Spain, and England, date from considerably earlier) (Lindow, 82). John Wycliffe (1320?-1384), who taught at Oxford and was an early translator of the Bible into English, along with his Lollard followers, represented a direct challenge to the Curia, canon lawyers, and the Roman Church, with its dependence upon, and advocacy of, Latin. Wycliffe is thus notable for his promotion of vernacular, or "vulgar," literature, and belongs in a developing tradition of like-minded authors, such as Dante, Chaucer, and (shortly after the publication of the Eulenspiegel stories) Martin Luther. Preachers and professors at the University of Prague were deeply influenced by Wycliffe and the Lollards, and sought for the first time to turn Czech into a literary language. John Huss (1370-1415), who received a master of arts degree from the University of Prague in 1396, was himself influenced by Wycliffe's ideas (see also Krofta, 46; Heer, 305-6; Lindow, 83).

29. Erfurt, noted here, was a university town from 1392 to 1816 (Lindow, 86).

31. Saint Brendan of Ireland (484-577?), mentioned here, is, in legend at least, reputed to have discovered America long before the Norsemen. Geoffrey Ashe, in *Land to the West* (New York, 1962), examines the legend of Brendan through investigations of both Irish history and the medieval European versions of Brendan's possible voyage.

33. The incorrect price of 28 pennies for eating at "the next table" is corrected to 18 in the 1519 edition.

34. The "old saying" cited here is unknown in the form in which Eulenspiegel presents it (Lindow 101), though variations were certainly familiar in pre-Reformation German-speaking areas, to wit, "Wer nach Rom zieht, sucht einen Schalk, beim zweiten Mal findet er ihn, beim dritten Mal bringt er ihn mit" [Whoever goes to Rome is looking for a rogue. On his second trip he finds the rogue, and on his third trip he brings the rogue along himself]. (Cf. also Lappenberg, 249.) The 1515 edition terms the Basilica of St. John in Lateran "Latronen," which means "thieves." The 1519 edition changes, or corrects, this to "lateran." Lindow (103) wishes to retain the satirical sense of what is most likely a printing error, and compares it with Eulenspiegel's possibly satirical apostrophe of the pope later in this tale as a "Servant Among All Servants." The latter is a translation of the conventional "servus servorum Dei," and as Eulenspiegel uses it, bowing elaborately, at least ironic. (Cf. also Sichtermann, 291.)

35. Various versions of this anti-Semitic tale appear in other contemporary jest-books, such as Heinrich Bebel's *Facetien* (Lindow, 104). Sichtermann, who finds the tale "unappetizing," remarks that it is the only tale in which Jews put in an appearance (292), finds "no trace" of anti-Semitism in the author of the tales, and attributes the bigotry exhibited here to Eulenspiegel himself. Eulenspiegel, however, is to be understood chiefly as satirizing superstitious beliefs (Sichtermann, 292) and gullibility, which is his frequent practice with all sorts of groups. What is more interesting than these reflections is the fact that the Eulenspiegel stories, in their rapidly multiplying editions after 1519, were popular among Jews themselves. A transliteration of the tales, specifically intended for Jewish readers, and done into Hebrew letters, was published on October 11, 1600, by Benjamin Merks (Tannhausen

and Augsburg), as *Wunderparlich und seltsame Historien Til Eulenspiegels* (a modern edition of this book, with transliteration into roman type, is John A. Howard ed., Königshausen + Neumann publ., Würzburg & Bamberg, 1983). This book contains tale 35 in full, though Eulenspiegel's reference to the Jews here as "dogs" is eliminated. Virtually no effort is made in Merks' edition to alter the numerous Christian references in the Eulenspiegel stories. Lappenberg (250) believes that the name "Alpha" in this tale is a variant of "Kaiphas."

37. Hoheneggelsen is fifteen kilometers northeast of Hildesheim. The bacon referred to here would have consisted of the meatless fat behind the ribs of the pig. It was both the cheapest and poorest tasting part of the animal. The commercial pig-slaughterers were those who slaughtered pigs for products other than food. The sudden entrance of a "third man," who overhears the priest in this story as he speaks with his servant-girl, is left a mystery.

38. Both the editions of 1515 and 1519 give the location here as "Rylßenburg," which makes no sense. Kissenbrück is a village south of Wolfenbüttel. The Duke of Brunswick mentioned here, may have been Henry the Strange, who died in 1322, or his son, Henry II (Lappenberg, 253).

41. Lindow (125) takes Eulenspiegel's verses addressed to the wife here, as well as his little speech in prose directed at the maid, as having erotic implications. The wife with "lots of white in her eye," who stands about looking at men all day instead of working, will want to go after them (Lindow notes that this is a version of a contemporary popular saying). The "beef" that the maid should "guard against" is a *double-entendre*.

43. Stade, mentioned here, was founded ca. 1150 (Lindow, 128).

44. Bootmakers should not be confused with shoemakers during this period (the late Middle Ages and the Renaissance). The two occupations were quite distinct (see also Lindow, 131). Eulenspiegel's target here is thus different from his target in those tales dealing with shoemakers.

45. The 1515 edition has "kalck" in the title here (the 1519 edition "Talck," or tallow), no doubt a typographical error (Lindow, 135).

46. Einbeck, mentioned here, was famous for its beer in the Middle Ages (Lappenberg, 225; Lindow, 137).

48. Honegger's discovery of the previously printed fragment of the tales (see also the Introduction) cites Bernburg as the location of this tale (Honegger, 38). Lindow and Lappenberg had thought that the "Brenburg" appearing in the 1515 and 1519 editions must be a misprint for "Brandenburg" (Lindow, 143; Sichtermann, 301).

49. Convocations of artisans, such as that of the tailors, which is described in this tale, were frequent throughout the North German towns belonging to the Hanseatic League. The league itself developed slowly during the High Middle Ages, as groups of merchants or Hansas, trading in foreign principalities, together with the towns and cities where they were located, began to cooperate for protection against competition and theft. The Hanseatic League dates formally from 1358. Despite its dissolution in the seventeenth century, Bremen, Hamburg, and Lübeck are still referred to as Hanseatic cities. (See also Lindow, 144.) Readers of Chaucer may recall the apropos and nearly contemporary description of the haberdasher, carpenter, weaver, dyer, and maker of tapestries in the General Prologue to *The Canterbury Tales*: they all belong to one "solempne and . . . greet fraternitee," or parish guild, with each of them seeming "a fair burgeys/To sitten in a yeldehalle on a deys" (ls. 364, 369-70).

50. Stendal, the site of this tale, was well known for its textiles and wool-weaving during the Middle Ages (Lappenberg, 257; Lindow, 148). The colloquialism "blue Monday," alluded to here as a labor-free day for wool-weavers' apprentices, apparently has its origin in the dyeing practices of the wool-weavers in the fourteenth century. When woad (from *Isatis tinctoria*, powdered and fermented) was used to dye the wool blue, it was necessary to allow twenty-four hours, at a minimum, for the process: twelve hours in the dye-bath and twelve hours of oxygenation in the open air. On Sundays, the entire day was allotted to the dyeing process, and an equal amount of time – in other words, all of Monday – was given over to the necessary oxygenation. As long as woad remained in use, the apprentices, therefore, could take Mondays off. The widespread introduction of indigo, in the sixteenth century, put an end to this custom, though the term "blue Monday" survives. (See also Lappenberg, 258; Lindow, 148.) The wool-weaver's admonition to Eulenspiegel to beat the wool "a little higher" is a bit of wool-weaver's slang, which Eulenspiegel of course takes literally. It refers to a taxing operation of beating the wool to induce its lightness and springiness, so that it is "higher" (see Sichtermann, 302).

51. Aschersleben, like Berlin (see Chapter 53) and Leipzig (see Chapter 54), was famous for its fur trade during the Middle Ages (Lappenberg, 258).

54. The humor of this tale depends on the absurd self-delusion of the furriers, in a city noted for its fur trade, Leipzig (see note on tale 51, above), allowing them to mistake the skin of a rabbit for the whole animal. The motif of mistaking one animal for another is common in folk tales (see Thompson, 494, motif J1757: Rabbit thought to be cow). This tale appears in a quite similar form in Hermann Bote's *Schichtbuch* (Sichtermann, 304). There is perhaps an echo here as well of the popular expression "eine Katze im Sack kaufen" (to buy a cat in a sack), and even of its English equivalent "to buy a pig in a poke."

55. Both Lappenberg (259) and Lindow (163) suggest that the absence of punishment, or even the suggestion that legal recourse is possible, in cases such as occur in this tale, in which Eulenspiegel destroys property gratuitously, reflects the difficulty of punishing criminals for petty crimes during the Middle Ages. It may also reflect a secret delight in such nasty activities. The delight, surely, is unquestionable for the audience reading Eulenspiegel's adventures, and remains part of the pleasure for the audience to this day: it is part of the audience's enjoyment too of Eulenspiegel's skill in evading the consequences of his bad deeds (see also Welsford, 50-51, and the Introduction, Artistic Achievement). Far more likely, therefore, is that tales such as this offer a specifically literary pleasure, usually denied in life, of simply "getting away with it," whatever the "it" may be. The opportunities of enforcing laws against petty criminals, however, varied considerably from place to place, as is shown in tale 56.

56. The name of the proprietor of the wine cellar near Lübeck's town hall, Lambrecht, who is specifically cited only in tale 57, is untraceable (Lappenberg, 260). The description of Lübeck's "justice," and indeed of the strictness of law enforcement in Lübeck, especially in cases of crimes of theft and against property, is accurate. The municipal code of laws, or town charter, of Lübeck dates from 1226, and became a model for similar charters of principalities in the Baltic area (Sichtermann, 306; Lindow, 164).

57. Lindow (167) notes that the punishment of "death on the gallows" for Eulenspiegel's rather trivial crime is harsh even for Lübeck. According to town statutes, capital punishment followed only when the property stolen amounted to at least four shillings. In an amendment to these laws of 1294, however, it is established that a thief operating in the Ratskeller may be hanged if he is found to have stolen property worth more than eighteen pennies. Honegger (64) speculates that the "weak" request Eulenspiegel makes toward the end of this tale – that only the wine-tapster and skinner kiss his arse – may be the result of censorship in Strassburg after 1512. Eulenspiegel would more likely have asked the city council and the mayor to administer the humiliating kisses: a far more persuasive means of escape for him. The censor, who apparently existed, may have toned down Eulenspiegel's last wish to avoid "complications" with the town council and mayor of the Hanseatic city of Lübeck. Kadlec (70f) traces Eulenspiegel's last wish to an earlier source, the *Mensa philosophica* (1470).

58. The satire here is clearly interwoven with motifs to be found in much earlier folk literature, as is often the case with Eulenspiegel's adventures. The theme of the bottomless purse appears, in variant forms, in ancient Greek folk literature as "the coin which keeps returning to the owner" and "magic self-supplying tables" (Thompson, 280; Type 745, Motifs D1602.11, cf. N211, and D1472.7).

60. This tale appears in various versions in other jest collections, to wit, in *Les repues franches* and Montanus' *Wegkürzer* (see the Introduction, Sources and Influence; also Lindow, 173).

61. The opening sentence, in which the Erfurt of the previous tale is misplaced in Hessen, is perhaps a printer's error, or the result of one (Lindow, 175). The description of Dresden as located "by the Bohemian Forest on the Elbe" harks back to a time when the Bohemian Forest was better known than Dresden itself (Lappenberg, 263).

62. In this, as in other tales in which Eulenspiegel manages a deception and a satire through eloquence, an echo of *maqama*, an Arab folk tale type, dating from the twelfth century, may perhaps be detected. In stories by al Hariri and al Hamadhani (Sternglass and Predergast trans.), tricksters who deceive through eloquence put in frequent appearances. Other historical references in this tale are, as is often the case, problematic. Frankfurt am Main became the site of the official election of Kaisers, according to an edict known as the "Golden Bull," in 1356 (Lindow, 179). The Count of Supplenburg, referred to here, may or may not be Lothar III, who was elected "Roman King" in 1125. Despite his description's matching rather exactly the account given of the newly elected King in this tale, Lappenberg (263) rejects Lothar on purely anachronistic grounds, while Lindow (178) finds him acceptable. Anachronisms are by no means infrequent in Eulenspiegel's adventures (see especially Chapters 27 and 31), so Lappenberg's rejection should probably be discounted. On Lothar III, see also Paul Fournier, "The Kingdom of Burgundy or Arles from the Eleventh to the Fifteenth Century," *The Cambridge Medieval History*, VIII (Cambridge, Engl., 1959), 312. Spectacle-making originates in Venice in the thirteenth century, and is established as a recognized craft in Nuremberg by 1482 (Lindow, 178). Eulenspiegel's mention of Brabant, in Flanders, no doubt has to do with the fact that Brabant had become an important center of spectacle-making by the fourteenth century. The Bishop of Trier, whom Eulenspiegel meets and entertains with his eloquence, may have been Archbishop Baldwin of Trier, who died in 1354 (Lappenberg, 263).

63. The "odd clothes" that Eulenspiegel is described as wearing in this tale remain unidentified. It is unlikely that they were the clothes of a fool or jester. In the woodcuts accompanying the 1515 and 1519 editions, Eulenspiegel never appears in jester's costume, not even in the sardonic woodcut on the title page. Honegger (133, n 351) bases his view, that Eulenspiegel commonly appears in riding clothes typical of the late fifteenth century, on comparisons of the woodcuts in the editions of 1515 and 1519. Eulenspiegel appears more consistently as a jester in Melchior Sachse's 1532 edition (Erfurt) for the first time (Sichtermann, 266-67). The wife's sarcastic remark to her husband here, that he has perhaps hired Eulenspiegel only because he was afraid that their bread might be molding, is to be understood as meaning that there was no one to eat it. On Eulenspiegel's names, Bartholomaus and "Doll" (or "Crazy"), in this tale, see Stieler, *Eulenspiegel-Jahrbuch*, 1976, 28. On Einbeck beer, famous in the Middle Ages, and mentioned here, see Lindow, 183. The Father Heinrich Hamenstede, referred to in the tale, is perhaps an actual person, a chaplain at Volkersheim, near Bockenem (twenty kilometers southeast of Hildesheim). Hamenstede was the priest of Goslar from 1474 to 1509, when he died (Sichtermann, 267; Lindow, 184). Lappenberg (266) suggests that the author's intention, in having Hamenstede driven under the gallows, is personally satirical.

64. Lindow (188) notes that "black magic," or indeed any sort of magic, receives scant attention in the Eulenspiegel stories. In the subsequent editions (after 1519), this tale is often altered so that Eulenspiegel is allowed to manage his deception by "natural" means.

65. The "pipemaker" here is a maker of wind instruments, who has become a wandering musician (Lindow, 191; Lappenberg, 267).

66. Lindow (196) wishes to argue that because Eulenspiegel is himself deceived in this tale, the tale itself cannot belong among the earliest versions of Eulenspiegel's adventures. For a contrasting view, see the Introduction, Artistic Achievement.

67. Exports of English fabrics, such as that cited here, were well known in German-speaking areas even earlier than the fourteenth century (Lappenberg, 269; Lindow, 197). Lindow (197) traces the motif of deception here, in perhaps its oldest written form, to India, and the *Panchatantra* (ca. 500 a.d.), and a story in which three con men trick a farmer into thinking that he has purchased a dog instead of a goat (on the *Panchatantra* see also Thompson, 69, and especially 376-78, in which the worldwide transmission of such motifs from India is discussed). Lappenberg (269) and Lindow (198) observe that the presence of Wends at a country fair in Uelzen is appropriate. "Wendland," an area distinguishable according to customs and language (and Slavic in the sources of both), extends through parts of east Saxony. The fact that the "Scottish priest" described here is a wandering monk of some sort probably means that he was in fact a Benedictine and originally Irish (Lappenberg, 269; Lindow, 198).

68. The phrase here having to do with "earth, ashes, and sand," which is meaningless, is perhaps the result of the omission of a line by the printer. Interestingly, this peculiarity occurs in both the 1515 and 1519 editions. (See also Lindow, 201.)

69. This particular prank takes various forms in jest-literature, appearing, for example, in Pauli's *Schimpf und Ernst* (Lindow, 203).

70. The episode with the twelve blind men forms the basis of Hans Sachs' Shrovetide play of 1553, *Eulenspiegel mit den Blinden* (Lindow, 205).

72. This tale, in which Eulenspiegel sows rogues in the street – with stones as seeds – may have satirical-political meanings. A broadside of 1606 presents the episode rather differently. Eulenspiegel sows decent citizens instead of rogues, and they rise in rebellion against local landowners. Lindow (213) suggests that in 1500 this tale may have had a meaning similar to that of the broadside. The Battle of Hemmingstedt, in 1500, saw the people of Ditmarschen, mentioned here, defending their freedom against the invading Dutch and Danish. The story as it appears in this and other early editions, however, cannot have had precisely these democratic implications. Eulenspiegel unquestionably sows rogues, and the satire takes aim at those "dishonest" citizens of the two cities in which he sows them – citizens who scarcely tolerate his mockery and in fact force him to perform his usual vanishing act.

73. The hops market mentioned here is reliably reported to have existed in 1353 (Lappenberg, 275; Lindow, 214).

75. The white jam here may also be either a milk pudding or a cabbage stew (Lindow, 219).

76. Saint Martin's Day, "when parties like this usually took place," falls on November 11, and in the Middle Ages was commonly followed by parties, dinners, and celebrations (Sichtermann, 318; see also the note on Chapter 5).

78. This tale also appears in Heinrich Bebel's *Facetien* and in Johannes Pauli's *Schimpf und Ernst* (cf. note on Chapter 6).

79. Variations on the notion of paying an innkeeper with the sound of his money appear in a good deal of folk literature. An extremely likely immediate source of this tale is the Italian *Le cento novelle antiche* (late thirteenth century; see also the Introduction, Sources and Influence).

80. Rostock is not in Saxony (where the previous tale occurs), a fact that suggests the misplacing of this episode. A nearly word-for-word repetition of the tale is to be found in Heinrich Bebel's *Facetien* (Lindow, 234). Eulenspiegel's remark at the end, "Whoever's last sweeps out the house," echoes the adage "Der Letzte muß die Zeche zahlen" [Whoever's last pays the bill].

81. According to Chapter 82, the village cited here must be near Staßfurt. A misprint typical of the frequent differences between the editions of 1515 and 1519 occurs when Eulenspiegel says (in the 1519 edition), "Ob ein Gast Euwer Kost Isset" [If a guest ate your food]. The 1515 edition repeats "gast," which is patently absurd.

82. Honegger (89) wishes to see a connection between the wheel (or "Rad") in this story and Hermann Bote's *Radbuch* (for another view, see my remarks in the Introduction, Date and Authorship). The symbolism of the wheel as a medieval torture instrument reserved for serious criminals is clear enough in any case. Sichtermann (320-21) believes that Eulenspiegel's description of himself as lying stretched on the wheel indicates a self-conscious perception of a powerful sort. Certainly the tale hints, if rather more delicately than Sichtermann maintains, at a sense of torment.

83. Familiar adages, such as the one with which this tale begins, are sprinkled throughout the tales (cf. Chapters 16 and 18, for instance, which lead off with similar popular sayings). Kadlec (187) and Roloff (129) see the last sentence here ("That's how to finish one's trip to Rome") as a clearly satirical remark directed against the Church. Sichtermann (321) disagrees. Unless the remark is construed as precisely the sort of anti-clerical satire that Kadlec and Roloff find it to be, it makes little sense, however.

84. This tale, like others (cf. the notes on Chapters 69 and 78), appears in Pauli's *Schimpf und Ernst* (Lindow, 242); it is eliminated from subsequent editions.

85. The word play here, on "Hochländer" and "Holänder," is puzzling (Lindow, 245). The texts do not make it clear whether the reference is to a Dutchman or a Highlander. On grounds of proximity and credibility, and because a choice is clearly required in translation, I have opted for the Dutchman.

86. Lappenberg (280) suggests that the Archbishop here may have been Burchard Grelle, who died in 1344, and whose character might indeed have led him to play the sort of trick described in this tale. The trick, at any rate, is, as Lappenberg suggests, quite in accord with the spirit of the times. See also Lindow, 247. Both the editions of 1515 and 1519 speak of the Bishop as receiving three times the money (30 guilders) that he gives Eulenspiegel for revealing his little secret. I have corrected the error.

87. The editions of 1515 and 1519 present Lübeck in the title here, but Einbeck in the story. Chapter 46, which also takes place near Einbeck, ought perhaps to follow this one. We are told that the "honest, simple peasant" who wishes to sell his plums was living at Oldenburg near Einbeck, but no such place exists near Einbeck. The three villages of Stadtoldendorf, Markoldendorf, and Kleinoldendorf are close to Einbeck, however. Lappenberg (281) suggests that N. may have had one of these in mind. Lindow (251) supports Stadtoldendorf, where in 1328 an Otto von Oldenburg is mentioned. Honegger ("Todsünden," 31f) argues that the peasant in this story is as much a sinner as Eulenspiegel, who ruins his plums. The peasant wishes to sell them at too high a price, or to engage in profiteering. He thus deserves what he gets. This seems a particularly weak argument in light of the "punishment" visited on him.

88. Lindow (252) notes that Marienthal, in the district of Helmstädt is a Cistercian abbey founded ca. 1136. He suggests that the abbey is described in this tale, and is confused with Marienwohlde, a nunnery founded in 1412 and located some two kilometers from Mölln–where (in Chapter 89) Eulenspiegel becomes ill and dies. This tale, at any rate, finds a close parallel in *Bruder Rausch*, published in 1515 in Strassburg (Lindow, 253); Lappenberg (282f) cites as well a poem of the fifteenth or sixteenth century, with comparable behavior.

89. The hospital "The Holy Ghost" (*Domus Sancti Spiritus Molne*) is mentioned in a Lübeck document of 1289 (Lappenberg, 287; Lindow, 256).

90. The origin of the term "beguines," which figures in this and succeeding tales, is unknown. Dayton Phillips, in his interesting study, *Beguines in Medieval Strassburg* (Stanford University Press, 1941), 2, suggests that the word is derived "from the Old French word *beige* or *bege*, referring to the gray-brown color of the penitent robe of undyed wool worn by 'beguines.' " Phillips believes that "a person wearing such a robe came to be called *beguinus*, through the addition of the Latin adjectival suffix *-inus* to the adjective *bege*, and that this combination in German-speaking provinces gave the *g* its hard sound." Beguines, in any case, is the name of certain laymen and laywomen who were first organized in Belgium and France during the twelfth century. While they devoted themselves primarily to charitable and religious lives, they were nonetheless free to marry. For a good history of the beguines in the Middle Ages, see Ernest W. McDonnell, *The Beguines and Beghards in Medieval Culture* (Rutgers University Press, 1954). Lindow (258) notes that beguines were for the most part attached to specific clerical orders, or lived on designated streets. They were active in charities after 1311. Eulenspiegel's unpleasant remark about a beguine's losing her piety when she is angry is in fact a medieval commonplace (Lindow, 259). On the contemporary fashion of letting one's coat hang below one's outer cloak–which Eulenspiegel mocks in this story, with the first of his last wishes–see Sichtermann, 325. For the sake of clarity, I have inserted the word "fashionably" into my translation here.

92. The custom of drawing up one's last will and testament in the manner described here was well in place by 1300 (Lindow, 262). Such documents were registered and deposited with local city officials.

93. Lindow suggests that the practice of strapping a body into a hollowed-out tree dates from the Bronze Age (265).

94. The word "wunderlich" is applied no less than three times to Eulenspiegel and his burial in this tale, as in the first sentence: "Bei Ulenspiegels Begräbtnis gieng es wunderlich zu." The word can mean "strangely," as well as "oddly," or even "amazingly" and "peculiarly." Each offers a slightly different critical emphasis, or in this case, interpretation of the events and of Eulenspiegel's life. I have opted for the more conservative "oddly," though all senses of the word are surely to be understood. Curiously enough, Ben Jonson, at his own request, was buried standing on his feet in Westminster Abbey. The parallel with Eulenspiegel's vertical position in his grave may not be accidental (Lappenberg, 289). Jonson mentions an "Howleglass" in his *Masque of the Fortunate Isles* (1626). On Jonson's posture in death, see Marchette Chute,

Ben Jonson of Westminster (New York, 1953), 347. Lindow (266) cites an inscription on a gravestone at Mölln, which while commemorating Eulenspiegel's death, may in fact have been erected only after the publication of the earliest editions of the *Volksbuch* (Sichtermann, 328).

95. This final chapter, numbered 96 in the editions of 1515 and 1519 (but see the note on the title page, above, for the probable reason for this error), presents a problem for the "acrostic" of Hermann Bote's name that Honegger wishes to establish. Obviously it does not continue the name with an expected additional letter (Sichtermann, 329). On the other hand, the chapter is clearly numbered as an additional adventure, and is introduced in the same manner as all the rest: "Die. xCvi histo:i sagt wie Ulen/spiegels EpithapCium onnd obergeschrifft zu Lünen/burg off seinem grab gehowen stot" [*sic*]. The chapter of course simply repeats, though with the important modification of the illustrative woodcut, the motif of the previous chapter. For this reason, Walther (67) believes it possible that this chapter marked the original final page of the book, and Honegger (109, n279) observes that the chapter is not in fact a true chapter. If the chapter is therefore omitted from consideration, it becomes superfluous to investigate – as has often been done – the mysterious identification of Lüneburg as Eulenspiegel's burial site. Sichtermann favors this approach (329), while recalling Lindow's conjecture on the matter. Lindow (266-67) suggests that Lüneburg in the title here may be the result of a confusion between Lüneburg and Lauenburg, which is the name of the duchy in which Mölln is located. All of this is sheer guesswork, to be sure, with the added disadvantage that it seems to eliminate evidence on the basis that it does not fit into an established hypothesis. What is perhaps more interesting, and certainly more consistent with the text itself, is a long-previous speculation of Lappenberg (289). Lappenberg reports that a Senator Albers of Lüneburg remembered (as recently as 1846) having seen a gravestone, in the Church of Saint Mary at Lüneburg, on which was carved an owl, but no mirror. As this cemetery has since been torn up, no confirmation of Albers' childhood memory is possible. Lappenberg himself believes that the confusion between Mölln and

Lüneburg is either a deliberate final joke of the author's or a misprint (of the sort to be found perhaps in Chapter 64, in which the title gives us a location for the tale that is at variance with the location given in the tale itself). The idea that the insertion of Lüneburg may be N.'s final joke is certainly tempting. Certainly too it is consistent with a text in which both the author and his hero seem to remain, in various important ways, not only jesting but invisible.

The Garland Library of Medieval Literature

Series A (Texts and Translations); Series B (Translations Only)

1. Chrêtien de Troyes: *Lancelot*, or *The Knight of the Cart*. Edited and translated by William W. Kibler. Series A.
2. Brunetto Latini: *Il Tesoretto (The Little Treasure)*. Edited and translated by Julia Bolton Holloway. Series A.
3. *The Poetry of Arnaut Daniel*. Edited and translated by James J. Wilhelm. Series A.
4. *The Poetry of William VII, Count of Poitiers, IX Duke of Aquitaine*. Edited and translated by Gerald A. Bond; music edited by Hendrik van der Werf. Series A.
5. *The Poetry of Cercamon and Jaufre Rudel*. Edited and translated by George Wolf and Roy Rosenstein; music edited by Hendrik van der Werf. Series A.
6. *The Vidas of the Troubadours*. Translated by Margarita Egan. Series B.
7. *Medieval Latin Poems of Male Love and Friendship*. Translated by Thomas Stehling. Series A.
8. *Barthar Saga*. Edited and translated by Jon Skaptason and Phillip Pulsiano. Series A.
9. Guillaume de Machaut: *Judgment of the King of Bohemia (Le Jugement dou Roy de Behaingne)*. Edited and translated by R. Barton Palmer. Series A.
10. *Three Lives of the Last Englishmen*. Translated by Michael Swanton. Series B.
11. Giovanni Boccaccio: *Eclogues*. Edited and translated by Janet Smarr. Series A.
12. Hartmann von Aue: *Erec*. Translated by Thomas L. Keller. Series B.
13. *Waltharius* and *Ruodlieb*. Edited and translated by Dennis M. Kratz. Series A.
14. *The Writings of Medieval Women*. Translated by Marcelle Thiébaux. Series B.
15. *The Rise of Gawain, Nephew of Arthur (De ortu Waluuanii Nepotis Arturi)*. Edited and translated by Mildred Leake Day. Series A.

16, 17. *The French Fabliau:* B.N. 837. Edited and translated by Raymond Eichmann and John DuVal. Series A.

18. *The Poetry of Guido Cavalcanti*. Edited and translated by Lowry Nelson, Jr. Series A.
19. Hartmann von Aue: *Iwein*. Edited and translated by Patrick M. McConeghy. Series A.
20. *Seven Medieval Latin Comedies*. Translated by Alison Goddard Elliott. Series B.
21. Christine de Pizan: *The Epistle of the Prison of Human Life*. Edited and translated by Josette A. Wisman. Series A.
22. *The Poetry of the Sicilian School*. Edited and translated by Frede Jensen Series A.
23. *The Poetry of Cino da Pistoia*. Edited and translated by Christopher Kleinhenz. Series A.

24. *The Lyrics and Melodies of Adam de la Halle.* Lyrics edited and translated by Deborah Hubbard Nelson; music edited by Hendrik van der Werf. Series A.

25. Chrétien de Troyes: *Erec and Enide.* Edited and translated by Carleton W. Carroll. Series A.

26. *Three Ovidian Tales of Love.* Edited and translated by Raymond J. Cormier. Series A.

27. *The Poetry of Guido Guinizelli.* Edited and translated by Robert Edwards. Series A.

28. Wernher der Gartenaere: *Helmbrecht.* Edited by Ulrich Seelbach; introduced and translated by Linda B. Parshall. Series A.

29. *Five Middle English Arthurian Romances.* Translated by Valerie Krishna. Series B.

30. *The One Hundred New Tales (Les Cent nouvelles nouvelles).* Translated by Judith Bruskin Diner. Series B.

31. Gerald of Wales (Giraldus Cambrensis): *The Life of St. Hugh of Avalon.* Edited and translated by Richard M. Loomis. Series A.

32. *L'Art d'Amours (The Art of Love).* Translated by Lawrence Blonquist. Series B.

33. Giovanni Boccaccio: *L'Ameto.* Translated by Judith Serafini-Sauli. Series B.

34, 35. *The Medieval Pastourelle.* Selected, translated, and edited in part by William D. Paden, Jr. Series A.

36. Béroul: *The Romance of Tristran.* Edited and translated by Norris J. Lacy. Series A.

37. *Graelent* and *Guingamor:* Two Breton Lays. Edited and translated by Russell Weingartner. Series A.

38. Heinrich von Veldeke: *Eneit.* Translated by J. Wesley Thomas. Series B.

39. *The Lyrics and Melodies of Gace Brulé.* Edited and translated by Samuel Rosenberg and Samuel Danon; music edited by Hendrik van der Werf. Series A.

40. Giovanni Boccaccio: *Life of Dante (Trattatello in Laude di Dante).* Translated by Vincenzo Zin Bollettino. Series B.

41. *The Lyrics of Thibaut de Champagne.* Edited and translated by Kathleen J. Brahney. Series A.

42. *The Poetry of Sordello.* Edited and translated by James J. Wilhelm. Series A.

43. Giovanni Boccaccio: *Il Filocolo.* Translated by Donald S. Cheney with the collaboration of Thomas G. Bergin. Series B.

44. *Le Roman de Thèbes (The Story of Thebes).* Translated by John Smartt Coley. Series B.

45. Guillaume de Machaut: *The Judgment of the King of Navarre (Le Jugement dou Roy de Navarre).* Translated and edited by R. Barton Palmer. Series A.

46. *The French Chansons of Charles D'Orléans.* With the Corresponding Middle English Chansons. Edited and translated by Sarah Spence. Series A.

47. *The Pilgrimage of Charlemagne* and *Aucassin and Nicolette.* Edited and translated by Glyn S. Burgess and Anne Elizabeth Cobby. Series A.

48. Chrétien de Troyes: *The Knight with the Lion,* or *Yvain*. Edited and translated by William W. Kibler. Series A.

49. *Carmina Burana: Love Songs.* Translated by Edward D. Blodgett and Roy Arthur Swanson. Series B.

50. *The Story of Meriadoc, King of Cambria (Historia Meriadoci, Regis Cambriae).* Edited and translated by Mildred Leake Day. Series A.

51. *The Plays of Hrotsvit of Gandersheim.* Translated by Katharina Wilson Series B.

52. *Medieval Debate Poetry: Vernacular Works.* Edited and translated by Michel-André Bossy. Series A.

53. Giovanni Boccaccio: *Il Filostrato.* Translated by Robert P. apRoberts and Anna Bruni Seldis; Italian text by Vincenzo Pernicone. Series A.

54. Guillaume de Machaut: *La Fonteinne amoureuse.* Edited and translated by R. Barton Palmer. Series A.

55. *The Knight of the Parrot (Le Chevalier du Papegau).* Translated by Thomas E. Vesce. Series B.

56. *The Saga of Thidrek of Bern (Thidrekssaga af Bern).* Translated by Edward R. Haymes. Series. B.

57. Wolfram von Eschenbach: *Titurel* and the *Songs.* Edited and translated by Sidney M. Johnson and Marion Gibbs. Series A.

58. Der Stricker: *Daniel of the Blossoming Valley.* Translated by Michael Resler. Series B.

59. *The Byelorussian Tristan.* Translated by Zora Kipel. Series B.

60. *The Marvels of Rigomer.* Translated by Thomas E. Vesce. Series B.

61. *The Song of Aspremont (La Chanson d'Aspremont).* Translated by Michael A. Newth. Series B.

62. Chrétien de Troyes: *The Story of the Grail (Li Contes del Graal),* or *Perceval.* Edited by Rupert T. Pickens and translated by William W. Kibler. Series A.

63. Heldris de Cornuälle: *The Story of Silence (Le Roman de Silence).* Translated by Regina Psaki. Series B.

64. *Romances of Alexander.* Translated by Dennis M. Kratz. Series B.

65. Dante Alighieri: *Il Convivio (The Banquet).* Translated by Richard H. Lansing. Series B.

66. *The Cambridge Songs (Carmina Cantabrigiensia).* Edited and translated by Jan M. Ziolkowski. Series A.

67. Guillaume de Machaut: *Le Confort d'Ami (Comfort for a Friend).* Edited and translated by R. Barton Palmer. Series. A.

68. Christine de Pizan: *Christine's Vision.* Translated by Glenda K. McLeod Series B.

69. *Moriz von Craûn.* Edited and translated by Stephanie Cain Van D'Elden. Series A.

70. *The Acts of Andrew in the Country of the Cannibals*. Translated by Robert Boenig. Series B.

71. *Razos and Troubadour Songs*. Translated by William E. Burgwinkle. Series B.

72. Mechthild von Magdeburg: *Flowing Light of the Divinity*. Translated by Christiane Mesch Galvani; edited, with an Introduction, by Susan Clark. Series B.

73. Robert de Boron: *The Grail Trilogy*. Translated by George Diller. Series B.

74. *Till Eulenspiegel: His Adventures*. Translated, with introduction and notes, by Paul Oppenheimer. Series B.